Teaching Comm
Skills and Competencies for the
International Workplace

Backed by evidence and research, this practical book presents an innovative yet comprehensive approach to teaching non-native English speakers the main communication and cultural competencies that are required to succeed in an international English-speaking workplace. Each unit includes strategies for teaching key skills, tasks to encourage reflection and notes on relevant cultural and technological issues. Practical features in each unit include lesson plans and materials, insights from research, extension tasks, reflection activities and further readings.

Supported by current learning theories, key teaching methodologies and assessment materials, the chapters address the challenges that non-native English speakers may face in the international English-speaking workplace. Areas of focus include:

- Job hunting
- Job applications
- Interviews
- Interpersonal, written and spoken communication
- Performance appraisals
- Applying for promotions

Written for pre-service, practicing and future teachers, with specific guidance for each role, this is an essential resource for all educators who want to confidently address the challenges that non-English speakers may encounter at work, including linguistic proficiency, cultural awareness and the use of technology.

Julio Gimenez is Principal Lecturer of English Language and Academic and Professional Literacies at University of Westminster, UK.

Teaching Communication, Skills and Competencies for the International Workplace

A Resource for Teachers of English

Julio Gimenez

Routledge
Taylor & Francis Group

NEW YORK AND LONDON

Designed cover image: © Getty Images

First published 2023
by Routledge
605 Third Avenue, New York, NY 10158

and by Routledge
4 Park Square, Milton Park, Abingdon, Oxon, OX14 4RN

Routledge is an imprint of the Taylor & Francis Group, an informa business

Library of Congress Cataloging-in-Publication Data
Names: Gimenez, Julio, author.
Title: Teaching communication, skills and competencies for the international workplace : a resource for teachers of English / Julio Gimenez.
Description: New York, NY : Routledge, 2023. | Includes bibliographical references and index.
Identifiers: LCCN 2022058658 (print) | LCCN 2022058659 (ebook) | ISBN 9781032254951 (hardback) | ISBN 9781032223599 (paperback) | ISBN 9781003283515 (ebook)
Subjects: LCSH: English language--Business English--Study and teaching. | English language--Study and teaching--Foreign speakers. | Business communication--Study and teaching.
Classification: LCC PE1115 .G56 2023 (print) | LCC PE1115 (ebook) | DDC 428.0071--dc23/eng/20230316
LC record available at https://lccn.loc.gov/2022058658
LC ebook record available at https://lccn.loc.gov/2022058659

ISBN: 978-1-032-25495-1 (hbk)
ISBN: 978-1-032-22359-9 (pbk)
ISBN: 978-1-003-28351-5 (ebk)

DOI: 10.4324/9781003283515

Typeset in Goudy
by SPi Technologies India Pvt Ltd (Straive)

Access the Support Material: Visit www.worldsofenglish.com for additional videos, audio, resources and activities for this book.

Support Material

Alongside the material featured in this book, there are also some additional resources that are freely available on the 'Worlds of English' website as downloadable Support Material. The specific resources that are available online are listed below. You can access these downloads by visiting www.worldsofenglish.com.

Support Material on the 'Worlds of English' website include:

1 Videos
2 Audio files
3 Downloadable scripts
4 Blogs
5 Supplementary activities

Contents

Illustrations

Figures

Tables

Preface

Dear Teacher

Teaching Communication, Skills and Competencies for the International Workplace has been designed as a resource book for new as well as experienced teachers of English for the workplace. Each unit of the book has been informed by key learning theories and teaching methodologies, as well as latest research in the field of workplace communication.

The core units of the book (Units 1–8) follow the *Teaching-and-Learning Cycle* presented and discussed in the Introductory Unit. The Cycle has four stages: 1. Reflection, 2. Lesson design, 3. Materials selection and 4. Assessment of learning, all of them orchestrated by you at the centre.

The distinguishing features of *Teaching Communication, Skills and Competencies for the International Workplace* include:

- **Reflection Activities**, which offer a strong link between the discussions presented in the book and your particular teaching context
- **Key Skills and Competencies**, which your students will need for the international workplace
- **Lesson Plans and Materials**, which have been tried and tested by teachers of English for the workplace in a number of countries
- **Extension Tasks**, which aim to provide further insights into the key topics of the units
- **Language Corner** boxes, which highlight the main linguistic features that your students will need to become active participants in workplace practices

- **Culture and Technology** observations, which aim to make your students aware of how cultural frames shape workplace practices
- **Insights from Research** notes, which summarise the key contributions that relevant research studies have made to particular work-related topics
- **Further Readings**, which accompany each unit to provide extra reading sources, and
- **Resources** (e.g., association, journals, ideas), which aim to support your own professional development.

I hope the book will prove a useful resource which will support your teaching practices as well as your professional development.

Julio Gimenez
Centre for Education and Teaching Innovation–
University of Westminster
London, United Kingdom

Acknowledgements

I am grateful to all the students who, along the years, took the module "Communication in the Workplace" at the University of Middlesex, the University of Nottingham and, more recently, the University of Westminster. They have provided invaluable comments and feedback on the materials and activities that eventually found their way into the book.

I am also thankful to my colleague Daniel Tomozeiu for teaching and piloting some of the materials, and for his comments, input and work in the initial stages of the project. I will be always grateful for his help and support.

A number of colleagues have also provided comments on previous versions of the materials in the book: my lifelong friend and colleague Nora Sapag, who read and provided me with feedback on the initial proposal; my dear colleagues at Donghua University, China, whose time, dedication and expertise helped to make this a better project; Mariangela Spinillo, who also made very useful comments on some of the materials; and the many teachers in Argentina, Brazil, Germany and China who kindly piloted some of the units, and provided incredibly useful feedback; to all of them, THANK YOU!

Karen Adler, my Commissioning Editor at Routledge, has been instrumental in taking the project to its final stage. Thank you for being such a supportive and enthusiastic editor.

Andrew Pitchford at the Centre for Education and Teaching Innovation (CETI)–University of Westminster made this project possible by providing me with much-needed support to complete the manuscript.

I am also grateful to the following for permission to reproduce materials: University of Sunshine Coast (p. 9); Tim Slade (p. 53); Accor careers (pp. 110-111); Ryan Spanger (p. 196) and Carrie Luxem (p. 260).

Last but not least, I feel indebted to my son Facundo, my daughter Maz, and my colleagues Katherine Mansfield, Richard Paterson and Mariangela Spinillo for their help with the recordings; and to my dearest friend Pablo Rodriguez for all his ideas and support with the technical side of this project.

London and Catania
November 2022

A roadmap for using the book

Teaching Communication, Skills and Competencies for the International Workplace has been designed in such a way as to offer a number of options for its use. In order to benefit from these options, you will need to take into account three key considerations:

- your experience as a teacher
- your students and their work-related experience, and
- the duration of the course you are teaching.

The following table is intended to serve as a guide into how the book can be used taking these considerations into account.

Key considerations for using the book

Key considerations	Suggested use	Observations
You as a teacher		
If you are new to teaching,	I'd suggest you started with the Introductory Unit before exploring the specific teaching units of the book (Units 1–8).	The introductory unit provides the basic principles of teaching and learning in general and English for the workplace in particular.
If you are a seasoned teacher but new to teaching English for the workplace,	I'd suggest you scanned through the Introductory Unit before you explore in more detail the specific teaching units of the book (Units 1–8).	Scanning through the Introductory Unit will make sure you are familiar with the pedagogical principles on which the rest of the units are based.

Key considerations	Suggested use	Observations
Your students		
If your students are pre-experience,	I'd suggest you work on all of the eight units with them. This, however, will also depend on the type of course you're teaching (see below).	Units 1–8 provide students with the complete work experience cycle; from applying for a new job to applying for promotion.
If your students are job-experienced,	I'd suggest focusing on units 5–8, especially if you are teaching a semester-long course (see below).	Units 5–8 highlight skills and competencies needed for active participation in the modern work environment; from internal communication to how to apply for promotion.
The course		
If you are teaching a year-long course,	I'd suggest you work on all of the eight units with your students unless they are job-experienced (see above).	Units 1–8 provide students with the complete work experience cycle; from applying for a job to applying for promotion.
If you are teaching a semester-long course,	I'd suggest you teach Unit 1–4 to pre-experience students and Units 5–8 to job-experienced students. Alternatively, you could split the 8 units into semesters 1 and 2.	If the course could be extended over two semesters, semesters 1 and 2 could be offered to pre-experience students, and semester 2 to only job-experienced students.
If you are teaching a short workshop (e.g., four weeks in length),	I'd suggest you take the type of students attending the workshop as the key factor to decide on its contents. A combination of units could be offered in this situation.	Possible combination would include: Units 1, 2 and 3 for pre-experience students; Units 5–8 for job-experienced students; and Units 4–6 for students interested in communication for the workplace.

As you can see, *Teaching Communication, Skills and Competencies for the International Workplace* offers you a great deal of flexibility for its use, depending on who you are as a teacher and, in particular, who your students are, and the type of course you are teaching. Whichever your situation, I'm sure you will be able to combine the considerations mentioned in the table above to better suit your needs and those of your students.

Part I
Getting ready

Introductory unit

Reflections for the (new) teacher

Learning Outcomes

By the end of the unit, you should be able to:

- identify the main learning theories that have influenced teaching and learning and apply them to your teaching situation
- assess lesson plans and design your own with confidence
- evaluate, select and adapt teaching materials in a principled way, and
- appraise relevant types of assessment for and of learning.

1.1 Introducing teaching principles

As a new teacher, you may be wondering where to start and what decisions to make in order to teach English for communication in the international workplace. This is something that

> all new teachers ask themselves. Even seasoned teachers of general English starting to teach English for the workplace would ask themselves some of these questions. So, let me tell you, *you are not alone in this.*

As a seasoned teacher and researcher of workplace communication, I always find that a good starting point to answer these questions is

DOI: 10.4324/9781003283515-2

reflecting upon my own views and beliefs about learning and teaching. Reflecting upon your views and beliefs is important not only to be able to make informed decisions but also to become a reflective teacher. Like in many other professions, reflection plays a central role in what we do as teachers. It provides both a window into our own thoughts, beliefs, and ideas, and an opportunity to improve our teaching practices.

Reflection

John Dewey's (1910) work on reflection has played an influential role in teaching and learning. He described reflection as "active, persistent and careful consideration of any belief or supposed form of knowledge in the light of the grounds that support it and the further conclusions to which it tends".

(p. 9)

Although written more than a hundred years ago, Dewey's definition is still relevant today. As you can see, his definition focuses on two elements: a. *your beliefs* about teaching in this case (e.g., how teaching should happen, the role that teachers and students should play, what teaching materials should look like); and b. *your knowledge* about teaching and obviously learning. Thus, reflecting upon your own views and beliefs about learning and teaching should be complemented with some form of knowledge. In our case, the three knowledge areas that should complement and inform reflection are:

- **learning theories** (e.g., cognitivism), which have defined how people learn
- **teaching approaches** (e.g., collaborative learning), which have developed out of learning theories, and
- **classroom techniques** (e.g., problem-solving tasks), which are used to put learning theories and teaching approaches into practice.

Learning theories, teaching methods and classroom techniques are all closely connected as should become clearer by the end of this unit. Such relationships can be seen from the macro perspective (from learning theories to classroom techniques) or from the micro perspective (from classroom techniques to learning theories). If you decided to plan your teaching following the macro perspective, then you would usually start thinking about which learning theories could inform your

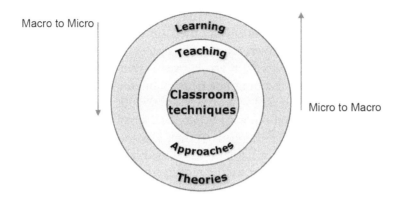

Figure I.1 The Relationship between Learning Theories, Teaching Approaches, and Classroom Techniques

other decisions (e.g., planning a lesson, choosing teaching materials). If, on the other hand, you chose to start with a classroom activity, you would probably consider which learning theory lies behind the activity and whether it would be appropriate for the type of students you are working with. In either case, teaching approaches are the linking element between the macro and micro perspectives. This is illustrated in Figure I.1.

We will now look at the key learning theories, teaching approaches and classroom techniques that have influenced the field of English language teaching.

I.2 Exploring learning theories, teaching approaches and classroom techniques

Over the years, there have been a number of key learning theories that have influenced how we teach. This section will discuss those that have been the most influential.

But before we take a look at learning theories, you may wonder: *why is it important for teachers to know about learning theories?* As we discussed above, most of what we do as teachers tends to be guided by our beliefs and views about learning. However, these beliefs are sometimes difficult to explain and rationalise. We usually explain what we do as teachers by saying things like "That's the way I have learnt/been taught", "I have always done it like that", and "That's what my students like." Important as our beliefs are, they are sometimes not enough to explain or justify our own teaching practices, let along reflect upon them. And this may create a gap between what we do and what we think we do in our teaching practices. Numerous studies (e.g., Wen, Elicker & McMullen, 2011; Wilcox-Herzog, 2002) have found inconsistencies between self-reported beliefs and actual classroom practices. What a teacher believes happens in their classroom may not always be a true reflection of what actually happens. For instance, some of the teachers in these and other studies reported to endorse student-centred practices, but, when observed, researchers found that their classroom practices were most often teacher-centred. That is why it is important to reflect upon what theories inform our teaching approaches and classroom practices to be able to find any inconsistencies between our beliefs and our actual practices.

So, let's pause for a moment to reflect. The first reflection activity of this unit (RA-IU.1) aims at guiding you on how to discover your views on learning and where they have come from. After you have completed the activity, you may want to read Wen, Elicker and McMullen's (2011) article that reports on their study on teachers' beliefs and practices (see Further readings list). Their study may also give you some further insights on why reflection is crucial.

Reflection Activity (RA-IU.1)

Take a few minutes to answer the following questions. You may want to take notes as you think about each answer. Keeping a reflection journal, where you can write notes on exercises like this one, could also be very useful for your professional development as a teacher.

- **How** do you think you learn best? Are there specific learning strategies that you use to help you to learn? Are there specific times of the day that you find more conducive to learning?
- **Where** do you think these views and beliefs come from? For example, from books or articles you have read? From observing other teachers teaching? From discussions with other teachers? From your own experiences as a learner?
- **Do you think** the way you were taught and learnt may have influenced your beliefs about teaching and learning?

Further reading: Wen, Elicker and McMullen (2011)

You have probably now realised that learning means different things to different people, including teachers. This is also why it is important to know about our own views and beliefs about teaching and learning. It is equally important to understand how learning takes place so that this understanding can inform our teaching practices.

Over time, learning has been theorised in different ways, resulting in a number of **learning theories**. The key learning theories that have had a significant impact on teaching languages in general and communication in particular are:

- **Behaviourism:** For this theory, human behaviour, including learning, is shaped by means of positive (e.g., praising) or negative (e.g., disapproving) reinforcement. For instance, learning will happen when the teacher praises a student with something like "Well done!" or when they disapprove of a learner's behaviour by saying "No, that's incorrect" and the student has to try again. This theory is based on the stimulus–response premise: if you are hungry (stimulus), you eat (response). In education, this has translated into the classroom as 'repetition/practice + feedback'. That is, students are given a verbal stimulus which they repeat, and the teacher provides either positive or negative reinforcement.

  Key names in behaviourism: I. P. Pavlov (1849–1936), J. B. Watson (1878–1957), and B. F. Skinner (1904–1990)

Extension Task (ET-IU.1)

Use the URL provided below to watch **video clip ET-IU.1** about Pavlovian conditioning and behaviourism. As you watch, think about these questions:

- Have you ever experienced the type of learning (stimulus–response–feedback) discussed in the video clip either as a teacher or a student? If so, how useful did you find it?
- Do you think "positive/negative reinforcement" plays a central role in learning? If so, how? If not, why not?
- What exercises are mentioned as typical examples of behaviourism?
- What would you say are the advantages of learning in this way? Any disadvantages?
  https://worldsofenglish.com/workplace-skills-extension-tasks/

- **Cognitivism**: Cognitivism originated as a reaction to behaviourism on the premise that learners are rational beings who need active participation rather than passive responses in order to learn. Cognitivism emphasizes inner mental activities such as thinking, memory and knowing as necessary for learning. Knowledge is a schema or mental construction that changes when learning takes place.

  Key names in cognitivism: J. S. Bruner (1915–2016), Ulric Neisser (1928–2012), Noam Chomsky (1928–present)

Extension Task (ET-IU.2)

Use the URL provided below to watch **video clip ET-IU.2** which describes cognitivism. After you have finished watching it, answer these questions:

- What are the pillars upon which cognitivism as a theory rests?
- How does it compare with behaviourism?
- Has any of your learning experiences been based on any of these principles?
  https://worldsofenglish.com/workplace-skills-extension-tasks/

- **Constructivism**: For constructivism, learning is an active and contextualized process by which learners construct rather than acquire knowledge, based on their previous personal experiences and hypotheses about reality. Learners formulate and test their hypotheses about reality and the world through social participation and interacting with others. Culture, thought and language all play a central role in the social construction of knowledge and therefore in learning.

  Key names in constructivism: J. Piaget (1896–1980), L. Vygotsky (1896–1934), E. Wenger (1952–present)

Extension Task (ET-IU.3)

Use the URL provided below to watch **video clip ET-IU.3**, and decide why (social) interaction is key to cognitive development in Vygotsky's social constructivism.
  https://worldsofenglish.com/workplace-skills-extension-tasks/

- **Connectivism**: Connectivism sees learning as a process of self-directed discovery within formal and informal networks that connect people, technology and information. By navigating across these networks, learners create opportunities for self-directed discovery and, in this way, knowledge emerges and learning takes place.

Key names in connectivism: G. Siemens (1970–present), S. Downes (1959–present)

Extension Task (ET-IU.4)

Use the URL provided below to watch **video clip ET-IU.4**. In the clip, the Centre for Support and Advancement of Learning and Teaching (C-SALT) at the **University of the Sunshine Coast** (Australia) interviewed Dr George Siemens about the origins and key principles of connectivism.

As you watch the clip, think how networked learning, the basis of connectivism, compares with the other three theories we have discussed so far?
https://worldsofenglish.com/workplace-skills-extension-tasks/

The four learning theories briefly discussed above deal with learning in general. While they have laid important foundations for learning, it was developments in the field of Second Language Acquisition (SLA) that had a direct impact on teaching languages. This is what we discuss next.

I.2.1 Second Language Acquisition (SLA)

In the 1970s the field of SLA developed, refuting behaviourist views of how students learn a second language. The main influences in the field were the study of errors (called 'error analysis'), acquisition of the order of morphemes (known as 'morpheme studies') and transitional stages in learning language skills (called 'interlanguage studies'). Although early influence was found in the studies of Pitt Corder and Larry Selinker, the main impetus for SLA theories and research was provided by the theories developed by Stephen Krashen in the 1980s. His theories, sometimes collectively referred to as the "Input Hypotheses", were based on the premise that learners develop a second language by being exposed to comprehensible input, that is, language input they can understand as it happens when we naturally learn our first language. By the 1990s, Krashen's theories were complemented by other theories such as the

- "Interaction hypothesis" developed by Michael Long. This hypothesis argues that language learning is promoted by face-to-face interaction and communication

- "Output hypothesis" put forward by Merrill Swain. The output hypothesis claims that learning happens when learners discover a gap in their knowledge of a language. As they notice this gap, learners become aware of it and are able to modify their output. In this way, they can learn something new about the language; and
- "Noticing hypothesis" developed by Richard Schmidt. Schmidt argued that learners cannot advance their language abilities unless they are able to notice input so that it then becomes intake. Intake is defined as the input that learners comprehend and act on to develop their knowledge.

Altogether, these theories of language learning have played an instrumental role in shaping the teaching of languages. A number of teaching approaches, such as 'The Natural Approach' and 'Communicative Language Teaching' (CLT for short), have been developed following SLA theories.

Key names in SLA: P. Corder (1918–1990), L. Selinker (1937–present), S. Krashen (1941–present), M. Long (1945–2021), M. Swain (1944–present), R. Schmidt (1941–present)

Now that you have read and watched video clips about the main learning theories that have influenced how teachers teach, it is time for another moment of reflection. In this second reflection activity of the unit (RA-IU.2), you will be asked to connect these readings and video clips with your own ideas and beliefs. After you have finished activity RA-IU.2, you may want to read Rosalyn Sword's blog on the role of communication in teaching (See Further readings list).

Reflection Activity (RA-IU.2)

- Which of the theories you have read and watched would you say best represents your views and beliefs about learning?
- Which do you think would be most appropriate for teaching workplace communication skills in the educational context you are teaching or considering to teach? Why?

Further reading: Sword (2020)

After having reflected upon how you see and understand learning, it is equally important for you to spend some time thinking about teaching. In particular, *what's the connection between theories of learning and approaches to teaching?* And *how do approaches to teaching translate into classroom techniques or activities?*

Theories of learning, like the ones we have discussed above, have been used to inform the development of a number of **teaching approaches** (sometimes called "instructional designs") that can be applied in different learning contexts. For example, *behaviourism* led to the development of approaches that favour mechanistic teaching through repetition. These approaches focus on accuracy, getting things right, and on the belief that mistakes have to be avoided, and, if they happened, they would have to be corrected immediately before they get fixed in the learners' mind.

Constructivism, on the other hand, was one of the main influencing theories in the design of approaches to teaching that support the development of communicative competence (Hymes, 1972) and communication skills. In this teaching approach, learners are exposed to activities that involve using communication and language for meaningful purposes. The typical example of this type of approaches is CLT.

By the same token, **classroom techniques** have been developed under the influence of particular approaches to teaching. For instance, extensive drilling and repetition are typical activities in teaching approaches that have resulted from behaviourism. On the other hand, classroom techniques, such as information gaps and problem-solving tasks, that have as their key aim fostering communication among students, are favoured in approaches based on the development of communication skills such as CLT.

There is, as you can see, a close connection between learning theories, teaching approaches and classroom techniques. Table I.1 shows how the three are connected together, and describes the roles teachers play and how students are seen in each one.

At this point in the unit, you may want to think about the connections explored in Table I.1. For instance, you can reflect upon which learning theories you align more closely with, which teaching approaches you would follow, and which type of classroom activities you wish your students to get involved in. This will help you to make informed decisions about your teaching practices, and to make sure they are coherent and cohesive. For example, if you believe that learning results from repetition of typical phrases or structures, then you will probably not include

Table I.1 Connections between Learning Theories, Teaching Approaches and Classroom Techniques

Learning theories (How students best learn)	Teaching approaches (How students are best taught)	Classroom techniques (How pedagogy can help learning happen)
Behaviourism Learning happens by external stimulus and reinforcement.	stimuli that can elicit the desired responses should be carefully chosen.	repetition practice + reinforcement
	situations should lead to practice and repetition.	multiple choice
	mistakes should be corrected as soon as they happen.	rote learning
	Role of the teacher: Provider of the appropriate stimuli and situations for practice, corrector of mistakes	Students are seen as: Passive recipients that react to a stimulus in a predicted way.
Cognitivism Learning happens through inner mental activities such as thinking, memory and knowing.	learning is an internal process.	critical analysis tasks
	long and short-term memory play an important role in learning.	problem-solving activities
	learning happens as new information is linked to information learners already have.	scaffolding activities
	Role of the teacher: Organiser of learning activities and provider of feedback	Students are seen as: Active organisers of new knowledge, searching for links between new and known information.

Learning theories (How students best learn)	Teaching approaches (How students are best taught)	Classroom techniques (How pedagogy can help learning happen)
Constructivism Learning is an active and contextualized process that happens through social participation.	learning happens through collaboration. active participation leads to learning. learning is always situated. Role of the teacher: Mentor to the learners by encouraging them to apply new knowledge to different situations	collaborative tasks group work case studies Students are seen as: Active participants in building new knowledge collaboratively, in pairs or groups.
Connectivism Learning is a process of self-directed discovery within formal and informal networks that connect people, technology and information.	learning results from self-directed discovery. learners make connections between different sources. links between people, sources and technology support learning. Role of the teacher: To empower learners to make new connections between sources of information	recognition activities synthesis of information⨯ technology-enhanced activities Students are seen as: Active seekers of (new) connections between networks of information.

(Continued)

Learning theories (How students best learn)	Teaching approaches (How students are best taught)	Classroom techniques (How pedagogy can help learning happen)
Second Language Acquisition Learning a language happens by exposure to comprehensible input, noticing such input and the production of comprehensible output. All these processes are influenced by the environment.	contextualised use of the target language language learning is learning to communicate. communicative competence is the desired goal. <u>Role of the teacher:</u> Motivators, encouraging communication from early stages, provider of opportunities for fluency development	communication activities gap activities and tasks exchange of information to solve problems <u>Students are seen as:</u> Individual users of the language, learning by trial and error; interactants with others for communicative purposes.

problem-solving tasks among the classroom activities for your students. On the other hand, if you adhere to the principles of connectivism, your teaching practices will probably exclude intensive drilling as a key classroom activity.

Coupled with these considerations, it is important that you take into account cultural aspects and technological developments that may also play a role in making decisions about teaching approaches and classroom activities, as we discuss in the first Culture and Technology Note of the unit (CTN-IU.1).

Culture and Technology Note (CTN-IU.1)

In some educational contexts (e.g., China, Hong Kong, Japan, Korea, many South American countries), rote learning or learning by heart may sometimes play a prominent role. This will also hold true for contexts where education, or a specific course, is largely exam-driven, that is heavily influenced by exams students must take. In such contexts and situations, teachers may be more concerned with students committing content to memory, and learning rules and exam-taking strategies than learning to become independent learners. In other contexts (e.g., France, the Netherlands, United Kingdom, the United States of America), education in general may be less influenced by final exams and teachers may need to place more emphasis on developing independent learning skills and collaborative work, for example. In these contexts, however, a course (e.g., IELTS preparation courses) may demand students to also learn rules and exam-taking strategies. This is why both national as well as institutional cultures and learning aims should always be taken into account when examining how learning takes place in a specific context.

By the same token, technology may also determine the choices you can make as a teacher. Some technology-based learning tools have been designed following behaviourist principles and will request a response to a stimulus provided. Such tools will obviously determine the type of pedagogical choices you can make. At the same time, you may also be asked to incorporate tools such as smartboards, presentation software, and classroom response systems, to enhance your students' learning experience. These will also influence your choices as a teacher. In contexts where teaching is delivered completely online, there will be an expectation for teachers to be familiar with teaching platforms, sometimes called Virtual Learning Environments (VLEs), such as ZOOM, Microsoft Teams, Moodle and Blackboard. If you are not familiar with these teaching platforms, most of them offer demo versions which you will be able to download and use for practice.

In all of these cases and contexts, it is essential that you familiarise yourself with both the educational tradition and beliefs of the country and the school where you are or will be teaching and their technological expectations. You will also need to be aware that sometimes the educational tradition and beliefs of a country and those of a school in that country may differ. If you teach in an international school located abroad, for instance, the teaching/learning culture of that particular school may or may not be in line with that of the country where it is operating.

It is time now to reflect on what we have been discussing so far. The third activity for reflection (RA-IU.3) is based on a video clip of a teacher of English teaching a group of young adult students. After the reflection activity, you may want to read Jack C. Richards's chapter, which offers a historical overview of the origins, development and applications of the CLT approach (see Further readings list).

Reflection Activity (RA-IU.3)

Use the URL provided below to watch **video clip RA-IU.3**. As you watch, consider the following questions:

- What classroom activities are the students on the clip involved in?
- Which teaching approach do you think has informed the teacher's decision to ask students to do this activity?
- What role(s) does the teacher play in this class? How are the students seen?
- Judging from your answers to these questions, how do you think this teacher sees learning a language (learning theory)?
  https://worldsofenglish.com/workplace-skills-extension-tasks/
  Further reading: Richards (n.d.)

This section has provided you with the basic features of key learning theories that have influenced teaching approaches and the classroom activities associated with them. It has also offered you opportunities to reflect upon your views and beliefs about learning and teaching, and upon the roles that education traditions and technological affordances may play in making pedagogical decisions. These decisions will find their way in your lesson plans. This is what we discuss in the next section.

I.3 Designing teaching lessons

Designing lessons lies at the heart of every teacher's professional activity. It allows teachers to reflect upon their own pedagogical principles and practices (learning theories, teaching approaches and classroom techniques), evaluate how they can best support their students' learning and assess their learners' progress. Before designing a lesson, among the questions you may wish to consider are:

- Why am I planning to teach this (e.g., a particular skill) **in this way**?
- What **teaching approaches** would be most suitable to teach it?
- What **classroom techniques** (or activities) will help my students to learn it?

As you can see, the three main considerations a teacher would normally make before designing a lesson are related to what we discussed in the previous section, that is, the:

- reasons behind planning learning in a particular way (learning theories)
- teaching beliefs and ideas (teaching approaches), and
- classroom activities students will be asked to do (classroom techniques).

As we have already discussed, these three considerations are connected to one another (see Table I.1). So, in designing a lesson, we have an opportunity to think deeply about and reflect upon the theories of learning that will inform our choices of methods and classroom techniques or activities. Lesson plans also offer us the opportunity to:

- **link** what we are planning to teach with **the curriculum of the course**
- think about what students already know and **can use to learn something new**, and
- **anticipate** what **challenges** they may face when attempting to do the classroom activities.

Lesson plans also serve a number of purposes for the teacher. They can help us to:

- feel more **confident**, especially when we are new to teaching
- plan the **sequence of activities** logically so learners get engaged in learning in a meaningful way
- determine the **suitability** of what needs to be delivered to learners and make informed choices about skills, materials, language, etc.
- make sure the lesson offers a **balance of activities**
- keep a tangible **point of reference** while delivering a lesson, and
- **reflect** upon the execution of the plan after the lesson has been delivered.

As you can see, lesson design is an important activity for both new as well as seasoned teachers. It may be a good idea at this point to take a minute to reflect upon how you see the role of lesson plans in your present or future teaching practices. Reflection activity RA-IU.4 presents you with a video clip and some statements for you to reflect upon.

Reflection Activity (RA-IU.4)

Use the URL provided below to watch **video clip RA-IU.4** about the importance of designing lesson plans and then think about your position in relation to the statements below:

https://worldsofenglish.com/workplace-skills-extension-tasks/

- lesson plans help teachers to be more organised.
- the plan is a guide to what teachers should be doing in class.
- the lesson plan is an answer to questions such as "Who and what am I teaching?", "How will I teach it?", "How will I assess learning?"
- lesson design allows teachers to take into account the needs and learning preferences of their students as well as the materials and the technology they can use to support teaching and learning.
- lesson plans can be informed by research on teaching and learning.

Let us now turn to how to actually design a lesson plan. We will draw a plan for a lesson on "reading information critically", one of the key skills for job hunting that we will be discussing in Unit 1.

The list below shows the six key elements that make up a lesson plan:

[1] **Learning outcomes/objectives**: Learning outcomes (LOs) or learning objectives outline what you want the learners to be able to do by the end of the lesson by focusing on a set of end results. Some of the questions you may want to consider before formulating LOs include:
- What do my students already know?
- What do they need to know?
- What did they do last class?
- How do they work best (e.g., by themselves, in pairs or small groups)?
- How motivated are they?

When designing LOs, it is useful to look at a taxonomy of learning aims (e.g., understand, apply, analyse, create) such as Bloom's or a model of significant learning such as Fink's (2013) to match the level of your students with what is required by the LOs. The categories in Bloom's taxonomy (see the Further reading list at the end of the unit) represent six levels of cognitive complexity that range from "remember" (e.g., recall basic concepts) to "create" (e.g., produce new work). Fink's categories are not hierarchical like Bloom's but interactive, and integrate cognitive, affective and meta-cognitive areas. They include categories like Foundational knowledge, Application, Caring and Learning how to learn (see the Further reading list at the end of the unit). An example of a LO would be "By the end of the lesson, students should be able to implement skills for reading information more critically."

[2] **Progression of teaching and learning**: This element is also called sequencing and grading activities. Here you list all the activities in which you will want your learners to engage in chronologically. This is also an

opportunity for you to see whether the activities are graded from easy to more difficult or simple to more complex.

Examples of activities that could be used to help learners to achieve the LO stated in [1] above include predicting content, verifying predictions, and reading between the lines. Note that in this case activities have been graded in terms of the challenges or difficulties that they will present for the learners. "Predicting content", for instance, is less complex and less demanding than "reading between the lines".

[3] **Strategies and materials**: In this section, you want to list the strategies that you will use to implement the series of activities in [2] and the materials that will accompany such strategies.

In the case of the reading critically example above, strategies could include "making predictions on content", and "reading the title and looking at the accompanying graphs". As to the materials in this case, we could make a note of the text that the learners will be asked to read.

[4] **Success criteria**: This section refers to how learner performance will be assessed. In other words, you specify here what behaviour your learners will need to exhibit to be successful in doing the activities in [2].

For the reading activities above, for instance, success criteria may include: "be able to predict ideas in the reading text correctly", and "be able to take down accurate notes of the ideas discussed in the text".

[5] **Assessment**: Here you specify how the LOs outlined in [1] will be assessed. It is important that these two sections of your lesson plan ([1] and [5]) speak to each other and that you only assess the LOs in section [1] and nothing else. For instance, in our reading example, you would avoid assessing their ability to remember details by heart, as this would be a test of memory rather than of critical reading skills.

[6] **Next steps**: This is an optional element as you may not want the learners to do any follow-up activities. If you do want them to do follow-up activities, homework and pre-class readings, they should be included here.

This template is just one of the many you can use for lesson design. There are, in fact, different models and templates for lesson plans that you can find on the Internet. I have chosen one that is detailed enough but still simple to design and follow (see Tables I.2 and I.3).

The next activity for reflection (RA-IU.5) discusses another template, taken from the British Council (UK) website.

Now, what does a lesson template based on the six elements presented above actually look like? Table I.2 shows a blank template that you can use to design your own future lessons, including the six key elements discussed above [1–6]. Table I.3 illustrates how the template has been used to design a lesson for teaching "critical reading for the workplace".

Reflection Activity (RA-IU.5)

Look at the plan for a lesson on "Multicultural UK" from the British Council website, and answer the questions below.

- How do the elements of this lesson compare with those discussed above?
- Would you choose to work with the elements on this sample lesson plan or would you prefer to work with the six mentioned above? Why?

https://www.teachingenglish.org.uk/sites/teacheng/files/TE_LP_Multicultural_UK_%28new%20template%29.pdf

Further reading: Bloom (1956)

Table I.2 A Lesson Plan Template

Course/Module:	Year group:	Date:
[1] Learning outcomes		
By the end of the lesson, students should be able to: (A) _____ (B) _____ (C) _____		
[2] Progression of teaching & learning		**[3] Strategies/ Materials**
Duration: ..... minutes	Introduction:	
Duration: ..... minutes	Main Activities:	
Duration: ..... minutes	Conclusion:	
[4] Success criteria	• • • Note: You could also develop a set of marking criteria for the lesson (see Section I.5)	**[5] Assessment**
[6] Next steps (e.g., homework, extracurricular activities)		

Table 1.3 A Lesson Plan for Teaching "Critical Reading" for the Workplace

Course/Module: Communication Skills for the International Workplace	Year group:	Date:
[1] Learning outcomes for critical reading for the workplace		
By the end of the lesson, students should be able to: (A) differentiate opinions from facts (B) interpret writer's intention; and (C) evaluate arguments presented in texts.		
[2] Progression of teaching & learning		**[3] Strategies/Materials**
Duration: 10 minutes	Introduction: T presents Sts with a short text and asks them how they would go about reading it.	Eliciting Sts' previous knowledge and experience of reading texts/short text on multinational/international companies
Duration: 40 minutes	Activity 1: 1. Sts underline what they think is an opinion and circle what they think is a fact. 2. Class discussion of 1 3. Agreement on 2	1. Work on a text/ Handout 1 2–3. Class discussion and agreement/Handout 4. Analysing a text/ Handout 2 5. Class discussion and agreement 6. Evaluating a text/ Handout 3 7. Class discussion 8. Identifying strategies, making a list/ Handout 3
	Activity 2: 4. Sts answer questions on writer's intention in pairs 5. Class discussion and agreement on 4	

(Continued)

	Activity 3: 6. Sts discuss the validity of the argument presented by the writer by using criteria (e.g., references) already known to them. T to add new criteria if necessary 7. Class discussion on 6 8. Discussion of new strategies learnt to become more critical readers and make a list	
Duration: 10 minutes	Conclusion: Sts are asked to wrap up by summarising what they did in class, highlighting what new knowledge they have acquired.	Class verbal summary
[4] Success criteria	• to be able to tell opinion from fact • to be able to discuss writer's intention from reading a text • to be able to apply (old and new) criteria to evaluate a text.	**[5] Assessment** Sts will do the same on a similar text and answer a set of questions
[6] Next steps (e.g., homework, extracurricular activities)	Read text in handout and answer the five questions for next class.	

All plans in the book have been designed for 60-minute lessons, but you could always adapt them to meet your own needs and teaching situation. If you have more or less than 60 minutes for your class, you will have to adapt the learning outcomes (e.g., add more outcomes for a longer lesson), the activities and the materials accordingly. Similarly, you will need to make sure that the assessment covers all of the learning outcomes that you have set up for a particular lesson or lessons.

As you can see from this example, a lesson plan can be a detailed class map for the teacher. However, it is important to keep plans flexible so that you can make space for students' needs and interests. As you become more experienced, you will not probably need so much detail but it is always a good idea to have a plan of what you want your students to do for the reasons we have already discussed. This is also considered in the next reflection activity (RA-IU.6). Once you have finished the activity, you may want to read Bonnie Murray's blog that presents useful questions and tips on how to draw lesson plans (see Further readings list).

Reflection Activity (RA-IU.6)

- How useful do you think lesson plan templates and examples like those in Tables I.2 and I.3 would be for you?
- How detailed do you think you would need your lesson plans to be?

Further reading: Murray's blog

In the previous sections of the unit, we read and reflected upon how learning theories and teaching methods influence lesson design and the choice of activities for your lesson plans. The next step is to think about another important element in the learning and teaching process: the teaching materials. This is what we explore in Section I.4.

I.4 Principles for evaluating, selecting and adapting teaching materials

Once you have decided on the LOs for your lesson (see [1] in the previous section) and the sequence of teaching and learning activities (see [2] in the previous section), you will have to give some consideration to the materials that you need to make those two things happen.

Sometimes, you would also want to work from the materials backwards. This is usually the case when we want students to be exposed to a particular set of materials.

Materials come in many shapes and forms. Instructional materials, sometimes called Teaching/Learning Materials, or TLMs for short, can be in print, audio or video format and are sometimes available on the Internet like YouTube videos.

Sometimes you will be provided with teaching materials for your class (e.g., a book, teaching handouts) that somebody else has already selected for you. Other times, you will be able to choose the materials yourself. Sometimes you will have a combination of both situations. Whichever situation you find yourself in, there are some principles for evaluating and selecting teaching materials that you could follow to help you to choose the right materials for your lesson. But before we examine such principles, let's look at the types of materials more closely.

As we have mentioned, there are different formats for teaching materials. The most typical ones are:

- **Printed materials**: Textbooks, handouts, flyers, study guides, etc.
- **Visual materials**: Blackboard, charts, drawings, flashcards, maps, photographs, real objects (also called 'realia'), and the like
- **Audio-visual materials**: Recordings, video clips, podcasts, filmstrips, presentations, and so on, and
- **Interactive**: Materials that combine text, images, audio, videos and animations.

The format that you choose for your lesson will be partly determined by the LOs, the teaching approaches you follow, the classroom activities you have chosen as well as your students and your teaching context (see CTN-IU.1). So, there should be a link between these three elements in your lesson and lesson plan (see [1], [2] and [3] in the previous section). If you take a look at Table I.3, you will realise that the LOs for that lesson (differentiate opinions from facts; interpret writer's intention; and evaluate arguments presented in texts) all require printed or textual materials for students to read and examine. It is no surprise then that the materials for the lesson include a text in the form of a class handout.

The next reflection activity (RA-IU.7) offers you another opportunity to think about the relationship between these three elements of a lesson.

Reflection Activity (RA-IU.7)

- How would you describe the relationship between [1] LOs, [2] progression of teaching and learning and [3] materials?
- What type of materials would you choose to teach a lesson where the main learning outcome were identifying relevant information in a presentation? Would they differ from those in Table I.3? How? Why?

Now, let's go back to the main principles for evaluating TLMs. Tomlinson (2003, p. 15) has stated that evaluating TLMs is "a procedure that involves measuring the value (or potential value) of a set of learning materials". As you can see, Tomlinson's definition suggests that evaluation happens before you choose the materials. However, other scholars (e.g., McDonough & Shaw, 2013; Rubdy, 2003) have suggested that evaluation can also take place in- and post-use. While they all serve different purposes, in- and post-use evaluations are equally important, in particular when establishing how successful the materials you chose pre-use are while you are still using them in class and for after-class reflection. After-class reflection will help you to decide whether the materials are worth using again or they need to be adapted. We will discuss adapting materials later on in the unit.

The following list of general categories and related questions should guide you through selecting and evaluating the right type of materials:

- **General appearance**: How do the materials look? Do they look well-designed? Attractive to the eye? Are they in bright colours? Are they written in a friendly tone?
- **Layout and design**: Do the layout and design reflect the approach/ methods suggested? Are they consistent in how they look? Is the design cluttered? Do the materials contain illustrations? Do the illustrations support the meanings/purposes of the materials? Are they of good quality? In case of handouts and copies, are they of good quality so that they can be easily read?

- **Teaching approaches**: Are the materials coherent with the teaching approaches suggested? Do they offer students an opportunity to practise what they are learning? In the case of video clips, how do they align with the LOs of the lesson?
- **Activities**: Do they offer a balance of activity types? Do they offer opportunities for different types of learning interaction (e.g., individual, pair and group work)? Are the activities in the materials challenging and engaging at the same time? In the case of audio-recorded materials or video clips, do they require some pre-listening/watching activities? Are these activities included or do you have to design them?
- **Skills**: Do the materials offer opportunities for developing different skills? Is there a balance of skills? Are some skills over-practised at the expense of others?
- **Content**: Are the contents of the materials up-to-date? Are they relevant to the students and the course they are taking? Are they biased? Are they culture-sensitive? Do they aim at making students aware of cultural differences?
- **Teachability and flexibility**: Are the materials easy for teachers to use? Do they provide notes/guidance for teachers? Are materials written at an appropriate level for your students? Can they be adapted easily? Do they provide extra materials (e.g., handouts, links to websites, recorded or video-taped materials)? Can they be used with mixed-ability classes? Can they be used to teach on a one-to-one basis?
- **Assessment**: Do the materials provide tests, quizzes, consolidation units, or progress tests? Do the assessment activities reflect the LOs of the lesson? Are they in line with the levels of the students? Are they easy to implement?

This list of questions should help you to decide whether the materials you wish to select are appropriate. In case the selection of materials has already been made for you, you may still want to use some of these questions to decide whether you will need to adapt them in order to meet your students' needs. We will discuss adapting materials in more detail later in the unit.

The next reflection activity (RA-IU.8) focuses on your views and ideas about evaluating and selecting materials. After you have finished the activity, you may want to read Rubdy's (2003) chapter (see Further readings list).

> **Reflection Activity (RA-IU.8)**
>
> - How useful do you think a list of categories and questions like the ones presented above is?
> - Would you use it for pre-, in- or post-use purposes?
>   Further reading: Rubdy's (2003) chapter on selecting materials

Whether you are selecting materials at the lesson-planning stage (pre-use), evaluating them during your lesson (in-use) or reflecting upon them after your lesson (post-use), you can still use the categories and questions presented above. They will need to be slightly modified to reflect these different stages in the evaluation process. Some such modified questions are shown in Table I.4.

Table I.4 Principles for Evaluating Materials Pre-, In- and Post-use

Categories	Pre-use	In-use	Post-use
General appearance	How do the materials look? Do they look attractive to the eye?	Are the students finding the materials attractive? Engaging?	Have the materials attracted the students' attention? Engaged them?
Layout and design	Is the design cluttered?	Are the students finding the materials confusing?	Can the design be improved easily?
Teaching approaches	Do they offer students an opportunity to practise what they are learning?	Are they helping the students to practise the new learning point?	Have the materials activated previous learning and helped students to acquire new knowledge?
Activities	Do they offer a balance of activity types?	Are the activities providing a variety of practice opportunities?	Have the students been encouraged to combine different activities? Do the activities need complementing?

(Continued)

Categories	Pre-use	In-use	Post-use
Skills	Is there a balance of skills?	Are the materials encouraging students to focus too much on one particular skill? Is this in line with the LOs?	Have they engaged students to use a combination of skills?
Content	Are they culture-sensitive?	Are the students being made aware of cultural issues through the materials?	Can they be made more culture-sensitive?
Teachability and flexibility	Are the materials easy to use?	How easy to teach are they proving to be?	Have they been easy to teach?
Assessment	Are they in line with the levels of the students?	Are students struggling to do the assessment activities?	How valid are the assessment activities in the materials?

Once you have used the materials and reflected upon their role in the classroom, you may decide that they need some adaptation. Adapting existing materials may be a better idea for a new teacher than trying to design teaching materials from scratch. Here is a list of things you need to take into account when adapting existing materials. You may decide the material need adaptation by:

- **Adding**: This means that something is missing from the materials. You may have realised that, for instance, the content needs updating as there have been some recent developments in the field the text refers to (e.g., science developments in relation to the global pandemic), there are not enough exercises provided in the original, or the teaching points in the original materials do not cover everything your students need. As a teacher, you will find yourself doing this very often in your professional career. Teachers often need to supplement the materials they are using. This is a good exercise that will give you the necessary skills to later move on to designing your own materials.

- **Deleting**: Deleting is the opposite of adding, but they usually go together as both processes aim at adjusting the materials to better meet the needs of your students. You usually delete when you find that the materials are really good but they may be too long for the time you have. Or, although relevant to the group of students you are teaching, the content is a bit repetitive and need shortening. Sometimes, there are too many exercises in the original material and some need deleting.
- **Simplifying**: This usually happens when the materials are a good match to your students' needs and the LOs of the lesson but the instructions in the original, for example, are too complex or not clear enough. In other cases, the contents of the materials are relevant and interesting and you think your students will find them motivating but they are a bit too difficult for their level. So, you may want to simplify the content to make it more accessible. In this case, you can simplify the content by reducing the length of its sentences, its grammar (e.g., the tenses, the voice), or any vocabulary items that may be too technical for your students.
- **Re-ordering**: This simply means changing the sequence in which the original materials have been presented. For example, a typical comprehension activity will have the reading or listening text followed by the comprehension activities (e.g., questions, quizzes, True/False statements). However, you may want your students to focus on the comprehension activities before reading or listening to the text. You may thus re-order the materials by putting the comprehension activities first. With materials for teaching presentations or business pitches which usually discuss what is needed to design a presentation and then provide an example, you may want to start with the example so that your students have "a model" to discuss before they learn how to design a presentation themselves.

As you can see, adapting materials have two main purposes. First, by adding, deleting, simplifying or re-ordering, you are making the materials more relevant to your students and thus meeting their learning needs more effectively. Secondly, by adapting materials you are also gaining experience and skills that will help you when you decide to design your own materials. It is important to remember that materials should always be culture-sensitive as we discuss in the following Culture and Technology Note (CTN-IU.2).

Culture & Technology Note (CTN-IU.2)

When you choose, adapt or design materials, you always have to be sensitive to the culture and cultural beliefs of the students you are teaching. This applies to multicultural and multilingual groups of students in particular. Ask the materials questions such as:

- Could the language and/or pictures in the materials cause offence to any of the students?
- Are the materials (its contents, language, illustrations) gender-biased?
- Are they respectful and inclusive?

Technology can help you to answer such questions. It is important that you research the culture and cultural beliefs of the students you are teaching so that the teaching materials you choose are respectful, compassionate and inclusive.

I.5 Assessing learning

Assessment is not a simple matter and all teachers, whether they are new or experienced, find assessing learning a bit of a challenge. However, there are certain principles (e.g., linking assessment to LOs; elements [1] and [5] in our lesson template in section I.3 above) that you can consider to guide you through assessing learner performance. The following list shows key principles for assessing learning.

Assessment will be:

- **Valid**
  This principle refers to the fact that any task or activity that you design or implement to assess your students' learning should measure whether and to what extent students have achieved the LOs of a particular unit or course. This may form part of the 'success criteria' included in your lesson plan (see Table I.2). As we have already mentioned, it is essential that assessment be closely linked to LOs. In other words, assessment should measure **whether** and **to what extent** your students have achieved LOs and **nothing else**.
- **Reliable**
  Reliability is the condition by which an assessment instrument (e.g., test, quiz) measures a particular ability of a student **over and over**

yielding the **same or very similar results** each time. Reliability results from having specific, clear and consistently applied assessment or success criteria, the fourth element in our lesson planning that we discussed in section I.3 above, and procedures that are followed every time an assessment instrument is used.

- **Equitable**

  An assessment instrument is equitable when it recognises that different students have different learning styles and preferences and so it **gives all students the same chances** of demonstrating whether and to what extent they have achieved the LOs. Therefore, assessment should consider different assessment methods (e.g., quizzes, presentations, project work) by which students can demonstrate learning and should avoid over-dependency on one particular method (e.g., essays or written reports).

- **Explicit and transparent**

  This double principle refers to the fact that before any assessment takes place, students should understand the procedures and requirements of the assessment and how their performance will be marked (see success criteria [4] in section I.3 above). This is achieved by **explaining such procedures and requirements** to the students and making the **success or marking criteria accessible** to them. It also refers to making feedback on student performance related to the LOs and the success criteria.

- **Part of the learning process**

  Assessment should inform learning. For this to happen, assessment should not only be summative (at the end of the course) but also formative (during the course). Formative assessment, as we will discuss in more detail below, will give students the opportunity to modify their existing performance to better achieve the LOs.

- **Efficient**

  This principle refers to the **ease** with which an assessment instrument can be administered and corrected so that marks and feedback are provided to the students in a timely fashion. This reinforces the idea that assessment should be part of the learning process. It also helps to avoid over-assessing any particular LO at the expense of others.

Now that we have discussed the key principles for assessing learning, you may want to turn to the next activity for reflection (RA-IU.9) to think more carefully about these principles.

Reflection Activity (RA-IU.9)

Using your experience as a learner or a teacher, answer these questions:

- How familiar are you with these principles for assessing learning?
- Do you recognise them as being part of the assessment tasks you have been involved in as a student or have designed as a teacher?
- How important do you think they are to inform your present or future assessment practices?

We often use two forms of assessment: formative and summative assessment.

Formative assessment aims to monitor rather than assess student learning and provide ongoing feedback to both students and teachers. Feedback, rather than marks, is a key element in formative assessment. Some call this type of assessment "assessment **for** learning" rather than assessment of learning (see the Cambridge Assessment blog in the list of Further readings below). Formative assessment helps students to identify what they can do well as well as what they need to still do or learn in order to achieve the LOs and be successful in learning.

There are a number of benefits of formative assessment. First, it can help students to improve their learning and performance before they are formally assessed (summative assessment). Important as summative assessment is, it gives no opportunity for students to improve on their past performance. Secondly, formative assessment also enables students to take control over their own learning process, helping them to become more independent leaners, and to take corrective action before they are assessed summatively. It also provides information to the teacher about what his/her students are struggling with and what content and skills may need further practice.

In order to implement formative assessment effectively, you need to make sure that:

- your students understand what role it plays in the learning process and what they can do with the feedback they receive so that they can take action before they are formally assessed, and

- your formative assessment instruments feed into the summative assessment activities or tasks so that there is a clear link between the two. For instance, before a presentation assessment, you could ask your students to share their presentation drafts with you and with the other students so that they can get formative feedback and make necessary adjustments to their performance before they present formally, and are assessed summatively.

Summative assessment, on the other hand, aims to evaluate what students have learnt and how well they have performed on a particular course. This is assessment **of**, rather than for, learning. It often means high stakes for the students (e.g., to enter a university, to get a job, to progress to the next level) and so in their eyes it may be more important than formative assessment. As we have discussed, it is essential, however, that you show your students the value of both types of assessment and how they relate to one another.

Formative assessment is forward-looking whilst summative assessment is backward-looking. It is, therefore, important that you achieve a balance between the two. Formative assessment provides a risk-free environment where your students can experiment and learn from their experiences and your and other students' feedback. Summative assessment, on the other hand, provides students with a final mark that reflects how and to what extent they have achieved the LOs of the course they have just completed.

The following Extension task (ET-IU.5) presents a video clip on the differences between these two forms of assessment.

Extension Task (ET-IU.5)

Use the URL provided below to watch **video clip ET-IU.5**, which discusses the main differences between formative and summative assessment. As you watch, think about these questions:

- What is the main purpose of using each of these two types of assessment?
- When do these assessments normally happen?
- How do students benefit from these types of assessment?
- How do teachers use these types of assessment?
  https://worldsofenglish.com/workplace-skills-extension-tasks/

The following Reflection activity (RA-IU.10) provides you with an opportunity to reflect on the role and place of both types of assessments in your teaching practices. This activity is complemented by the Culture & Technology Note (CTN-IU.3) that follows.

Reflection Activity (RA-IU.10)

Think about your experience of assessing learning before you answer the following questions:

- What is your experience with both types of assessment?
- Do you also think that summative is more important than formative assessment?
- How can you address this situation?

Culture & Technology Note (CTN-IU.3)

As we discussed in the first Culture & Technology Note (CTN-IU.1), the culture of the country and of the institution where you work may determine the type of assessment you will be expected to implement. In some educational traditions around the world and for some types of courses, and therefore for their students as well, summative assessment is all that matters. However, as a teacher you can also implement formative assessment without losing sight of the importance given to summative assessment in such contexts or situations.

Technology can actually help you with the design and implementation of formative assessment instruments. There are a number of quiz creation tools (e.g., ClassMarker, Raptivity) that allow you to create and customise quizzes and tests that can provide students with formative feedback.

You could also ask your students to video-record their task (e.g., presentation practice), for instance, on a smartphone and send you their video clips for feedback. Another alternative is to use survey design tools (e.g., Microsoft forms) to create multiple choice tests that your students can submit and even get feedback on their performance.

Another aspect of assessment that is as important to keep in mind relates to marking or success criteria (see also Tables I.2 and I.3). It is always a good idea to design a set of marking criteria at least for the module if there is no time to design one for each lesson. The template below (Table I.5) shows an example of marking criteria that, like the template for lesson plans, you can adapt to match your teaching needs.

Table 1.5 A Template for a Set of Marking Criteria

Skills/ Competencies	Proficient user		Independent user	
	(C2) (100%–80%)	(C1) (79%–60%)	(B2) (59%–50%)	B1 (49%–40%)
Understanding of input in various forms (spoken, written, etc.)	Can understand practically any type of input.	Can understand demanding texts.	Can understand complex as well as technical ideas.	Can understand key points in input.
Responding to situations	Can respond to almost any situation with ease and fluency.	Can respond to situations with ease.	Can respond to situations with certain degree of ease.	Can produce simple responses to basic situations.
Reading written texts of different kinds	Can read and understand virtually any type of texts.	Can read and understand a variety of demanding texts.	Can read and understand complex as well as technical texts.	Can read and understand basic written texts.
Speaking in different situations	Can interact with fluency and precision in a number of situations.	Can interact effectively in a number of situations.	Can interact in a number of situations with a degree of fluency.	Can describe simple experiences.
Producing a variety of written texts	Can produce complex texts from a variety of sources.	Can produce clear and well-structured texts.	Can produce texts in detail and with supporting viewpoints.	Can produce a number of basic written texts.

Marking criteria should make it clear to the students skills and competencies they should demonstrate proficiency in for the module or lesson, and how their performance in such skills and competencies is going to be assessed qualitatively (feedback) or quantitatively (marks). As Table I.5 shows, skills and competencies are normally laid out in the first column on the left-hand side, and marks/feedback on performance on the top, across the table. This set of criteria has been designed based on The Common European Framework of Reference for Languages.

I.6 Summary

In this unit, we have discussed and reflected upon the key principles for teaching and learning that will help you to make informed decisions about your teaching practices. At the same time, these principles will guide you through reflecting upon your practices before, during and after teaching. All this could inform your professional development as a teacher.

These principles can be represented as forming a teaching-and-learning cycle which includes the four elements we have discussed in the unit:

1. **reflecting upon teaching and learning principles** that apply to what you are planning to teach
2. **designing lessons** where these reflections are put into practice
3. **selecting materials** that you think will facilitate the elements of the lesson you have planned, and
4. **assessing** whether and to what extent learning took place.

This cycle is illustrated in Figure I.2. These considerations will be supported, and sometimes even determined, by the culture of your students and the institution you are working for, and the technological affordances you will have at your disposal.

It is important to keep in mind that learning and teaching form a cyclical process. As you can see from Figure I.2, after a class has been delivered, you can always go back to reflecting upon both how the class went and whether your choices were appropriate or need adjusting.

And don't worry if the lesson you planned, the materials you chose or the assessment instrument you used did not actually work as expected.

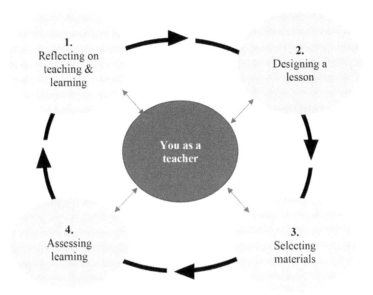

Figure I.2 The Teaching-and-Learning Cycle

What is important here is that you take time to reflect upon what has happened and keep a record of things that really worked and of those that need adjusting. After each lesson, you can always take corrective action based on your reflection. After all, you are at the centre of the cycle, orchestrating how learning can be best facilitated for your students.

This is the cycle around which *Teaching Communication, Skills and Competencies for the International Workplace* has been designed. In the next units, you will find that the four stages are followed to cover the different skills that your students will need for successful communication in the international workplace.

Further readings: An annotated bibliography

Bloom, B. S. (1956). *Taxonomy of educational objectives, handbook 1: Cognitive domain*. Addison-Wesley Longman.

Although published in the second half of the 1950s, this taxonomy is still being used to design learning outcomes and pedagogical materials. Bloom's Taxonomy uses a multi-tiered scale ranging from less to more complex (remembering, understanding, applying, analysing, evaluating, creating) to represent the level of expertise required to achieve each learning outcome in a measurable way. Applying this taxonomy will help you to select appropriate classroom techniques and assessment tasks for the course.

In 2001 a revised version of Bloom's taxonomy was edited by Lorin W. Anderson and David Krathwohl under the title: *A taxonomy for learning, teaching, and assessing: A revision of Bloom's taxonomy of educational objectives*. The revised version presents a more dynamic approach to cognitive activity.

Getting started with assessment for learning https://cambridge-community.org.uk/professional-development/gswafl/index.html

This blog offers an extensive introduction to assessment for learning (AFL) or formative assessment. It provides a thorough discussion of what AFL is, the processes in it, and how it relates to summative assessment; all illustrated with a plethora of examples.

Dewey, J. (1910). *How we think*. Heath and Co.

This is John Dewey's classic book. The central premise of the book, and Dewey's seminal contribution to education, lies in what he termed 'critical thinking' and/or 'reflective thinking'. Although critical thinking and reflection play an important role in many professions, it has become one of the pivotal activities in which teachers in particular engage with their teaching practices, and the basis for their professional development.

Fink, L. D. (2013). *Creating significant learning experiences: An integrated approach to designing college courses*. Wiley.

This is the updated version of Fink's classic which provides invaluable conceptual and procedural tools for instructional design. In its practical section, Fink presents a step-by-step guide on how to implement his taxonomy of significant learning to produce powerful learning experiences, making learning a more meaningful experience for students.

McDonough, J. and Shaw, C. (2013). *Materials and methods in ELT*. Blackwell.

This is a practical guide for those interested in evaluating and designing instructional materials. It features sections on IT applied to teaching and technology for materials design. It is particularly useful for ideas for the under-resourced classroom.

Murray, B. P. (n.d.) The new teacher's guide to creating lesson plans. https://www.scholastic.com/teachers/articles/teachingcontent/new-teachers-guide-creating-lesson-plans/

In this blog, Bonnie Murray presents eight useful questions any teacher should ask before sitting down to create a lesson plan and some very useful tips on how to go about doing it.

Richards, J. C. (n.d.). Communicative language teaching today. https://www.professorjackrichards.com/wp-content/uploads/communicativelanguage teaching-today-v2.pdf

Jack C. Richards offers a historical overview of the origins, development and applications of Communicative Language Teaching (CLT) since its beginnings in the 1970s and how it has influenced teaching practices until the present day. Although it focuses on language teaching, many of the principles discussed also apply to teaching communication skills for the workplace.

Rubdy, R. (2003). Selection of materials. In: Tomlinson, B. (Ed.), *Developing materials for language teaching* (pp. 37–57). Continuum.

In this chapter, Rani Rubdy discusses the aims of pre-use evaluation and presents a number of arguments as to what both teachers and learners can do with learning materials in the classroom.

Sword, R. (November 16, 2020). *Effective communication in the classroom: Skills for teachers.* https://www.highspeedtraining.co.uk/hub/communication-skills-for-teachers/

In this blog, Rosalyn Sword outlines the key reasons why classroom communication is so important for both effective teaching and effective learning. The blog discusses and illustrates some useful strategies that teachers can use to help students to achieve their communicative aims.

Tomlinson, B. (2003). *Developing materials for language teaching.* Continuum.

This volume offers a comprehensive coverage of the main processes and procedures involved in developing instructional materials. It looks at these processes and procedures from the perspective of both developers and users of materials, and shows practical ways of designing and evaluating materials.

Wen, X., Elicker, J., McMullen, M. (2011). Early childhood teachers' curriculum beliefs: Are they consistent with observed classroom practices? *Early*

Education and Development, 22(6): 945–969. https://doi.org/10.1080/1040
9289.2010.507495

In this study, 58 preschool teachers completed a survey about their
professional backgrounds and curriculum beliefs before their classroom practices were observed. Most participating teachers endorsed
child-initiated learning beliefs strongly. However, the most frequently-
observed teacher behaviours in their classrooms included: giving direc-
tions to children, responding to children's initiations, and engaging
in non-interactive classroom management activities. The authors concluded that teachers' beliefs and observed teaching practices correlated
rather weakly.

Wilcox-Herzog, A. (2002). Is there a link between teachers' beliefs and behaviors? *Early Education and Development*, 13(1): 81–106. https://doi.
org/10.1207/s15566935eed1301_5

In her study, Amanda Wilcox-Herzog examined the link between beliefs and behaviours in primary school teachers. Forty-seven teachers
completed a self-report questionnaire and their teaching practices were
assessed via videotape. The results showed that there was not a close relationship between teachers' beliefs and their actions in the classroom.

Part II
Preliminaries

Unit 1

Teaching skills and competencies for job hunting

Learning Outcomes

By the end of the unit, you should be able to:

- identify key skills and competencies needed for job hunting
- use data collection tools for finding out your students' learning needs
- make pedagogical decisions about designing lessons, selecting materials, and assessing job-hunting skills and competencies, and
- select effective vocabulary items required for successful job hunting.

1.1 Introducing job hunting

Today's international job market is extremely competitive, and, like many local markets, it is very sensitive to uncertainty periods and turbulent times (e.g., a global pandemic) which can have a significant impact on global labour markets (International Labour Organisation, 2022).

This makes it imperative that students wishing to work internationally are equipped with a strong set of skills, competencies and strategies that will help them to achieve their goals. Finding a job on the international job market requires careful planning, great perseverance and complete dedication.

DOI: 10.4324/9781003283515-4

Potential applicants have to be well-prepared from the moment they start hunting for a job. To this end, they will need to be able to search strategically for a relevant position (e.g., the place where to search, the industry they want to work in), become effective and critical readers (e.g., what are international organisations really looking for?), and become truly aware of their own skills and competencies (e.g., what can they offer? What do they still need to do before applying?).

This unit introduces the key skills and competencies your students will need to have or develop for finding a job in the international workplace. As these heavily depend on their ability to read and write strategically, the first aim of the unit is to suggest different ways in which you can help them to become critical readers and strategic writers.

The second aim of the unit is to discuss the importance of finding out what your students already know, and what skills and competencies they need in order to achieve specific learning goals. This is especially important in the case of job-experienced students (students with previous work experience), although it will also be of benefit to pre-experience students (students with no previous work experience). The unit focuses on two data collection tools you can use: Needs Assessment (NA) and SWOT (Strength, Weaknesses, Opportunities and Threats) Analysis.

Before doing the activities for the unit, you may want to begin by reflecting upon your own job-hunting experiences. Activity RA-1.1 includes a few questions which will guide your reflection process. Reflecting upon your own personal experiences can also help you to become aware of what your students may need in order to be successful when searching for a job themselves.

Reflection Activity (RA-1.1)

Based on your previous job-hunting experiences, think how you would answer the following questions. You may want to make brief notes about your answers.

- How did you go about hunting for this teaching job?
- How did you learn about it? Where was it advertised?
- Did you consider your professional goals before applying for the job?
- Did you do any kind of exercises or analyses to determine how your skills matched the job requirements?
- If you did, what did you learn from the process?

Now that you have reflected upon your job-hunting experiences, you may want to compare your own experiences with how other people see the process of searching for a job. Extension task ET-1.1 provides a short video about the processes involved in searching and applying for a job.

Extension Task (ET-1.1)

Use the URL provided below to watch **video clip ET-1.1**, which discusses the stages involved in job hunting and job application:

https://worldsofenglish.com/workplace-skills-extension-tasks/

As you watch the clip, think about the similarities and differences between your views and experiences and those expressed in the video. You can use the table below to guide your comparison.

Process/Step	From your own experience	Offered in the video
Formal aspects		
Goals		
Story/Narrative		
Documents		

After having reflected upon your experiences (Reflection activity RA-1.1) and compared them with the views of other job hunters (Extension task ET-1.1), you are now ready to identify the key skills and competencies needed for successful job hunting.

1.2 Key skills and competencies for job hunting

This section of the unit explores three steps needed prior to planning a lesson to teach skills for job searching:

- identifying key skills and competencies for job hunting (Section 1.2.1)
- collecting information about your students (Section 1.2.2), and
- turning skills and competencies into LOs (Section 1.2.3).

1.2.1 Identifying key skills and competencies for job hunting

It is important to differentiate between the terms 'skills' and 'competencies':

- **skills** are the specific abilities that your students will need to do something well. For instance, being able to speak English fluently is an important skill to succeed in the international workplace. Skills are often divided into <u>hard skills</u> (e.g., coding for computer programming) and *soft skills* (e.g., effective verbal communication)
- **competencies** refer to the necessary knowledge and expected behaviours required to do something well. For example, "effective planning" is an essential competency for managing a project well.

In the case of job hunting, the following set of skills and competencies are essential

Table 1.1 Key Skills and Competencies for Job Hunting

Skills/Competencies	Needed for
1. Searching strategically **(skills)**	**Looking for a job**
2. Reading **(skill)**	**Reading job ads**
3. Being an effective reader **(competency)**	**Identifying key requirements** for a particular job
4. Critical reading **(competency)**	Reading job ads **critically** (e.g., who the advertiser is, what they expect from applicants, what they're offering)
5. Writing **(skill)**	Making a list of **your existing skills**
6. Matching skills and competencies with requirements **(competency)**	Comparing **existing and required skills/ competencies**

You may want to add other related skills and competencies to the list presented above to better meet the needs of the group of students you are teaching. If you are teaching a new group or this is the first time you teach English for the international workplace, you will need to collect information about your students before you actually design your lessons for them. This is what we discuss in the next section.

1.2.2 Collecting information about your students

There are a number of tools that you can use to collect information about the skills and competencies for job hunting that your students already have or need to develop. Apart from information about what they know and need to know, these tools can also be used to provide you with information about your students' learning styles, preferences and motivations. One such tool is what is known as a 'Needs Analysis' or 'NA' for short.

As its name suggests, a NA exercise can help you to identify what the learning needs of your students are and, possibly more importantly, what they are capable of doing, what the required or desired level of linguistic performance is, and how motivated about learning they are. Some people call this 'Training Needs Analysis' (TNA), which is finding out the existing 'training gap' (target performance minus present performance) for a particular person or group. This is why collecting information about your students (e.g., their level, needs and aspirations, motivations) is an important step before you set up the learning outcomes for a lesson.

There are different types of NA exercises that range from very simple (e.g., giving students a list of course aims for them to prioritise) to more complex (e.g., a survey for them to complete about skills and competencies, learning preferences, and motivation levels). Whichever type of NA you decide to use, it is important to note that conducting a NA with your students is also part of helping them to build their awareness and autonomy as learners. A NA can provide students with valuable information about themselves (e.g., their language level, what they need to learn, how motivated they feel) which they can use to make decisions about their own learning.

The typical format of NA exercises include (in order of complexity):

- Lists of items to rank
- Surveys
- Questionnaires
- Focus groups
- Observations

The following are two examples of NA exercises that aim to find out students' views on the importance of a particular set of skills and competencies.

Table 1.2 A NA Exercise Based on Course Skills and Competencies

Needs Analysis (NA) exercise	Student's name	
These are the main skills and competencies that you will learn on this course. Read the list and rank each item from 1 to 9 in order of importance (e.g., 1 = most important, 9 = least important). Then, add the contexts/places in which you think you will need the items ranked.		
Skills/Competencies	Rank	Contexts/places of use
Reading general texts		
Becoming a critical reader		
Writing application letters		
Writing reports		
Preparing for interviews		
Answering interview questions effectively		
Making presentations		
Listening for specific information		
Negotiating		

After your students have finished doing the exercise, you may want to discuss their answers either on a one-to-one basis or as a whole class. The following example of NA shows a more complex exercise based on a survey. The type you decide to use will depend on the level of your students, the time available, and, in particular, the possibility of using the NA results to shape your course. If you are unable to use the results to inform course decisions, it may not be a good idea to ask your students to do the exercise as they may feel frustrated to discover that their views and opinions have not been taken into account for designing the course they are taking.

Table 1.3 A NA Exercise Based on a Survey

Needs Analysis (NA) exercise	Student's name:
For each of the following statements, tick the option (1 = very much, 4 = not at all) that best represents your learning needs.	

Skill/Competency	Options			
	1	2	3	4
1. Reading highly technical texts				
2. Writing technical texts or specific reports				
3. Making highly specialised presentations				
4. Listening to technical presentations				

You can also ask your students to work in pairs to conduct the NA exercise themselves. This is called 'Peer Needs Analysis' (Anderson, 2017). As Anderson suggests, Peer Needs Analysis can provide an opportunity for meaningful communication among learners, and foster understanding of other students' needs and interests.

Another typical tool for collecting information about your students is what is known as a 'SWOT analysis'. Although mostly used to analyse businesses, this tool can also be applied to find out the **Strengths** and **Weaknesses** of students, and the **Opportunities** and **Threats** that learning a particular skills or competency can afford them. Here is a more detailed explanation of the components of a SWOT analysis for teaching purposes:

- **Strengths** can refer to what a student can do (skills), what they know or behaviours they already possess (competencies), courses they have taken, and experiences they have had. These are considered "internal" to the student.
- **Weaknesses**, on the other hand, refer to what the student is still unable to do, knowledge they haven't yet acquired, experiences they haven't had so far. These are also considered "internal" to the student.
- **Opportunities** are "external" elements or situations that offer a student the possibility to turn weaknesses into strengths. For instance, a course may offer them the opportunity to acquire knowledge or experiences they still don't have.

- **Threats**, as opposed to opportunities, are negative situations that can put the student or their opportunities in danger. Other applicants for the same job, for example, can pose a threat, especially if they are stronger candidates. Threats are also considered "external" to the student.

A SWOT analysis will help your students to find out both their strengths and weaknesses and decide what opportunities they may need to turn the latter into the former and the possible threats they may face when applying for a new job (see Figure 1.1). Different from a NA exercise, a SWOT analysis examines broader skills or competencies. There are different SWOT analysis templates. Table 1.4 shows one of them which you can use with or adapt for your students.

As shown in Figure 1.1, one advantage of doing a SWOT analysis is that it may help your students understand what opportunities (1) they need (e.g., take a course) to turn a weakness (2) (e.g., lack of certain skill) into a strength (3), and use their new strength to fight against a possible threat (4). It will also show them the level of control they can exercise over each of the areas. This is exemplified in Table 1.5.

Table 1.5 shows another example of a SWOT analysis, this time for negotiating skills.

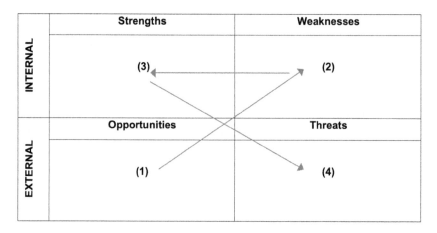

Figure 1.1 Turning Weaknesses into Strengths

Table 1.4 A SWOT Analysis Template

INTERNAL	Strengths	Weaknesses
	I can... 1. _____ 2. _____ I know... 3. _____ 4. _____ I have experience in... 5. _____ 6. _____ My attitude towards this is... 7. _____ 8. _____	I am unable to... 1. _____ 2. _____ I would need to know... 3. _____ 4. _____ I need experience in... 5. _____ 6. _____

EXTERNAL	Opportunities	Threats
	I can learn to (see weaknesses 1–4 above) by... 1. _____ 2. _____ I can gain experience in (see weaknesses 5-6 above) by... 3. _____ 4. _____	The possible threats are 1. _____ 2. _____ 3. _____ 4. _____

Table 1.5 A SWOT Analysis for Negotiation Skills

Negotiation Skills			
S **Strengths**	**W** **Weaknesses**	**O** **Opportunities**	**T** **Threats**
• Good skills I have developed	• What I still don't do well or don't know about negotiating	• What I can learn on this course	• What others can do better
• What I do well when negotiating	• Skills or competencies I still lack	• Practice in a safe environment before real life situations	• Negative results from previous negotiations
INTERNAL TO THE STUDENT		**EXTERNAL TO THE STUDENT**	
More <<<<<<<<<<<<<<<<<<<CONTROL>>>>>>>>>>>>>>>>>>>>>>Less			

We can now make a pause here to reflect upon these tools for collecting information about your students. Reflection activity (RA-1.2) presents three questions to help your process of reflection.

Reflection Activity (RA-1.2)

Thinking about the NA exercises and SWOT analysis shown above, how:

- useful do you think they would be for planning your classes?
- interested would your students be in doing them?
- would you use the results to inform your pedagogical decisions?

To the activities and tasks of the previous unit, "Language corner" sections are added to this and the rest of the units. The aim of the language corner is to highlight some of the key language items (e.g., vocabulary, collocations, structures) your students will need to do the tasks suggested. You may want to teach these items before the activities you design for your students, or highlight these if they appear in the materials you use.

The first Language Corner activity (LC-1.1) should help you to identify such key language items in relation to NA exercises and SWOT analyses. When teaching or revising the items with your students, you may want to bring their attention to the typical collocations (group of words that usually go together) and frequent structural elements associated with 'NA exercises' and 'SWOT analyses', as suggested in the language corner. You may also ask your students to do their own search for typical collocations and structures. One online collocation dictionary that may help them with their search is **Ozdic** (https://ozdic.com/). If you ask your students to use a collocation dictionary (e.g., Ozdic), you may want them to share and discuss the results of their searches with the rest of the class.

Language Corner (LC-1.1)

In order to complete and discuss the results of NA exercises and SWOT analyses, your students will probably need some language items that are specific to them. The list below provides some such items, but you may also want to add a few more that you think will be relevant to your own teaching context.

- To conduct/do an NA exercise/a SWOT analysis
- To identify/find out strengths, weaknesses, opportunities, threats
- To become aware of/conscious of
- To make someone aware of
- To address/meet the needs of
- (At the moment,) I am able to (verb)/capable of (verb+ING)
- According to the results, I should
- What I need to learn
- (I think) My strengths/weaknesses are/lie in
- (I believe) There are (good) opportunities for
- The main threats (I can see) are
- I feel (highly) motivated to/(very) interested in
- I like/prefer learning/I'd rather learn by

Collocations

You may want your students to search for collocations for the following key words:

- **Strength** (e.g., adjectives = great, real, etc.; verbs = gain, play to; preposition = in)
- **Weakness**
- **Opportunity**
- **Threat**
- **Motivation**

Structural elements

- **Simple present** (e.g., I feel....)
- **Would rather** + Verb (e.g., I'd rather learn by...)
- **Expressions of tentativeness** (e.g., I think I should...)

It is now time for our next extension task. Extension task ET-1.2 presents a video clip, where Tim Slade from http://timslade.com/ defines NA, explains its benefits, and describes how to conduct one.

Extension Task (ET-1.2)

Use the URL provided below to watch **video clip ET-1.2**, where Tim Slade from http://timslade.com/ explains how to conduct a NA. As you watch the clip, think of the following questions:

- According to Tim Slade, what is a NA?
- Why is it important to conduct one before designing a lesson or a course?
- What are the three stages for conducting a NA?

https://worldsofenglish.com/workplace-skills-extension-tasks/

You can also use social media applications to collect information about your students. However, if you decide to use any of the available applications (e.g., Facebook, WeChat), you should take cultural and social conventions into account. The first Culture and Technology Note (CTN-1.1) of the unit offers a few tips on using social media to collect information about your students.

Culture and Technology Note (CTN-1.1)

Besides using the typical social media platforms such as Facebook, WhatsApp and WeChat in the class to improve communication among the students and between students and you, these applications can also be used to conduct surveys which may feed into your NA or SWOT analyses. A Facebook, WhatsApp or WeChat account can be set up for your class and ask students to vote for a lesson or a particular aspect of a lesson they consider interesting or important, or for a specific skill they want to acquire or develop. This could be done outside class time to give you the opportunity to plan ahead.

A few tips to remember when you decide to use social media in your class:

- **Review local policies**. Familiarise yourself with the national and school policies about the use of social media in class or with students
- **Discuss your ideas** with your line manager in order to explore institutional policies in connection with using social media
- Keep in mind **privacy issues**. It is always a good idea to discuss privacy settings with your students before making a final decision. Always set up the account as **private** so that only the students (invited members) will have access to its contents
- **Be transparent**. Always be clear about the aims and purposes of setting up a class account and discuss this with your students
- **Opting in/out**. Always provide an option for students to opt in and out of the group. Let them initiate the request for joining the class social media account.
- **Protect information**. Do not share any of the contents or discussions with anyone outside the class group.

So far, we have discussed the key skills and competencies for searching for a job and explored various tools you can use to collect information about your students' learning needs. It is time now to discuss how we can turn the skills and competencies we have identified into LOs for your lessons.

1.2.3 Learning outcomes (LOs)

As we discussed in the previous unit (see Section I.3 of the Introductory Unit), LOs specify what you want your learners to be able to do by the end of a lesson. So, turning skills and competencies into LOs requires that you give some consideration to questions such as:

- what do my students already know?
- what do they need to know?
- how do they work best (e.g., by themselves, in pairs or small groups)?
- how motivated are they?

These four questions can be answered by looking at the results of your NA exercise or SWOT analysis. The results will tell you what your students can do already and what they need to learn to achieve a specific LO, their preferred way of learning and how motivated they are to learn or further develop the required skills or competencies.

So, a set of LOs based on the skills and competencies listed in Table 1.1 would look something like:

By the end of the lesson/unit, students should be able to

- search for job ads strategically in appropriate places
- read job ads critically and effectively
- write a list of their existing skills and competencies and compare them with those required for the job, and
- decide what they need to do to develop the required skills they still do not have.

These can be further broken into smaller LOs (e.g., write a list of their existing skills and competencies relevant to a chosen job; compare existing skills and competencies with those required for the job), depending on the level of your students and the time available.

It is always important to keep in mind the close relationship between the key skills and competencies for a particular task (e.g., job hunting) and the LOs you want to set up for a lesson. Table 1.6 shows such relationship together with sample questions that have facilitated the link between the two.

Table 1.6 Relationship between Skills/Competencies and LOs

Skills/ Competencies	Questions	Resulting LOs
Searching for job ads strategically	Where do they normally look for jobs? Do they need to look somewhere else depending on their own skills and expectations?	By the end of the lesson, you should be able to search for job ads in the right places.
Reading critically	Can they read critically and for detail? Can they identify key elements in a job ad?	By the end of the lesson, you should be able to read job ads critically by identifying key elements in them.
Listing own existing skills and competencies	Are they aware of the relevant skills and competencies they already have? Can they list such skills and competencies?	By the end of the lesson, you should be able to write a list of your existing skills and competencies.
Identifying required skills and competencies	Can they identify the skills and competencies required for a specific job?	By the end of the lesson, you should be able to identify the skills required to do a specific job.
Comparing existing skills with those required for a particular job	How do their existing skills and competencies compare with those required for the job they have chosen?	By the end of the lesson, you should be able to compare your existing skills and competencies with those required for the job you have chosen to apply.

1.3 Designing lessons for job hunting

Before starting to think of a lesson plan for teaching job-hunting skills and competencies, you may want to review the main theories, approaches and techniques we discussed in the Introductory Unit (see Section I.2). This will help you to choose the most appropriate components for your lesson. The following list of questions should also help:

- how do you think your students **would best learn** job-hunting skills and competencies? (e.g., In a mechanistic way? By getting engaged in tasks with other students?)
- as a teacher, how **would you like to teach** these skills and competencies? (e.g., By providing your students with a series of stimuli for them to respond to?)
- in your view, are there **specific activities that would facilitate** learning or developing such skills and competencies more effectively? (e.g., Problem-solving tasks? Group work?)

Once you have given some thought to these questions, you will be in a better position to make decisions about how to design your lesson plans. You may find the template for lesson planning introduced in the Introductory Unit (see Section I.3) also helpful in guiding your decisions.

Table 1.7 shows one example of what a lesson for teaching job-hunting skills and competencies would look like.

Table 1.7 A Lesson Plan for Teaching "Reading Job Ads Critically"

Course/Module: Communication Skills for the International Workplace	Year group:	Date:
[1] Learning outcomes for reading job ads critically		
By the end of the lesson, students should be able to: (A) read job ads critically and summarise the key aspects in them (B) fully understand job requirements and make lists of such requirements (C) compare required and existing skills and competencies.		

(Continued)

[2] Progression of teaching & learning		[3] Strategies/ Materials
Duration: 10 minutes	Introduction: T presents students (Sts) with a few job ads and asks them how they would go about reading them.	Eliciting Sts' previous knowledge/experience in reading job ads
Duration: 40 minutes	Activity 1: 1. Sts identify what they think the key information pieces in the ads are 2. Class discussion of 1 (Why do they think this information is important?) 3. Agreement on 2	1. Working on job ads individually/ Handout 1 2–3. Class discussion and agreement/ Handout 1 4. Answering specific questions/ Handout 2 5. Class discussion and individual writing/ Handout 2 6. Profiling skills and competencies/ Handout 3 7. Writing a list/ Handout 3
	Activity 2: 4. Sts identify the specific requirements for the job in each ad (e.g., formal qualifications, skills, languages) 5. Sts discuss their choices and write a summary of key requirements in ads	
	Activity 3: 6. Sts make a list of their own relevant skills/competencies 7. Sts compare required and existing skills and competencies (profiling) and draw a comparison list.	

Duration: 10 minutes	Conclusion: Sts wrap up by summarising what they did in class, highlighting new knowledge they have acquired.	Class verbal summary
[4] Success criteria	• To be able to read job ads critically • To be able to sum-marise key informa-tion in ads verbally and in writing • To be able to make lists of job requirements • To be able to com-pare required and existing skills and competencies.	[5] Assessment Sts will do the same activities on a similar ad and answer a set of questions
[6] Next steps (e.g., homework, extracurricular activities)	Read a new set of ads and choose one they are interested in. They should be prepared to answer questions for next class.	

For the activities in the lesson plan shown in Table 1.7, your students will probably need some specific language items. Language Corner LC-1.2 provides some such items but you may also want to add a few more that you think will be relevant to your own teaching context.

Language Corner (LC-1.2)

- I (normally/usually) search for job ads (place) (e.g., **on** the inter-net, **in** the local newspaper)
- I pay (close) attention **to**
- I am (particularly) interested **in**
- The job requires/demands
- The (key) requirements **of** the job are
- **For** this (particular) job it's necessary to have

- A (leading) company based **in** (city/country)
- They are looking **for**
- To fill a position/the position **of**
- If you want/wanted to apply **for** this job, you will/would need
- (I think/believe) I am good **at**
- To specialise **in**
- To be able to provide/lead/work with
- Keep **in** mind that
- My list is/shows
- To make an application (**through** the company's website)
- I have learnt that

Collocations

As noted in LC-1.1, you may want to draw your students' attention to specific collocations such as

- **pay attention to**
- **keep in mind**
- **be good at**

Structural elements

- **simple present** (e.g., I normally search for jobs in...)
- **present progressive** (e.g., They are looking for...)
- **present perfect** (e.g., I have learnt that...)
- **conditionals** (e.g., If you want to....; If you wanted to...)
- **prepositions** (e.g., I am good **at**).

The next Reflection activity (RA-1.3) provides you with an opportunity to reflect upon the relationship between NA, teaching approaches, LOs and lesson planning. To this end, a list of questions has been provided to aid your reflection.

Reflection Activity (RA-1.3)

- How can the results of a NA exercise inform your decisions about teaching approaches and classroom techniques?
- Where would you obtain information that can feed into the LOs of a lesson?
- How are LOs and lesson planning related?

So far, we have looked at the relationship between the components of the pedagogical strategies we implement when teaching a particular lesson. A central element in all this is the LOs. The next extension task (ET-1.3) discusses how the taxonomy developed by Bloom (see Introductory Unit) has been revised and can be adapted to account for the latest developments in technology.

Extension Task (ET-1.3)

Use the URL provided below to watch **video clip ET-1.3** which describes how Bloom's taxonomy has been revised and how activities developed following the taxonomy can incorporate digital technology. As you watch the clip, think about these questions:

- How are lower- and higher-order thinking skills represented in the taxonomy?
- What do you think are the main contributions of the updated version?
- How can recent digital developments be applied to the taxonomy?

https://worldsofenglish.com/workplace-skills-extension-tasks/

To explore "searching for job ads strategically", another of the LOs listed in Table 1.6, you could present students with a list of questions for them to discuss in pairs. Such a list could include questions such as "Where do you usually search for a job?" (For job-experienced students), "Where would you search for a job?" (For pre-experience students), "What kinds of jobs are normally advertised there?", "Why is that a good place to look for a job?".

You would also want to teach or revise the language items they may need to answer such questions. Language Corner LC-1.3 provides a list of possible items.

Language Corner (LC-1.3)

There are a number of language items that your students will need to be familiar with when searching for a job. The list below provides some such items. You may also want to add a few more which you think will be relevant to your own teaching context.

- To be/go job hunting/employment searching, to be in a/n (active) job search
- To look for, hunt for, search for or seek (no preposition after 'seek') a job
- To do a job search
- Job hunter, job seeker, applicant
- A/n (effective) job search
- A job search starts/finishes with/when
- A phase/stage of the process/job search
- A vacancy, vacancy position, an opening, an open position, a job opportunity, an opportunity for employment
- A temporary/permanent job
- A full-time/part-time job
- Demanding, time-consuming, stressful
- To take into account professional/personal considerations
- To identify one's (own) skills, goals, aspirations
- Desirable, required skills, skill sets
- To set short/long-/mid-term goals

Collocations

- Job hunting/job search = To **go job hunting** (not to do job hunting) but to **do a job search**, to **be/go job hunting**, to **be in a job search**
- Job = **ideal, dream, top, well/badly-paid, challenging, demanding, boring**
- Considerations = To **take into account** (professional/personal) **considerations**
- Goals = **To set** (short/long-/mid-term) **goals**
- Skills = **required, desirable, essential, important,** (skill) **set**

Structural elements

- Simple present (e.g., This vacancy **requires** candidates to have....)
- Adverbs of frequency (e.g., I **always** have a look at....)
- Prepositions (e.g., look/search/hunt **for** a job **in** the local newspaper; an opening **in** the marketing department)

Now that we have discussed ideas for lesson planning, it is time to explore teaching materials that can be used to teach job hunting skills and competencies.

1.4 Materials for teaching job-hunting skills and competencies

Before, you examine the contents of this section, you may want to revisit what we discussed in relation to principles for evaluating, selecting, and adapting teaching materials in the Introductory Unit (see Section I.4).

This section of Unit 1 presents materials for teaching how to read job ads (1.4.1), how to understand job requirements (1.4.2) and how to compare existing skills and competencies and those required for a job (profiling) (1.4.3).

1.4.1 Materials for teaching how to read job ads critically

One of the main LOs of a lesson on job hunting is to help students to become critical readers of job ads as shown in the lesson plan provided in Table 1.7. To this end, you may want to start by asking students what they think the key information in a particular job ad is. This is exemplified in Handout 1.

Handout 1: Key Information in Job Ads

Read the following three job ads and:

1. circle the information that you think is key in each of the ads
2. think why this information is important for you
3. be prepared to discuss your choices with other students.

2

JOB OPENINGS - JOB OPENINGS - JOB OPENINGS
The **RightNow!** Team is looking for creative and self-starting candidates to fill the positions of:

PROGRAMME ASSISTANT	DEVELOPER
JOB DESCRIPTION	JOB DESCRIPTION
A programme assistant who can provide excellent operational and administrative support to the Programme Leader and his Staff. He/She should be able to also provide logistical services to the team.	A front-end developer who specialises in client-side web applications, including those needed for clients to interact with businesses.
REQUIRED SKILLS	REQUIRED SKILLS
Multi-tasking	Javascript
Excellent organisation	CSS
Good at meeting deadlines	HTML

APPLY NOW!
Applications should be made through our dedicated website: RightNowjobs.com

VACANCIES
New Future Secondary School is a leading public school in Berkshire, England. Our success over the past few years has led to rapid expansion. The School is now offering the following vacancies:

Teachers
We require experienced teachers in the following subjects: English, Mathematics, and Business Studies. Applicants must be qualified teachers with a minimum of three years of teaching experience. The ability and commitment to help the School achieve even higher results will be an advantage.

Applications, including a cover letter and an updated curriculum vitae, must be sent to:

The Principal
New Future Secondary School
Enfield Road
Berkshire, England

3

4. You can use the table below to record your answers.

Ad 1	Ad 2	Ad 3

[with a focus on writing summaries = reading into writing]

Before or after reading the ads in Handout 1, you may want to teach or revise key language items included in them. Language Corner LC-1.4 lists a few of them.

Language Corner (LC-1.4)

These are key vocabulary items present in the ads. You may also want to revise those in the previous Language Corner (LC-1.3).

- experienced/creative/self-start staff/candidates/applicants
- with a minimum of (time) experience in
- a related industry/business/area
- (interested) applicant should apply by
- position/vacancy will be filled on an on-going basis
- multi-tasking
- (excellent) organisation (skills)
- (due to) rapid expansion

Collocations

- To apply by (Verb+ING)
- On an on-going/that basis/on the basis of
- Invited to (an interview)
- Be good at (something/doing something)
- To interact with
- To lead to

Structural elements

- **Present progressive** (e.g., is looking for, is offering)
- **Passive voice** (e.g., are required for (position), are required to/ are requested to (do something), will be filled, will be invited)
- **Modal verbs** (e.g., who can + Verb (infinitive without 'to', be able to (Verb), must be)

1.4.2 Materials for teaching how to understand job requirements

Another important competency related to job hunting that you may want your students to develop is understanding what is required for a particular job. This competency demands paying close attention to the expectations that the business, company or institution advertising the job has about the potential applicants. Handout 2 illustrates some activities for developing this competency.

Handout 2: Profiling Skills and Competencies

Go back to the ads in Handout 1 and now answer the following questions:

1. What particular skills are required from the applicants in each ad?
2. Do these vary with the job advertised?
3. Do the ads mention any formal qualifications required?
4. How about the location of the job? Would it require working on site? Can you work remotely/from home?
5. Do they require speaking foreign languages? Is it specified in the ads?
6. Do they mention the salary offered?

You can use the following to write lists of bullet points with your answers. Be prepared to discuss your choices with the rest of the class.

Ad 1	Ad 2	Ad 3
Particular skills		
•	•	•
•	•	•
•	•	•
Formal qualifications		
•	•	•
Location		
•	•	•
Foreign languages		
•	•	•
•	•	•
Salary offered		
•	•	•

Depending on the proficiency level of your students, you may want to draw their attention to the following language items shown in Language Corner LC-1.5 that they would need to do the exercises in Handout 2. Add other items of vocabulary you think your students may need.

Language Corner (LC-1.5)

- They require/seem to require
- They don't require/don't seem to require
- The requirements vary/change/are similar to/different from
- ... is/are not mentioned
- The position/job/vacancy offers/doesn't offer the possibility of

Collocations

- Have/has the ability to (Verb)/Be able to (Verb)/Be capable of (Verb +ING)
- A qualification/degree in

Structural elements

- **Simple present tense** (e.g., They require a qualification in...)
- **Passive voice** (e.g., The salary is not mentioned...)

1.4.3 Materials for teaching how to profile

Once your students have learnt to identify and isolate particular skills and competencies required for a job, they will find it useful to do a profiling task. Profiling refers to matching their existing skills, competencies, formal and informal education (what they can offer) with those needed for the job (what skills/competencies they are requested to exhibit). This kind of SWOT analysis will help them to find out how they fare in respect of the expectations and requirements of the job advertiser and, possibly more importantly, to decide whether they are ready to apply for the job. They may also use the results of the profiling task to decide what they need to do (e.g., take a particular course) if they realise they are not ready to apply now, but would like to do so for a similar position in the future. Handout 3 shows an example of a profiling task for job hunting.

Handout 3: Profiling Skills and Competencies

Look at the ads in Handout 1 again and choose the one for the job you are most interesting in. Then, look at the requirements you identified in Handout 2. In the following task, you need to match the requirements for the job you chose (what they are looking for) with your own skills, competencies and aspirations (what you have to offer). This is called "profiling". You can use the table below to help you to complete the profiling task.

Ad		Myself
Particular skills		
•		•
•		•
Formal qualifications		
•		•
Location		
•		•
Foreign languages		
•		•
Salary		
•		•

What could you do to fulfil those requirements you can't meet at present?

The next Language Corner (LC-1.6) shows some of the language items your students may need to do the profiling task in Handout 3.

Language Corner (LC-1.6)

These are some language items that your students may need to complete the profiling task.

- I can/can't
- I am/am not able to
- I am/am not capable of
- I would need to
- This job requires/demands... and/but I
- I am/am not looking for

Collocations

- Speak (language/s) fluently
- To be qualified in

Structural elements

- **Simple present tense** (e.g., They require a qualification in...)
- **Present progressive** (e.g., At the moment I'm doing a course in...)

Now that you have examined some examples of materials for teaching job-hunting skills and competencies, you may want to reflect upon these examples. A few questions have been provided to guide your reflection for the next activity (RA-1.4).

Reflection Activity (RA-1.4)

- How useful did you find these examples?
- Would they be suitable to teach your students?
- Would they require any adaptation before you can use them?
- How would you need to adapt them?

Similarly, you may want to draw your students' attention to the need to acquire new or further develop their existing communication skills, in particular those for digital and multimodal communication. These are explored in some detailed in the next Culture and Technology Note (CTN-1.2).

Culture and Technology Note (CTN-1.2)

Although most students would be very familiar with social media and applications they use for every day communication, they may not be aware of how these work for particular purposes in more formal contexts like educational institutions and the workplace. The term "digital literacies" is usually used to refer to this. The term was coined by Paul Gilster, who defined it as "the ability to both understand and use digitised information" (Gilster 1997, p. 2). Digital literacies include:

- **media literacy**: Critically read and produce communications using a variety of media
- **information literacy**: Find, interpret and evaluate information
- **ICT literacy**: Use, adopt or adapt digital devices
- **digital communication**: Take part in digital networks.

In a similar vein, students may need to become aware of the growing importance of multimodal communication in the international workplace. As its name suggests, multimodal communication refers to the different "modes" in which communication can take place: visual, aural, written and kinaesthetic. People receive messages in different ways and thus a multimodal message, which may combine text, images, motion, and/or audio, will be more effective in reaching different audiences while being more accessible to most of them. Therefore, workplaces in general and international workplaces in particular, require staff to be able to use, or at least to understand and evaluate, a wide range of modes of communication. This skill is sometimes called "multimodal literacy".

At the same time, digital and multimodal communication in the workplace may require your students to be able to "multi-communicate". According to Gimenez (2014, p. 1), multi-communication means "holding multiple, face-to-face and electronically mediated conversations at the same time". (Multimodal and multi-communication will be explored in more detail in Unit 5.)

This and the following units incorporate Insights from Research notes. These notes aim at summarising contributions made by research relevant workplace skills and competencies. Insights from Research (IR-1.1) explores the concepts of culture and organisational culture. It also offers some pedagogical ideas for helping students develop a deeper understanding of both concepts.

Insights from Research (IR-1.1): Understanding Culture and Organisational Culture

Culture with a Big C, also called national culture, is a very complex term to define and researchers have to date not agreed on a single definition. This is partly due to the fact that, as Bremner (2018) has argued, cultures are complicated, ambiguous, diverse, and always changing. To avoid a monolithic view of culture, some researchers have described it as a continuum rather than a dichotomous concept. One very influential such descriptions was advanced by Hall (1976) who placed culture on a continuum ranging from high-context (e.g., Japanese, Latin) to low-context (e.g., German, Swiss) cultures. High-context cultures value relationships and take context very much into account. Low-context cultures, on the other hand, value results and tend to disregard context. Obviously, this view of culture has important implication for communication within these cultures. Another model was advanced by Beamer (2000). Her model includes eight cultural dimensions (e.g., individualist vs. collectivist, learning from experience vs. learning from authority, rules-observing vs. rules-bending), each of which can be placed on a continuum.

Most of these considerations also apply to organisational culture. Denison (1990: 2) described organisational culture as "the underlying values, beliefs, and principles that serve as the foundation for the organization's management system as well as the set of management practices and behaviors that both exemplify and reinforce those basic principles".

It stems from this definition that each organisation will have a particular set of values, beliefs, and principles that will guide their own practices, i.e., how they go about doing their business. This also means that organisational culture will have a shaping effect on how an organisation communicates as we will discuss later on.

The difficulty of defining both culture and organisational culture deserves careful attention at the time of designing pedagogical materials (Bremner, 2018; Gimenez, 2014). Barnes and Smith (2013), for example, have designed a number of assignments that require students to have access to a real organisation to analyse its culture and communication patterns by means of a battery of tools (e.g., interviews, surveys, observation). Similarly, Bremner (2013) has created a set of similar assignments that his work-experienced students have to complete on their own workplaces. If you are teaching pre-experience students, it would then be more difficult for them to access real companies. However, they can be asked to work with business cultural artefacts, such as reports, advertisements, and surveys, which can be accessed from the websites of a variety of organisations (see the Resources section of the book).

Organisational values, a central element of organisational culture, also present a degree of difficulty to any observer, seasoned or inexperienced. The main difficulty with values is that they are not always articulated, that is, "explicitly formulated in corporate documentation" (Bjørge, Sandvik and Whittaker, 2017: 403). In fact, there may be a number of equally important values that are implicit and which students will have to discover as they gradually become more familiar with the culture of their workplace. Explicit values are normally expressed in abstract nouns (e.g., initiative, honesty, loyalty, integrity) and serve as guidelines for desired and expected behaviour. Students should be made aware of how values are normally linguistically articulated so that they can develop some insights into what behaviour is expected of them.

When working internationally, students should also be made aware that, they will probably be expected to embrace the values of the international company they are joining. Understanding the new values, especially when they differ from their own or from those of their previous workplace, and what is expected of them as new employees will not always be easy and will take time and effort. What is more, interpretation of corporate values has been discovered to be closely connected to cultural background. Thus, local employees would interpret corporate values differently from international employees (Bjørge, Sandvik and Whittaker, 2017). However, being aware of this and of the skills and competencies needed to discover explicit and implicit values is an excellent starting point. As it is impossible to cover in one course all existing possible organisational cultures and their explicit values-let alone the implicit ones, it is important that teachers help students to develop an awareness of these issues and a set of skills and competencies for analysing how workplace behaviours reflect both types of organisational values.

These considerations are equally important when it comes to communication in the international workplace. As Pan, Wong Scollon and Scollon (2002: 5) have observed, "successful communication in the international workplace requires a self-reflective understanding of the process of communication", particular to each organisation. Their observation encapsulates two important elements which we have already touched upon in various parts of the book: "a self-reflective understanding" and "the process of communication". The former can be fostered by exposing students to examples and case studies that reveal the different elements that influence communication in the international workplace (e.g., cultural orientations and understandings, technology, relationships), and which will ultimately equip them with a set of critical skills to enhance their reflective understanding. The latter will require students' attention to be drawn towards how communication happens in their workplace and the different elements that constitute it (e.g., preference for written or spoken communication, mostly face-to-face or on the telephone, choice of informal over formal register, relationship with the audience as a defining factor for preferences and choices). Together these skills and competencies will help students to be better prepared to face the possible challenges of working in the international market.

1.5 Assessing learning

This section offers two tasks you may want to use to assess your students' achievements in relation to the LOs set up for the unit. The first is a self-assessment task which present students with a list of Can-Do statements for them to consider in relation to the skills developed in this unit. The second task is an integrated (reading into writing) task that assesses the same skills and competencies as the Can-Do statements: reading a job ad critically, identifying what is required for the job advertised, and matching existing and required skills for your students to decide whether to apply or not. The first task can be used for formative assessment and the second for either formative or summative assessment. (See the discussion on formative or summative assessment in the Introductory Unit).

1.5.1 Self-assessing job-hunting skills/competencies

Self-assessing skills and competencies for job hunting				
Use the following list of Can-Do statements to self-assess the skills and competencies you have learnt in this unit. In case you are not sure or think you have not yet acquired the skill or competency referred to, make a note on what you can do about it.				
I can	Yes	No	?	I'm planning to
1. search for a job in the right places.				
2. read job ads with little difficulty.				
3. identify and list key requirements in a job ad.				
4. identify my existing skills and competencies in relation to specific jobs.				
5. match my existing skills and competencies with those required for a particular job.				
6. identify what I need to do to match the requirements of the job more effectively.				

1.5.2 Assessing job-hunting skills/competencies

Read this job ad and do the two tasks that follow.

Customer Service Advisor –

TUDOR Central London
    You will be an advocate for the TUDOR values, and will do
    all you can to meet customer expectations—from serving on the till
    and the collection counter, to providing assistance on the shopfloor,
    to picking stock in the stockroom.

    You will have:

   • A passion for fantastic customer service
   • Previous experience within a retail or hospitality environment is
       beneficial but not essential

- Great communication skills
- Keen to develop and progress your career with TUDOR

Benefits include:

- £9.50 per hour (£9.18 if under 21)
- An initial holiday allowance of 22 days per year pro rata (which increases with service)
- TUDOR pension scheme

As a Customer Service Advisor you will be working in an exciting environment with the potential to develop your skills in our Academy for a career that fits with your own aspirations.

At TUDOR we're a proud equal opportunities employer that values diversity at every level of our business. Inclusion and Diversity are fundamental to our culture and values, fostering an innovative, collaborative and fast paced work environment that means we can build a better future for our colleagues and our customers.

If you think you are the right person for the job, send us your CV to

TUDOR
Human Resources Manager
101 New Cavendish St,
London
W1W 6XH

1. Complete the following table with what you consider to be the specific requirements for the job advertised in the TUDOR ad.

Ad	Specific requirements, be as detailed as you can
Customer Service Advisor – TUDOR Central London	

2. How do you, as a potential applicant, meet the specific requirements you identified to complete task 1 above?

Specific requirements	Myself as a potential applicant

The next Reflection activity (RA-1.5) provides you with some questions to help you to reflect on the appropriacy of these two assessment tasks for your students.

Reflection Activity (RA-1.5)

Considering the two assessment tasks above, how would you:

- rate them in terms of appropriacy for your own teaching context?
- adapt them if necessary?
- design new assessment tasks following these examples?

Finally, it is also important to remember to design a set of marking criteria as we discussed in the Introductory Unit (see Section I.5).

1.6 Summary

In this unit, we have discussed and reflected upon how to teach skills and competencies for job hunting.

As mentioned in the Introductory Unit, the sections in this unit have followed the teaching-and-learning cycle. Thus, we started by identifying key skills and competencies for job hunting so that we could then set appropriate LOs and reflect upon the key **teaching and learning principles** that could inform our pedagogical decisions. Based on this, we considered an example for **designing a lesson** to teach job-hunting skills and competencies and also analysed samples of materials to accompany the lesson plan we designed. Finally, we examined

assessment tasks which can be implemented for formative and summative assessment.

These considerations were complemented by reflection activities, extension tasks and culture and technology notes. The unit also introduced the 'Language corner' which highlights relevant language items
that your students may need to be able to complete the activities in the
unit successfully. It also introduced 'Insights from Research' notes that
aim at summarising relevant research views on the topics discussed in
the unit.

The next unit, Unit 2, looks at teaching skills and competencies for
applying for a job, following the teaching-and-learning cycle. It also offers reflection activities, extension tasks, culture and technology notes,
the language corner and insights from research notes.

Further readings: An annotated bibliography

Anderson, J. (2017b). Peer needs analysis: Sensitising learners to the needs
of their classmates. http://www.jasonanderson.org.uk/downloads/peer_
needs_analysis.pdf

In this article, Jason Anderson discusses Peer Needs Analysis as a tool
to raise students' awareness of the needs of other students in their class,
thus turning a NA exercise into a social activity.

Bennet, J. (n.d.-b). *SWOT analysis: Generating ideas.* https://www.teaching
expertise.com/articles/swot-analysis-generating-ideas/

In this blog, Julie Bennett looks at the ways in which SWOT analysis
can be used for brainstorming and exploring projects, ideas, change and
decisions together with the students.

Gilster, P. (1997b). *Digital literacy.* Wiley.

In this book, Paul Gilster explores basic thinking skills and core competencies needed to thrive in an interactive environment. Although
many developments in the area of digital literacies have been advanced
since its publication, Gilster's book is the first discussion on the topic.

Gimenez, J. (2014b). Multi-communication and the business English class:
Research meets pedagogy. *English for Specific Purposes*, 35(1), 1–16. https://
doi.org/10.1016/j.esp.2013.11.002

In this study, I investigated multi-communication (MC) practices at four London-based multinationals specialising in telecommunications, management consultancy, marketing and banking. The article presents a revised definition of MC as "the act of holding multiple conversations at the same time" (Gimenez, 2014, p. 1), expanding the coverage of the term 'conversation' to include not only face-to-face but also electronically mediated communication (e.g., talk over the telephone, email and IM). The study also expanded on previous research by examining the underpinning role of digital media in workplace interactions, and thus managed to reveal a set of interactional skills, such as 'thematic threading', 'presence allocation', 'media packaging' and 'audience profiling', needed to communicate effectively in the contemporary workplace. See also Unit 5 of this book.

Unit 2
Teaching skills and competencies for job applications

Learning Outcomes

By the end of the unit, you should be able to:

- identify key skills and competencies needed for job applications
- turn these skills and competencies into LOs
- make pedagogical decisions about designing lessons, selecting materials, and assessing job application skills and competencies, and
- select effective vocabulary items your students will require for applying for a job.

2.1 Introducing job applications

As we mentioned in Unit 1, the global job market is becoming increasingly competitive and employers or their employment agencies have countless job applications to consider. Therefore, students will need to prepare their job applications carefully, and clearly demonstrate that they possess the skills and competencies employers are looking for.

Depending on the type of job, industry and organisational culture, some jobs will require applicants to submit a Curriculum Vitae (or CV) and cover letter, others may ask them to fill in an application form. Most will request applications to be submitted via the company's

DOI: 10.4324/9781003283515-5

website, although, in some contexts, paper forms are still accepted and sometimes preferred.

Whichever the case may be, to produce a strong job application your students will need a number of skills and competencies such as doing research on the organisation advertising the job, identifying the specific documents required for applying, and drafting such documents by using effective language and appropriate register.

This unit focuses on the key skills and competencies your students will need in order to write and submit a successful job application. We will look at the different ways in which such skills and competencies can be taught and practised.

Like Unit 1, this unit begins by identifying the key skills and competencies for performing a particular task for the international workplace—in this case writing a successful job application. These generic skills and competencies may be applied to a number of different cultural settings, while taking into account the specifics of the country or region and industry where the job is advertised. As we have mentioned before, you will probably also want to adapt the identified skills and competencies to meet the needs of your students more effectively. To this end, you can consider specific aspects of the country/region and particular industries or business sectors your students are interested in, and thus make the skills and competencies you select more relevant for their situation.

We will also consider appropriate theories, teaching approaches and classroom activities to inform pedagogical decisions as discussed in the Introductory Unit. In order to do this, we will start by turning the identified skills and competencies into teachable LOs.

Next, we will examine sample lesson plans for teaching some of the skills and competencies for making effective job applications, as well as suggestions on how other lesson plans could be designed, together with some sample materials you could either adopt or adapt. Finally, assessment will be discussed and possible assessment tasks for evaluating students' skills and competencies for job applications will be considered.

Let's then begin by identifying some core skills and competencies needed for making a job application in an international context.

2.2 Key skills and competencies for job applications

Before teaching your students the skills and competencies needed for successful job applications, it's important to get a sense of how experienced they are in applying for jobs. You may want to start by exploring this with your work-experienced students. If you are teaching pre-experience students only, you may want to ask them to do a brief survey among their friends and family. At the same time, it is important for them to realise that work experience is sometimes determined by cultural norms as briefly discussed in the first Culture and Technology Note of the unit (CTN-2.1).

Culture and Technology Note (CTN-2.1)

In some cultures, high-school and university students typically work part-time, or at least during the summer holidays. In other cultures, young people who study are discouraged to seek part-time jobs, the idea being that they need to focus on their studies. You probably know already what the norm is in the place where you are teaching. Starting from that, you can find out about the experience of your own students by doing a simple NA exercise (see Unit 1). The NA can simply ask them whether they have had any experiences in applying for jobs, who has or has had a job, and how they got that job. These questions would provide a good starting point for planning your lessons.

At this point it is also important to consider other cultural aspects relating to professional networks. In some cultures, professional connections may be more important than formal degrees or previous work experience. This may be an advantage for inexperienced young people. In other cultural contexts, the opposite is true. Many international and multinational companies take pride in being meritocracies and therefore skills, knowledge, attitude and experience tend to count the most. Again, consider the local culture and, if possible, the culture of the organisation your students are interested in (see also Unit 1), and whether this is something you need to discuss with your students in a culture-sensitive way. By the same token, consider the possible differences between recruitment in the country/region where you are teaching and international recruitment.

International recruitment involves hiring someone from overseas to work at an international company. In most cases, the company will need to arrange a visa for the overseas employee to work and live in the company's country. Although, international recruitment is not always an easy process due to the number of issues involved in it (e.g., visa red tape, work permits,

> moving costs), many international companies embark on it for the benefits it may bring: A broader talent pool to choose from, higher diversity, market insights, inclusivity and multiple languages, among others. These are important aspects of working for an international company that both work-experienced and pre-experience students need to take into account when considering applying for a job in the international marketplace.

As we read in CTN-2.1, one of the benefits of international recruitment is hiring staff who can speak more than one language. The first Insights from Research of the unit (IR-2.1) provides some views of multilingualism in the contemporary workplace.

Insights from Research (IR-2.1): Multilingualism in the Workplace

In the past few years, research on multilingualism in the workplace (e.g., Gunnarsson, 2013; Hewitt, 2008, 2012) has identified a number of tendencies in the use of a variety of languages for work purposes despite the supremacy of the English language as a lingua franca in many contexts. Due to global migration, technological advances and social mobility, many international organisations have adopted English as a workplace lingua franca alongside other languages. As Gunnarsson (2013: 162) has argued, many "transnational companies and organizations [...] use English, or another global language, as their corporate language and employ multilingual people who can move between jobs, between branches, and between countries". For some researchers (e.g., Hewitt, 2008, 2012), the adoption of English as a corporate language has, however, created a situation in which certain tasks are linked with a particular language based on the prestige associated to it. In his London study, for instance, Hewitt (2008), found that whereas other languages than English were used for most work-task and social purposes, English only was used for tasks that were considered strategically more important, such as interaction with customers, suppliers, and banks. Despite this, knowing different languages is undeniably a clear advantage for graduates wishing to become part of the global job market. As Hewitt (2012: 275) concludes, "today's workplaces are 'plurilingual' and successful communication is of utmost importance [and this] places heavy demands on graduates' language skills across the board".

Now, to help you to think about international recruitment, here is a list of skills and competencies your students will need to develop to apply for a job at an international company:

- researching the profile (e.g., history, type of business, values) of the company/business advertising the job
- identifying the specific documents required for a job application
- understanding the role of the different documents for job applications
- drafting a successful cover letter
- drafting a generic CV and adapting it to the specifics of the job advertised
- securing recommendations and other documents
- using effective language and appropriate register to draft the cover letter and CV.

Let's pause here for a minute and reflect on these skills and competencies. Activity RA-2.1 has been designed to help you with this.

Reflection Activity (RA-2.1)

- How aware do you think your students are about these skills and competencies? How can you help them to become (more) aware?
- Based on your experience, what other skills or competencies, relating to job applications, you would like to add to the list above?
- How do you think your students will best develop these skills?
- How would you go about teaching them?

As suggested by the questions in this reflection task, your choice of what skills and competencies to teach will always be determined by who your students are and the type and location of the job they want to apply for.

The next important aspect to focus on is how to turn the skills we have already identified into measurable LOs. In order to move from skills to teachable LOs, you can do a NA exercise, as we have mentioned before. This could be done by means of a survey that asks your students about their previous experiences, skills and competencies and goals and aspirations, or by means of scenarios that present them with options to choose from.

As we discussed in Unit 1, LOs are formulated using the phrase "By the end of the lesson, you should be able to…", where "should be able to" refers to the new skills and competencies they will acquire through the lesson. Remember that Bloom's or Fink's taxonomies can guide you through deciding what specific verbs (e.g., recalling, interpreting, inferring, implementing, producing) to use for formulating LOs (see also the Introductory Unit).

In the case of the skills and competencies we have identified for this unit, Table 2.1 shows how they can be turned into LOs. As we saw in Unit 1, the questions in the middle column exemplify the thinking process involved in transforming skills and competencies into LOs.

Table 2.1 Turning Skills and Competencies into LOs

Skills/Competences	Questions	Resulting LOs
Researching the profile (e.g., history, type of business, values) of the company/business advertising the job	How can students find out about the profile (e.g., history, type of business, values) of the company/business advertising the job? What search tools can they use for researching company profiles?	By the end of the lesson, you should be able to identify effective ways and use appropriate tools for finding information about international companies/businesses you would like to apply for.
Identifying the specific documents required for a job application	How can students find out what documents are required to apply for a job at an international company/business? What search tools can they use for researching the required application documents?	By the end of the lesson, you should be able to identify what application documents are required for a specific job by using a variety of search tools.
Understanding the role of the different documents for job applications	What role(s) does each application document serve in the location/industry students are considering?	By the end of the lesson, you should be able to identify the key roles played by specific documents required to apply for a job.
Drafting a successful cover letter	What does a successful cover letter look like? What information should it provide?	By the end of the lesson, you should be able to evaluate, discuss and draft a successful cover letter.

(Continued)

Skills/Competences	Questions	Resulting LOs
Drafting a generic CV and adapting it to a specific job ad	What should a generic CV include? How can a generic CV be adapted for a specific job, following a particular job ad?	By the end of the lesson, you should be able to draft a comprehensive generic CV. By the end of the lesson, you should be able to adapt your generic CV by editing it to suit a specific job vacancy.
Securing recommendations and other documents	How can students identify who is in a position to write a recommendation for them? How can students go about asking for a recommendation?	By the end of the lesson, you should be able to consider and identify who you should ask for a recommendation. By the end of the lesson, you should be able to approach the identified person and confidently ask them for a recommendation.
Using effective language and appropriate register to draft a cover letter and a CV	What appropriate language items will students need to draft application documents? What specific vocabulary items will they find useful to achieve these particular LOs? What is the general tone and level of formality needed for the documents? Are there any key structural elements they will need?	By the end of the lesson, you should be able to draft a cover letter and a CV, using effective language and appropriate register.

Now that we have considered the relationship between skills and competencies and LOs outlined in Table 2.1, it is time to reflect upon such a relationship. The questions in the next activity aim at guiding your reflective process.

Reflection Activity (RA-2.2)

- How useful do you find Table 2.1?
- How would the LOs in it need to be adapted so that they meet the particular needs of your students?
- Do you think the supporting questions are also relevant to your students/teaching situation? If not, how could you adapt them to make them more relevant?

Table 2.1 shows the LOs that students would need in order to ultimately feel confident when evaluating and drafting the necessary documents to apply for a job at an international company/business. However, you may need to devote a number of lessons to cover all of them as there are too many objectives for one lesson alone. The LOs shown in the table have been graded from less to more complex, so you may want to start with the less complex ones depending on the proficiency level in English of your students.

At the same time, your students will probably need particular language items to engage in the activities that would help them to achieve these LOs. The first language corner of the unit (LC-2.1) shows some such items.

Language Corner (LC-2.1)

There are a number of language items that your students will need to be familiar with when searching for a job. The list below provides some such items. You may also want to add a few more which you think will be relevant to your own teaching context.

Company profile

- This company/business was founded in
- They believe in
- Their core values are/include

Specific documents and their role

- They are asking for/require
- If you want to apply for this job, you'll need to submit...
- The key role of a cover letter/CV is
- Your cover letter/CV will have to show/demonstrate...

Drafting documents and effective language

- The key sections in a cover letter/CV are...
- An effective cover letter/CV has/contains...
- Use/Don't use...
- A useful phrase/sentence/expression for ... is...

Collocations

- Draft/write a cover letter/CV
- Post/fax/email a cover letter/CV
- Send a cover letter/CV by post/email
- Reply by letter
- In your letter/job ad of (date)...
- Concerning/regarding your job ad of (date)...
- A letter of application/an application letter

Structural elements

- **Simple present** tense (e.g., They believe in..., Their core values are)
- **Present progressive** tense (e.g., They are asking for...)
- **Conditionals** (e.g., If you want to apply for this...)
- **Passive voice** (e.g., The company was founded in...)

Before moving on to lesson design, you may want to revisit the learning theories and teaching approaches we discussed in the Introductory Unit to decide which ones would be most appropriate given these LOs and your own teaching context. For example, **Connectivism**, which encourages learning by self-discovery, is one of the theories that could be applied here. Students could be encouraged to search the internet or ask family and friends for models of successful cover letters and CVs. They could then be guided as to how to adapt these documents for their own job applications. Have a look at the other learning theories and teaching approaches discussed in the Introductory Unit, and consider whether they could also be useful in designing activities and tasks to help your students.

2.3 Designing lessons for job applications

This section presents some sample lesson plans to teach two of the skills we have identified for this unit. Together with this, the section shows some ideas for you to consider when developing your own lesson plans for the other skill sets and competencies explored in the unit.

The first lesson plan has been designed to teach "drafting a successful cover letter" and the second to teach "drafting a generic CV and adapting it to a specific job ad".

Before we discuss in detail the lesson plan for "drafting a successful cover letter", here are a few ideas for activities you could do to help your students with "understanding the role of the different documents for job applications". You may want to engage your students in such activities before you help them with drafting a successful cover letter and CV.

- bring to class sample cover letters, CVs and other application documents (you could find a variety of samples on the Internet or use the samples in this unit) and ask your students to compare and contrast them in either pairs or small groups,
- based on this comparison, ask them to consider what role(s) each document might serve in the application process (you may want to guide them by providing them with a few questions)
- get the different pairs/small groups to feed back to the entire class their ideas on the role(s) of each document
- have a general class discussion around document type and roles.

At this point, you may also ask your students to consider cultural aspects that could shape their decisions as to how to best write application documents. This is discussed in Culture and Technology Note CTN-2.2.

Culture and Technology Note (CTN-2.2)

Writing documents to be used for a job application is a highly cultural matter that depends both on the national culture (that of the country where the company is located) and the local culture (that of the industry or the company advertising the job) (see also Unit 1). It is therefore important to consider the locality, the industry as well as the company or business advertising the job when deciding which job application documents to focus on. In some contexts, formal documents, such as a letter of application addressing how the candidate meets the requirements of the job, a CV or Resume, and other supporting documents such as letters of reference are normally required. In other contexts and depending on the industry, portfolio of previous activities and experiences may be required as application documents. In many international contexts, an online application, usually in the format of a template, is required. The online application usually needs to be accompanied by a series of documents, such as a CV and a purpose statement, which should be also submitted online.

Technology can be very helpful in exposing students to the typology of documentation needed for job applications, especially when they are planning to apply for a job located internationally. Depending on the level of internet access and the level of privacy in the culture regarding personal documents such as cover letters and CVs, students can be encouraged to use the internet and/or their personal connections or professional networks in order to identify or request suitable models of job application documents.

It is essential, however, to remind students that models serve illustrative and guiding purposes, but should not be used to apply for a particular job. Specific documents should be drafted for each particular job for which they wish to apply, taking into consideration what is required in the job ad and, if possible, making some intelligent cultural choices (see also Table 2.4).

The second Insights from Research (IR-2.2) explains the concept of cultural intelligence. You may also want to draw your students' attention to interpersonal communication and emotional intelligence (See Unit 4).

Insights from Research (IR-2.2): Cultural Intelligence

Cultural intelligence requires both awareness of oneself as a cultural being and awareness of others also as cultural beings. It develops from general knowledge about culture and how people as social agents normally interact as well as specific knowledge about a particular culture based on real-world examples, a mix that Tuleja (2021) calls culture-general and culture-specific knowledge. However, she warns us that for knowledge to contribute effectively to cultural intelligence, it needs to go beyond facts and move towards analysing and reflecting upon one's cultural behaviour.

It is equally important to be aware that overarching claims and generalisations about culture and cultural behaviour should be counterbalanced with localised micro perspectives (Bargiela-Chiappini, Nickerson & Planken, 2007), especially when we refer to large countries or geographical regions. Latin America is one example in case. As Spillan, Virzi and Garita (2014: 2) explain, although many important changes in information and technology and democratisation have taken place in the region, they have not all happened across the board, and so a "one-size-fits-all" approach to applying for jobs in Latin American countries would not actually work. Therefore, some specific cultural knowledge about the particular area one intends to work in is essential for a successful application.

Searching for general cultural behaviour on the internet is a good starting point to develop one's cultural awareness and knowledge of a particular country or region, what Tuleja (2021) refers to as 'culture-general knowledge'. However, this is not enough. Knowledge about the specific cultural behaviour of the country and of the company (e.g., values and beliefs) one is interested in should also be gained. This, which would exemplify 'culture-specific knowledge' (Tuleja, 2021), could also be developed through the internet.

We can now return to lesson planning. To design a lesson plan for drafting a successful cover letter, you can use the blank template provided in Table 2.2 of the Introductory Unit. This is illustrated in Table 2.2.

As we mentioned in Section 2.2, the cover letter and the CV are two crucial documents in the job application process that need to complement each other. They also need to reflect the personal characteristics

Table 2.2 A Lesson Plan for Drafting a Successful Cover Letter

Course: Communication Skills for the International Workplace	Year group:	Date:
Learning outcomes for drafting a successful cover letter		
By the end of the lesson, students should be able to: • evaluate and discuss the key characteristics of cover letters, • assess the appropriacy of a sample cover letter in relation to a job ad, and • draft a successful cover letter for a job of their choice.		

(Continued)

Progression of teaching & learning		Strategies/Materials
Duration: 5 minutes	Introduction T asks Sts to discuss in pairs what they think a cover letter should look like, and what information it should contain.	Eliciting Sts' previous knowledge/experience
Duration: 15 minutes	Activity 1 1. Sts read a sample cover letter and discuss key characteristics (format, length, register, language, opening and closing expressions, etc.). 2. Sts make lists of key characteristics and discuss their choices. 3. Sts agree on key characteristics as a class.	1. Considering key characteristics of cover letters/Handout 1 2. Listing and discussing 3. Agreeing on key characteristics
Duration: 15 minutes	Activity 2 4. Sts individually read two job ads and decide for which ad the cover letter they have just read would be most appropriate, and why. 5. In pairs, Sts compare and discuss their views. 6. Pairs share their discussion with class.	4. Considering strengths and weaknesses of the sample cover letter in relation to a job ad/Handout 2 5. Discussing results in pairs 6. Reporting results to the class

Duration: 15 minutes	Activity 3 7. Sts individually rewrite the cover letter based on their own profile as a possible applicant (see Unit 1 for profiling activities). 8. In pairs, Sts swap the amended cover letter and write supportive comments on what is good in the letter and what could be improved. 9. Sts re-write their cover letter based on the comments from their peer.	7. Re-writing a cover letter 8. Providing peer feedback 9. Amending a cover letter
Duration: 10 minutes	**Conclusion** Sts reflect on the activities of the lesson and summarise what they have learnt.	
Success criteria	• To recognise the key characteristics of a successful cover letter • To identify strengths and weaknesses of a sample cover letter in relation to job ads • To draft a cover letter based on their own profile	**Assessment** Sts will adapt the cover letter they rewrote (see Point 9) for a different job ad.
Next steps	Write brief reflective comments (200–300 words) on how the cover letter and a particular job ad should be connected.	

and skills mentioned in the job ad. As a more personal piece of writing, the cover letter may offer candidates an opportunity to be creative and present these characteristics and skills in the manner they wish. The CV, on the other hand, is a bit more rigid. That being said, the type of CV preferred may depend on the culture and the location of the job and the company advertising it (also see Culture Note CTN-2.2). There are several different models of CVs that can be used and so it's important to share with your students the relevant ones.

Some of these considerations are further explored in the next Culture and Technology Note (CTN-2.3).

Culture and Technology Note (CTN-2.3)

There are several different models of CVs. For example, there is a model endorsed by the European Union. This is very much based on a southern European model in which details such as age or marital status are included. This, and other personal information (e.g., gender, number of children and their ages), is also commonly found in Chinese CVs. However, these types of details tend to be omitted in the Anglo-Saxon world as they may lead to discrimination based on age or marital status. On the other hand, in the UK and the US a section on hobbies and personal interests is often included, as employers in these countries tend to believe it is important to 'consider the candidate as a whole person'. Similarly, in Anglo-Saxon CVs experiences and developed skills tend to be in the same section, while in EU CVs, for example, they are included not only in different sections but even on different pages. In many countries in Latin America, a CV usually includes a very long list of previous jobs and courses taken by the applicants, but two-page resumes summarising key previous experiences and skills, common in countries like the US and China, are often discouraged. In other countries, such as Japan, you may be asked to produce both a CV and a resume (also see ET-2.1). The reason for asking for both documents is that for some a CV is a long list of all the experiences and skills an applicant can offer, similar to the typical Latin American CV, whereas a resume is a summary of those experiences and skills relevant only to a particular job.

These considerations make it really crucial for your students to consider what type of CV or resume would be the most appropriate for the job they wish to apply for before they write their own. It is equally important for them to keep in mind that different industries might be using slightly different types of CVs or resumes, as we mentioned earlier (see also 2.4).

When searching the Internet for examples, it is always a good idea to "contextualise" the search so that more appropriate samples are returned. For instance, a search containing the following key words "sample CVs" will always return less specific examples than "sample CV for engineering jobs" or "sample CV for engineering jobs in Brazil".

Let's now have a look at the second lesson plan for this unit. This plan, shown in Table 2.3, aims at helping students to develop skills for "drafting a generic CV and adapting it to the specific job application". As mentioned in Unit 1, the plan was designed for a 60-minute lesson but you could always adapt it to meet your own needs and teaching situation. If you have more or less than 60 minutes for your class, you will have to adapt the learning outcomes, the materials and the assessment activities accordingly.

Table 2.3 A Lesson Plan for Drafting a Generic CV

Course: Communication Skills for the International Workplace	Year group:	Date:
Learning outcomes for drafting a generic CV		
By the end of the lesson, students should be able to: • analyse, evaluate and discuss the key elements of generic CVs, and • draft a comprehensive generic CV taking into account cultural specificity in terms of structure, level of detail, and language.		
Progression of teaching & learning		**Strategies/Materials**
Duration: 10 minutes	Activity 1 1. T provides Sts with an example of a generic CV and Sts analyse its structure in pairs. 2. Sts identify the elements in each section of the structure. 3. Pairs share results of their analysis with class.	1. Analysing a CV/Handout 3 2. Identifying specific elements/ Handout 3 3. Class discussion

(Continued)

Duration: 20 minutes	Activity 2 4. T shows an example of a different generic CV. 5. In pairs, Sts compare the new type of CV with the previous one in Handout 3 (e.g., different sections, levels of detail, language used). 6. Sts take down notes on their analysis and discussion. 7. Pairs share the results of their discussion with the class.	4. Looking at a different CV/Handout 4 5–6. Writing discussion notes 7. Reporting results to the class
Duration: 25 minutes	Activity 3 8. Sts individually start drafting their own generic CV by deciding what sections to include. They may use the notes they made in Activity 2. 9. Sts list bullet points with the information they want to include in each section. 10. In small groups, Sts present their choices of structure and bullet points with information to each other and provide feedback.	8. Writing an outline for a generic CV 9. Selecting information for CV sections 10. Sharing work and providing feedback

Duration: 5 minutes	Conclusion Sts reflect upon the type and amount of work needed in order to write a successful CV.	
Success criteria	• To be able to analyse, evaluate and discuss the key elements of generic CVs • To be able to draft a generic CV, taking into account cultural specificity in terms of structure, level of detail, and language.	**Assessment** None at this stage
Next steps	For homework Sts could be asked to write out the bullet points and edit the generic CV into one coherent document.	

The lesson plan above can be combined with the one shown in Table 2.4. However, the tasks presented in both lessons are labour-intensive and require a great deal of attention to detail, as well as drafting and possibly editing. For the students that have never drafted and adapted a generic CV, this can be rather demanding. This is why they are presented here as two separate lessons.

Table 2.4   A Lesson Plan for Adapting a Generic CV

Course: Communication Skills for the International Workplace	Year group:	Date:
Learning outcomes for adapting a generic CV to a specific job ad		
By the end of the lesson, students should be able to: • modify the format/content of a generic CV to suit a specific job vacancy, and • edit the final copy to meet specific job requirements.		

(Continued)

Progression of teaching & learning		Strategies/Materials
Duration: 10 minutes	Introduction T reminds Sts of the importance of tailoring their CV to the specific job ad. Using a specific example, T demonstrates how the language of a specific job ad should be reflected in the CV. T could focus on a specific section of the job ad (for example the "person specifications" section)	Introducing topic to Sts
Duration: 20 minutes	Activity 1 1. T shows an example of a CV and new job ad. 2. In pairs, Sts mark on the sample CV what should be removed, what should be rephrased and what should be added to make the generic CV appropriate for the job ad. 3. Pairs are rotated so that each student has a new partner to share their suggestions with.	1. Distributing paper or digital version of one CV and a new job ad/Handout 5 2. Analysing sample CV 3. Exchanging suggestions
Duration: 25 minutes	Activity 2 4. T discusses language items (pre-teach if necessary) 5. Sts focus on the sections of the CV that need redrafting. 6. Sts individually redraft/edit the language to reflect the specific job ad.	4. Discussing language items 5. Examining CV sections 6. Editing a CV 7. Sharing linguistic choices 8. Supporting Sts

	7. Sts read to the class their chosen phrasing for the rephrased section(s). 8. T supports Sts with vocabulary, phrases and grammatical structures.	
Duration: 5 minutes	<u>Conclusion</u> Sts reflect on skills and competencies required for writing/redrafting a CV and identify areas of their own CV they would like to work on.	
Success criteria	• To be able to modify the format/content of a generic CV in order to suit a particular job ad • To be able to edit a CV to meet specific job requirements.	**Assessment** None at this stage.
Next steps	Sts could be given a new (yet related) job ad and asked to amend their CVs to meet the requirements included in it.	

Extension Task ET-2.1 offers some views on the differences between a CV and a resume.

Extension Task (ET-2.1)

Use the URL provided below to watch **video clip ET-2.1** on the differences between a CV and a resume. As you watch, think of the following:

- According to the clip, what are the main differences between the two documents?
- How relevant for your students do find these differences?
- What type of activity or task could you design for them to learn to draft both documents?

https://worldsofenglish.com/workplace-skills-extension-tasks/

Another activity for writing an effective CV in which you can engage your students starts with some reflection on their strengths and their work experiences. You could start by asking your students to think about what impression they would like to create for the readers of their CV or resume. You could also ask them to think about:

- their strengths: what they are good at and can be considered a good contribution to their new job and organisation (see SWOT analysis in Unit 1)
- their work story and highlights of any achievements they've had
- how they can support their work story by providing concrete evidence (e.g., how they solved a problem and the positive results from their intervention)
- how they can group their skills and competencies so that they show a more rounded picture of themselves (e.g., soft skills such as effective communication skills and emotional intelligence together)

Once the discussion is over, you could ask them to do the following task.

2.3.1 Task

Before writing your CV or resume, you may want to use a table like this to organise the relevant information for the job you are planning to apply for.

Area	Your notes
STRENGTHS & ACHIEVEMENTS	
Your **strengths** (refer back to your SWOT analysis in Unit 1)	
Achievements to highlight	
Evidence in support of achievements (concrete examples, data, new opportunities resulting from achievements)	
SKILL SETS	
Soft skills (e.g., communication skills, emotional intelligent, negotiation skills—see Unit 8)	

Area	Your notes
STRENGTHS & ACHIEVEMENTS	
Hard skills (e.g., knowledge of IT packages, subject knowledge)	

The third Insights from Research (IR-2.3) reminds us of the importance of keeping culture in mind when developing a specific CV to apply for a job.

Insights from Research (IR-2.3): Culture and Example CVs

It is important to always keep in mind that the templates and examples of CVs and resumes provided in a number of sources were created for a specific purpose and within a particular cultural frame, and that the contextual practices they represent may not travel well across contexts. As Pan, Wong Scollon and Scollon (2002:73) reminds us, writing resumes "is never a standardized practice across cultural boundaries and across professional fields". This clearly points to the need to help our students to develop research skills and a critical mind so that they can use their technological and human networks to find the most appropriate examples of the specific professional area and the particular cultural framework for the job they wish to apply. The importance of tailoring their CVs to meet the specific requirements of a job cannot be emphasised enough.

2.4 Materials for teaching job application skills and competencies

The following sets of materials present a number of possibilities for their use in class. You can use them as materials for a lesson similar to that in Tables 2.2 and 2.3 or to exemplify cultural notes such as those presented in the Culture and Technology Note CTN-2.3. Alternatively, you can use them to design activities and tasks such as the ones suggested below.

Handout 1: A Cover Letter

Look at the sample cover letter below. After you have examined its characteristics (e.g., format, sections, register), find the errors it contains and either underline or highlight them.

Dear Sir/Madman,

I am writing to you in order to apply for the position of Sales Representative advertised by ABC Inc. in the Guardian newspapers on 15 March.

I am a recent graduate in marketing and communication from the university of south asia. I terminated top of my class due to my dedication to study and my interpersonal skills. My communication skills is very good and I am sure I can be a successful sales representative. Also, I spend a lot of time on the computer so I know a lot about softwere. This will help me in selling the software that ABC Inc make.

Last summer I took an internship with a gaming company as a tester. I tested a lot of their video games so I have good understanding of video games to. I look forward to working for an important and cerebral company like ABC Inc.

I look forward to elaborating on the above-mentioned points in a meeting.

Kind regards,
Tony Thomas

Here is the same cover letter, now with the errors underlined. How many of these errors did you identify?

Dear Sir/<u>Madman</u>,

I am writing to you in order to apply for the position of Sales Representative advertised by ABC Inc. in the Guardian <u>newspapers</u> on 15 March.

I am a recent graduate in marketing and communication from the <u>university</u> of <u>south asia</u>. I <u>terminated</u> top of my class <u>due to</u> my dedication to study and my interpersonal skills. My communication skills <u>is</u> very good and I am sure I can be a successful sales representative. <u>Also</u>, I spend <u>a lot of</u> time on the computer so I know <u>a lot</u> about <u>softwere</u>. This will help me in selling the software that ABC Inc make.

Last summer I took an internship with a gaming company as a tester. I tested a <u>lot of</u> their video games so I have good understanding of video games <u>to</u>. I look forward to working for an important and <u>cerebral</u> company like ABC Inc.

I look forward to elaborating on the above-mentioned points in an interview.

Kind regards,
Tony Thomas

Exercise 1
In the space below say what type of errors they are and provide the correct version.

Example:

1. Spelling error: It should read *Madam*, not *Madman*
2. _____
3. _____

Exercise 2
The sample cover letter starts with the phase "I am writing to you in order to apply for the ....". Search online for other cover letter **opening phrases** and write them in the space below. Once you have finished, compare your list with that of another student.

Example:

1. I would like to apply for the...
2. _____
3. _____

Exercise 3
Similarly, the cover letter ends with the phase "I look forward to elaborating on the above-mentioned points in an interview." Search online for other cover letter **ending phrases** and write them in the space below. When you have finished, compare your list with that of another student.

Example:

1. I would appreciate the opportunity to elaborate...
2. _____
3. _____

Handout 2: The Right Cover Letter for the Right Job

Now, consider for which of these two jobs ads the cover letter you have read in Handout 1 would be most appropriate. Be ready to give reasons for your choices. Then, compare your set of reasons with that of another student and share the results of your comparison with the rest of the class.

Job ad A	Job ad B
Our Sales Department is currently seeking to appoint a senior manager to lead the new software division of the company. Previous experience is required as well as knowledge of the computer gaming market. Foreign travel may be required.	Our company is looking for an experienced and dynamic Sales Representative for our new software division. Excellent communication skills. Background in marketing an advantage as well as knowledge of a foreign language.

Handout 3: The EU-Endorsed CV Template

Look at the following CV template. It is very frequently used in many European countries. As you read, pay particular attention to its features (e.g., format, sections, length, language). Discuss the results of your analysis with another student and be prepared to share the results of your discussion with the rest of the class.

PERSONAL INFORMATION	Insert: First name(s) Surnames(s) Insert: Address (house number, street, city, postcode, country) Insert: Telephone number, mobile number (add country and area codes) Insert: Email Insert: Date of birth (DOB), nationality, marital status Insert: Gender Insert: Job/position applied for Insert: Personal statement
EDUCATION AND TRAINING	Insert: Qualification awarded Insert: Name of institution, city, country Insert: Principal subjects studied
PERSONAL SKILLS	Insert: First language Insert: Other languages and levels (A1/A2 Basic user; B1/B2 Independent user; C1/C2 Proficient user) Insert: Communication skills and context where acquired/developed (e.g., good communication skills gained through my experience as hotel receptionist) Insert: Organisational skills and context where acquired/developed (e.g., co-ordinator of small team of 4 at present company) Insert: Digital skills and levels (Basic; Independent; Proficient user)

Experience	Insert: Any relevant previous work experience you have had, indicating how long (from/to) and main responsibilities.
Additional Information	Insert: Publications Insert: Presentations Insert: Projects Insert: Honours and Awards Insert: Memberships Insert: References (Provide: name(s) and surname(s); company and position; contact details (address, email and telephone number)

Handout 4 shows a template commonly used by British graduates who have no or very limited work experience.

Handout 4: Template for a British Graduate CV

Forename and Surname

Location:_____

Telephone(s):_____

Email: _____

Professional profile

Provide a summary of your skills and competencies that you have to offer employers, including your educational achievements (especially your degree), grades, courses and projects.

Add any industry or sector-related knowledge and workplace skills that you have gained or developed so far (e.g., communication, teamwork, interpersonal, IT skills and the like). Include any relevant extra-curricular activities.

Education and qualifications

- **Name of university** – dates attended (from – to)
  - **Degree subject**
- **Name of college** – dates attended (from – to)
  - **Qualification** and grade
  - **Qualification** and grade
  - **Qualification** and grade
- **Name of school** – dates attended (from – to)
  - **Qualification** and grade
  - **Qualification** and grade
  - **Qualification** and grade

Placements and projects

Provide as much information as possible and examples of skills and competencies that could be transferred to the workplace. Give details of any projects you have been part of.

Project/placement: from mm/yyyy   to mm/yyyy

Give a summary of project or placement, explaining its goal and your involvement in it

Key responsibilities

- List responsibility and provide examples that explain it.

- List responsibility and provide examples that explain it.

- List responsibility and provide examples that explain it.

Key achievements

- Describe key achievements you've made that have had an impact of the project/placement and its users or customers.

Hobbies and personal interests
Briefly describe your hobbies and personal interests that you think may be somehow connected to the position you're applying for. For example, include 'team sports' if the job requires teamwork.

The following is an example of a Japanese CV. Depending on the preference of your students, you may want to use this template for any of the activities suggested in the previous handouts.

Sample Japanese CV

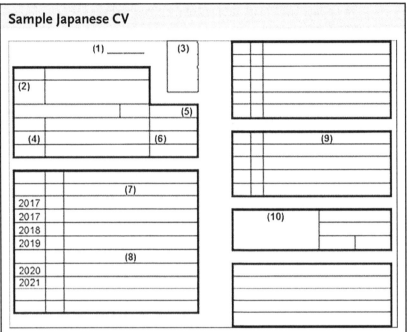

1. Date; 2. Name in full; 3. Photograph; 4. Address/Contact Information; 5. Telephone Number; 6. Email Address; 7. Education; 8. Professional Experience; 9. Licenses and Certifications; 10. Personal Statement

Handout 5: Adapting a Generic CV

Choose one of the templates provided in the previous handouts and try to match it with the following job ad. Working with another student, mark on the CV what needs to be changed to make it more suitable for the job advertised.

Job ad
English/Mandarin-speaking Graduate Media Sales Administrator

Fantastic opportunity for a recent graduate to join an international media company in central London as a Sales Administrator to develop advertising sales opportunities to companies in China and the UK.

Duties & responsibilities

- To assist the company in all aspects of China-based media groups (print, TV and radio)
- To update and create profiles of the titles/websites/TV channels/ and radio stations
- To prepare presentations and mailings intended for clients
- To send general information concerning the titles to clients
- To maintain client relationships and develop new business
- To send orders to publishers in China

Candidate background, skills & experiences

- Fluency in English and Mandarin
- Graduate—be educated to university level—essential
- Previous experience in sales position or administration is an advantage but not essential
- Good abilities in calculating invoices
- Ability to prioritise tasks

Now that we have examined a number of examples of CV, we are ready for the next Reflection activity (RA-2.3).

Reflection Activity (RA-2.3)

Taking into account the materials we have explored above, how would you

- rate them in terms of their relevance to your students?
- modify them to make them more relevant to them and appropriate for the job they would like to apply for?
- exploit the formal and cultural differences shown in them?

It is time for another extension task. Extension Task (ET-2.2) provides you with further ideas about how to write a successful resume and what common mistakes your students should avoid. You may also wish to use the video clip with your students.

Extension Task (ET-2.2)

Use the URL provided below to watch **video clip ET-2.2**, where a career advice expert talks about the typical mistakes she usually finds in submitted resumes. As you watch the video, consider the following questions:

- When should a candidate start a resume by listing their education?
- Why should they only include relevant information?
- Should a resume contain a photo? Do you think this may vary from culture to culture? How about in your culture?
- Is it a good idea to organise the content of a resume in columns?
- How about spelling and grammar mistakes?
- Do you agree with what she says about first impressions? Why? Why not?
- How much of what she considers a mistake is, in your view, culture-specific?
      https://worldsofenglish.com/workplace-skills-extension-tasks/

The following are examples of activities that you can use in conjunction with the learning materials presented above. You may need to adapt some of them to meet the level and needs of your students.

Activity 1 Make a list of similarities and differences between the European, British and Japanese CV templates.

Similarities			Differences		
European	British	Japanese	European	British	Japanese

Activity 2 Search for more CV templates for other countries you may be interested in working in the future. Then, complete the following table and be ready to make an informal presentation to the class on the results of your search.

Characteristics	Country 1: _____	Country 2:_____	Country 3:_____
Length			
Number of sections			
Information provided			

Characteristics	Country 1: _____	Country 2:_____	Country 3:_____
Chronology of education			
Chronology of jobs			
References			
Language			
Others			

2.5 Assessing learning

This section of the unit offers two possible tasks for assessing the skills and competencies identified in the unit. The first is a self-assessment task (2.5.1), and the second an integrated task (2.5.2).

2.5.1 Self-assessing skills and competencies for job applications

Self-assessing skills and competencies for job applications				
Use the following list of Can-Do statements to self-assess the skills and competencies you have learnt in this unit. In case you are not sure or think you have not yet acquired the skill or competency referred to, make a note on what you can do about it.				
I can	Yes	No	?	I'm planning to
1. understand the key documents needed to apply for a particular job.				
2. identify the key elements of such documents.				
3. draft a cover letter to accompany a particular job of my choice.				

4. draft a CV to accompany a particular job of my choice.				
5. draft a resume to accompany a particular job of my choice.				
6. identify what I need to do to produce more effective application documents.				

2.5.2 Assessing skills and competencies for job applications

The following integrated task provides students with an opportunity to show the skills and competencies they have learnt in this unit. You could use it to complement the self-assessment exercise in 2.5.1, as a formative assessment exercise or for summative assessment. Alternatively, you can use it as a model for designing another task that would meet your students' needs more closely.

2.5.2.1 Applying for a job

Instructions: Read the following ad for a hotel job in Spain, published on the Accor website (https://careers.accor.com). Supposing you wanted to apply for it, how would your cover letter and resume for this job look like?

Would you like to join our teams as an intern? This is a great opportunity to be part of a 5^* Resort in Sotogrande and develop your skills.

Providing friendly, sincere and personalised service is one of the ways our colleagues turn moments into memories for our guests at SO/ Sotogrande.

What you will be doing:
- Ensure a smooth and efficient experience delivered to all guests at registration, during their stay and at check out.
- Accurately and efficiently receive and process guest reservations whilst observing policy and procedures for the hotel operation.
- Attend to all incoming calls in a professional and polite manner, constantly striving to provide Total Customer Satisfaction.
- To record and distribute all guest and employee messages accurately and efficiently.
- To ensure that the highest level of customer satisfaction & service is offered and maintained at all times in relation to welcoming guests to the hotel complex, the transfer, storage and handling of guest luggage and property as well as responding to guest requests for assistance and or information.
- Take responsibility to ensure all required tasks are completed accurately and within given time frames.
- Participate in scheduled training and development programs provided by the Hotel to improve self and department standards and attend departmental meetings as required.

What we need from you:
- Availability during, at least, 6 months.
- Languages: perfect English and Spanish.
- Person with strong written and verbal communication skills.
- Great attention to detail.
- Proactive and reactive, with a positive attitude, and a good disposition to work as a team.

- Be highly responsible and reliable.
- Ability to focus on the needs of the guest, always remaining calm and courteous.
- Have knowledge of OPERA.
- Own vehicle.

From **Accor careers**: https://careers.accor.com/global/en/job/22030254/ Front-Office-Internship (reproduced with permission)

As we discussed in the Introductory Unit (see Section I.5), assessment tasks can be accompanied by a set of marking criteria which clearly indicate the skills and competencies the students should demonstrate proficiency in, and how their performance in such skills and competencies is going to be assessed.

2.6 Summary

In this unit, we have focused on the key skills and competencies your students will need to make a successful job application. In particular, we have emphasised those skills and competencies needed for drafting a cover letter and a CV or resume, two key documents needed for job applications.

The unit started by identifying the key skills and competencies for making a successful job application. In so doing, we have explored and discussed some of the cultural specifics relating to the countries or regions and industries where a particular job may be advertised.

We then looked at how the identified skills could be turned into teachable LOs. We also considered appropriate theories and teaching approaches which can be used to inform the pedagogical decisions for helping students to reach such LOs successfully.

We then examined sample lesson plans together with some sample materials. Finally, possible assessment tasks for both summative and formative assessment have been considered.

In Unit 3, we will be discussing skills and competencies for job interviews. This will be done following the teaching and learning cycle presented and discussed in previous units.

Further readings: An annotated bibliography

Bremner, S. (2018). *Workplace writing. Beyond the text.* Routledge.

Bremner's text offers a comprehensive view of the issues relating to writing for the workplace. It presents a balanced discussion of the theory and pedagogy of workplace writing with a plethora of examples for classroom applications.

How to apply for jobs abroad

https://www.gooverseas.com/blog/how-apply-for-jobs-abroad

This blog provides four useful steps to find and apply for a job abroad. It also shows some of the key industries that some countries advertise in and considers key cultural aspects for the international applicant.

How to get a job in another country

https://www.indeed.com/career-advice/finding-a-job/how-to-get-a-job-in-another-country

This article from indeed.com explains how to get a job in another country and offers tips and other considerations for working abroad. It discusses six steps, from deciding the type of job to applying for it.

Unit 3
Teaching skills and competencies for job interviews

Learning Outcomes

By the end of the unit, you should be able to:

- identify the types of interview formats usually used across a number of business sectors
- recognise the key skills and competencies needed for job interviews
- turn these skills and competencies into LOs
- make pedagogical decisions about designing lessons, selecting materials, and assessing job interview skills and competencies, and
- select effective vocabulary items your students will require for job interviews.

3.1 Introducing job interviews

Job interviews, whether conducted face-to-face or online, are an integral part of any hiring process, and implemented in most industries and business sectors. For the company looking to hire, interviews represent an opportunity to meet the short-listed candidates and decide who is right for their needs. Interviews also allow hiring companies to identify whether the person they are interviewing is a good fit for them; that is, if the candidate aligns or is likely to align with the goals and culture of the

DOI: 10.4324/9781003283515-6

company. Interviews are essential for companies that engage in "forward hiring", that is, hiring someone that is suitable not only for the present but also for a few years ahead. For applicants, interviews give them a chance to expand on any relevant information they could not include in the documents they submitted with their application, and to judge whether they will fit into the values and culture of the hiring company.

There are different types of interview formats; each of them has its own components and follows specific procedures. The most common types are:

- **behavioural interviews** (to assess how candidates have handled specific employment related situations in the past)
- **case interviews** (to evaluate candidates' problem-solving skills and competencies given a specific situation)
- **competency-based interviews** (to assess candidates' soft and interpersonal skills and competencies), and
- **panel interviews** (to evaluate whether candidates are a good fit by gathering information provided by multiple interviewers from the same company)

All of these interview formats will require a series of questions and tasks short-listed candidates will be asked, and required to perform. Different types of interview questions may be asked, but the most common are: Ice-breaking questions, skills/experience-based questions, behaviour-related questions, and situational questions. We will explore them in more detail later on.

Short-listed candidates may also be required to perform a series of tasks. These will vary among companies and business sectors. However, most task-based interviews will include one or two of the following:

- **technical tasks**, which are used to gather specific technical information about the candidate's areas of expertise
- **problem-solving tasks**, which test a candidate's ability to identify a problem and solve it
- **personality tasks**, which are used to determine a candidate's cultural fit
- **communication tasks**, which assess a candidate's ability to communicate complex ideas to, for instance, other team members; and
- **confidence tasks**, which test a candidate's ability to talk confidently and react on their feet.

Now that we have explored typical interviews formats, question and task types, we are in a better position to identify the key skills needed to be successful at job interviews, and turn the skills and competencies identified into LOs. This is what we will do in the next section.

3.2 Key skills and competencies for job interviews

Many interviews will combine questions and tasks, so it is important that you help your students develop and practise the underlying skills and competencies needed to answer and ask questions successfully as well as perform well in interview tasks. The following is a list of key skills and competencies for job interviews. As we have already mentioned, you may want to add others to the list based on the needs of your students and teaching context:

- recognising types of interviews
- identifying question types
- asking for clarification
- replying questions successfully
- using research to make interesting questions
- recognising interview task types
- completing tasks successfully

Let's reflect for a moment on these skills and competencies. Task RA-3.1 has been designed to help you with this.

Reflection Activity (RA-3.1)

- How aware do you think your students are of the different types of interviews? Would their level of awareness vary depending on whether they are pre-experience or job-experienced? How can you help them to become (more) aware?
- What other skills or competencies you would like to add to the list above based on your teaching context?
- How would you go about teaching them?

As suggested by the questions in this reflection task, who your students are and the type of context (e.g., English school, business college) in which you are teaching will always determine the choice of skills and competencies you need to focus on.

Next, we need to turn the skills and competencies we have listed above into measurable LOs. As we discussed in previous units, listing necessary skills and competencies, together with information about your students' abilities and needs from a NA exercise or SWOT analysis, will facilitate the transformation of skills and competencies into measurable LOs and actual teaching activities when it comes to designing lessons (see Unit 1, Section 1.2.2).

In the case of the skills and competencies we have identified for this unit, Table 3.1 exemplifies how they can be turned into LOs. As in previous units, the questions in the middle column show the thinking process involved in transforming skills and competencies into LOs.

Table 3.1 Turning Skills and Competencies into LOs for Job Interviews

Skills/ Competences	Questions	Resulting LOs
Recognising interview types	What are the different types of job interviews normally conducted in most business sectors? How can students learn to identify such types?	By the end of the lesson, you should be able to identify different types of job interviews.
Identifying question types	What types of job interview questions are commonly asked? How can students learn to identify such types?	By the end of the lesson, you should be able to identify different types of job interview questions.
Asking for clarification	How can students ask for clarification when they don't understand a question? What appropriate language do they need to use?	By the end of the lesson, you should be able to use appropriate language to ask for clarification.
Using research to make interesting questions	What information researched and gathered in preparation for the interview can be used to ask interesting questions?	By the end of the lesson, you should be able to use information gathered in preparation for the interview to ask interesting questions.

Skills/ Competences	Questions	Resulting LOs
Replying questions successfully	What strategies can students deploy to answer questions successfully?	By the end of the lesson, you should be able to deploy a number of strategies to answer questions successfully.
Recognising interview task types	What types of tasks are usually used in job interviews? How can students learn to identify such types?	By the end of the lesson, you should be able to identify different types of job interview tasks.
Completing tasks successfully	How can students learn to identify key requirements of an interview task? How can interview tasks be completed successfully?	By the end of the lesson, you should be able to identify key requirements of an interview task to complete it successfully.

We can now pause here to reflect upon the contents of Table 3.1. The questions in the next Reflection Activity (RA-3.2) aim at guiding your reflective process.

Reflection Activity (RA-3.2)

- Would you need to adapt the LOs in Table 3.1 so that they best meet the particular needs of your students? If so, how would you do it?
- Do you think the supporting questions in the table are also relevant to your students? If they are not, how could you adapt them to make them more relevant?
- Based on the resulting LOs, can you anticipate the teaching method or approach that would be most appropriate?

Now, you are in a position to do the extension task for this unit. In Extension Task ET-3.1, you will watch a video clip published by **Indeed** (www.indeed.com) where a recruitment consultant is speaking about interview questions.

Extension Task (ET-3.1)

Watch the following video clip about interview questions by Indeed.com. As you watch, think of the following points the presenter is making:

- The value of doing some research on the company advertising the job
- The importance of demonstrating alignment of their goals and values with yours
- The relationship between the skills and competencies mentioned in the job description and those the candidate has to offer
- The role of self-awareness and self-improvement in relation to a candidate's weaknesses
- Strategies for speaking about one's potential, future goals and career development.

https://www.youtube.com/watch?v=rcrnHWv-wHc

When either asking or answering questions, your students will probably need particular language items. Language Corner LC-3.1 shows some such items.

Language Corner (LC-3.1)

There are a number of language items that your students will have to be familiar with when dealing with interview questions. The list below provides some key items, but you may want to add a few more which you think will be relevant to your own teaching context.

Answering questions

- That's an interesting/a tough question.
- I was hoping you would ask that. I think...
- Well, I believe...
- The main reason (to apply for the job) was...
- I'm interested in this job because...
- What attracts me (the most) about this job actually is...
- Well, (I think/believe/in my experience) [question theme (e.g., conflict management)] is a difficult aspect/an interesting example of...
- A (clear) example of that would be when I...

Asking for clarification

- Could you repeat (the question), please?
- Could you clarify that for me, please?
- Are you asking whether...?
- Am I right in thinking that you're asking me...?
- So, you're saying...? So, are you saying...?
- If I understand the question correctly,...

Asking questions

- I've read that you value (name value). What/How would you say...?
- What would you say is (the most important value of the company)?
- If I were offered the job, what would...?
- Would you describe the job as...?
- What promotion opportunities are there in the department where the job is?
- When will I hear about...?
- Is there any other information I could facilitate?

Collocations/Expressions

- Interesting/difficult/tricky/tough question
- A question about
- An example/instance of
- To be interested in
- To be shortlisted
- To be good at...
- To be a good example/instance of...
- To be a perfect fit for the job/position
- To harness the (company) data
- To explore their social media/financial reports/competitors.

Structural elements

- **Simple present** (e.g., I'm interested in this job because...)
- **Simple past** (e.g., On that particular occasion, I simply asked the team to...)
- **Past progressive** (e.g., I was hoping you would ask that. I think...)
- **Modals** (e.g., Could you clarify...?; Would you describe...?)

Similarly, when engaging with interview tasks, your students will need to have readily available a particular set of vocabulary items. Some of these are shown in the next language Corner (LC-3.2).

Language Corner (LC-3.2)

The list below provides some relevant language items relating to interview tasks. Again, you may also want to add others to match your own teaching context.

- I think a good example/instance of that is...
- As an example, I'd say that...
- I've always been interested in...
- I have three years' experience in (job/role/sector). During that time, I....
- My previous experience includes...
- My responsibilities include/d (verb+ING)...
- I am/was responsible for...
- As a fluent speaker of (language/s), I would say...
- Considering this situation, I'd say/start by (verb+ING)...
- This is a typical problem/issue in...
- I think I'd solve the problem by (verb+ING)...
- In that particular case, I would...
- At that time, I resolved the situation by... (verb+ING)...
- In my previous job, I collaborated with.../I led (a team of) ...
- As a result of that (action/my intervention), we...

Expressions

- To ace the interview/task
- To share responsibilities
- To take initiative to
- To take responsibility for
- To lead on (project)
- To communicate effectively

Structural elements

- **Simple present** (e.g., I think a good example of that is...)
- **Present perfect** (e.g., I've always been interested in...)
- **Conditional structures** (e.g., As an example, I'd say that...)

Before exploring possible lesson plans for teaching job interview skills and competencies, you may want to revisit the learning theories and teaching approaches in the Introductory Unit (Section I.2) to decide which ones would be most appropriate given these LOs and your own teaching context.

Some of the questions you may ask yourself are:

- Would a mechanistic approach to answering questions best help my students?
- Would working in pairs and on real-world simulations be appropriate?
- Would they benefit from discussing previous experiences with other students, family and friends?

These and other similar questions will help you make decisions about the most appropriate teaching approach for your students, and about the most helpful classroom activities you would need to design your lessons. This is what we explore in Section 3.3.

3.3 Designing lessons for job interviews

This section of the unit offers lesson plans for dealing with interview questions (Table 3.2) and engaging with interview tasks (Table 3.3).

Table 3.2 A Lesson Plan for Dealing with Interview Questions

Course: Communication skills for the international workplace	Year group:	Date:
Learning outcomes for dealing with interview questions		
By the end of the lesson, students (Sts) should be able to: • identify different types of interview questions, and • select appropriate vocabulary items to deal with interview questions.		
Progression of teaching & learning		**Strategies/Materials**
Duration: 10 minutes	Introduction T asks Sts to discuss in small groups (3-4) their knowledge and experiences of interview questions (e.g., types of questions)	Eliciting Sts' previous knowledge/experience

(Continued)

Duration: 25 minutes	Activity 1 1. T presents students with a text on interview question types and discuss them with the Sts. 2. Sts watch a video of a simulated job interview. As they watch, they pay attention to the types of questions asked and jot down examples from the video. 3. In their groups, Sts classify the questions on the clip following the text presented by the T, paying attention to relevant vocabulary items. They then report their results to the class.	1. Discussing interview question types/Handout 1 2. Watching a video clip, identifying different question types, and jotting down a few examples/ Handout 1 3. Classifying questions and sharing results with the class.
Duration: 15 minutes	Activity 2 4. Sts watch the video again and focus on the applicant's questions for the interviewer. 5. Sts complete a table, make a list of relevant vocabulary items, and discuss their answers in pairs. 6. Pairs share the discussion on their answers with the class.	4. Considering the structure and the content of the applicant's questions/ handout 2 5. Discussing answers in pairs 6. Reporting results to the class
Duration: 10 minutes	Conclusion Sts reflect on the activities of the lesson and summarise what they have learnt.	

Success criteria	• To identify different types of interview questions, and • To select appropriate vocabulary to ask and answer interview questions.	**Assessment** In pair or small groups, Sts will make a list of possible questions for applicants to a specific job ad given by the T.
Next steps	Sts will ask family and friends about typical questions for job interviews. They will report the results of their survey back to the entire class.	

Table 3.3 A Lesson Plan for Engaging with Interview Tasks

Course: Communication skills for the international workplace	Year group:	Date:
Learning outcomes for engaging with interview tasks		
By the end of the lesson, students should be able to: • identify the key elements (e.g., requirements, language) in an interview problem-solving task • perform an interview problem-solving task with confidence, and • select appropriate vocabulary items to deal with interview tasks.		
Progression of teaching & learning		**Strategies/Materials**
Duration: 10 minutes	<u>Activity 1</u> 1. T introduces interview task types to Sts and presents them with examples.	1. Analysing interview task types/ Handout 1 2. Analysing a problem-solving task/Handout 1 3. Identifying specific vocabulary/ Handout 1 4. Class discussion

(Continued)

	2. Sts focus on a problem-solving task and analyse its content and structure to identify the key elements of problem-solving tasks. 3. Sts identify the vocabulary items they will need to perform the task. 4. Sts share results with class.	
Duration: 20 minutes	Activity 2 5. Individually, Sts make a list of the possible answers to the requirements of the problem-solving task. 6. In pairs, Sts compare and contrast their lists taking into account their content, relevance, level of detail, and language used. 7. Sts take down notes on their discussion. 8. Pairs share their discussion with the class.	5. List making/Handout 2 6. Comparing notes/Handout 2 7. Writing discussion notes/Handout 2 8. Reporting results to the class
Duration: 25 minutes	Activity 3 9. Sts choose a problem-solving task from those presented to them by their T.	9. Choosing a task/Handout 3 10. Discussing and jotting down notes/Handout 3 11. Simulating a job interview task.

(Continued)

	10. In pairs, Sts discuss the possible ways in which the task can be done, taking into account appropriate language. 11. Sts simulate a job interview in which such a task is given to the candidate.	
Duration: 5 minutes	<u>Conclusion</u> Invite Sts to reflect upon the activities of the class and what they have learnt.	
Success criteria	• To identify the key elements in an interview problem-solving task • To perform an interview problem-solving task with confidence, and • To select appropriate vocabulary items to perform interview tasks.	**Assessment** None at this stage
Next steps	For homework Sts could be asked to read further on interview problem-solving tasks (see materials in the next section), and be prepared to share with the rest of the class what they have discovered by reading the text.	

Now that we have looked at these two possible lesson plans for teaching students how to deal with interview questions and interview tasks, you may want to pause and reflect upon such lesson plans. Activity RA-3.3 provides some questions to help you think about the relevance of the plans for your own teaching context.

Reflection Activity (RA-3.3)

- How would the lessons in Tables 3.2 and 3.3 need to be adapted so that they best meet the particular needs of your students?
- Would they go well with the teaching approach that you reflected upon in Section 3.2?
- If not, how would they need to be changed to sit well with the approach you chose?

As we have already discussed, national and corporate culture will play an important role in determining both the format and the content of job interviews. The following Culture and Technology Note (CTN-3.1) provides you with a few insights into this.

Culture and Technology Note (CTN-3.1)

It is essential to discuss with your students how culture (national and corporate) will be a main factor influencing the interview format and the type of questions and tasks included in it. You may want to bring to their attention things such as:

- Ice-breaking or small talk at the beginning of a job interview is typical in many cultures. Small talk takes different forms and it may vary in terms of topic and length. Although it plays an important role in certain workplace communication instances, it is always about unimportant or uncontroversial matters.
- Similarly, the emphasis on skills and/or experience is typical of Anglo-Saxon cultures. Other cultures around the globe might focus on qualifications rather than skills and experience (this tends to be the case in southern Europe, for example). Yet, in other cultures the focus might be on family connections (this may be the case in cultures where the concept of social groups such as family plays an important role in society).
- Many cultures value job interview answers that provide specific examples. Sometimes it can be difficult for recent graduates to come up with good examples that demonstrate their skills. However, recent graduates can always use examples from their part-time jobs, volunteering activities and school positions. Even as a recent graduate it is ideal to have some examples that relate to the world outside school ready to be used at an interview.

Cultural notes like these could then be followed by reflection questions such as "How are job interviews conducted in your context?" If you are teaching pre-experience students, they could conduct a brief survey to family and friends. They could then share the results of their surveys with the rest of the class. Following this, the whole class could write lists of typical trends in different work environments and sectors.

So far, we have identified key skills and competencies relating to job interviews and have looked at ways to turn them into LOs. We then examined how these LOs could be realised by means of teaching lessons. In the next section, we examine sets of materials that can be used for the lesson plans in this section.

3.4 Materials for teaching job interview skills and competencies

The following sets of materials have been designed to teach dealing with interview questions (Section 3.4.1) and engaging with interview tasks (Section 3.4.2).

3.4.1 Dealing with interview questions

Handout 1: Types of Interview Questions

There are different interview question types. The most common ones are: Ice-breaking questions, skills/experience-based questions, behaviour-related questions, and situational questions. The following text and exercises illustrate these types of questions.

- **Ice-breaking questions**
  These questions are asked at the beginning of the interview, after the formal greetings and introductions. They aim to put the candidates at ease before the proper interview starts. Some examples include:
  - Why did you apply for the job?
  - Why are you interested in the job?
  - What attracted you (the most) about this job?
  As you can see, these are general questions that give candidates the possibility of describing their reasons for applying and relaxing at the start of the interview. So, it is important that you think why you have applied and have a few key ideas in mind in case these or similar questions are asked.

- **Skills/Experience-based questions**
  These questions aim at knowing more about what you can do in relation to specific aspects of the job you have applied for. They tend to be practical in nature (e.g., what you can do, your experience in doing something).
     These are some examples of skills/experience-based questions:
  - Have you ever been involved in designing a new product?
  - Can you tell us about how spreadsheets work?
  - Have you ever done any professional presentations?
  As these examples show, these questions are not about what you know (theory) but what you can do or have been involved in the past (practice). A SWOT analysis should give you an idea of your strengths in terms of your skills and experiences and what you can do in relation to the job you have applied for. Use the results of a SWOT analysis or profiling exercise to think of possible skills/experience-based questions and how you could answer them.

- **Behaviour-related questions**
  These questions explore a candidate's attitude to and motivation for the job, their work ethics, work style, and commitment. Examples include:
  - How do you manage conflict in the workplace?
  - Can you tell us how you tackle difficult tasks?
  - Describe an example when you took your own initiative for a task given to you.
  As you can see, these questions are more complex than the previous type as they focus on intangible things such as motivation, attitude and ethics. It is important that you take some time to think about you and your work-related behaviour. This will help you understand who you are as a job seeker and make it easier for you to answer such questions.

- **Situational questions**
  These types of question give you an opportunity to show what you would do in a specific scenario or situation. They normally involve a background situation followed by a question. They are used to explore your confidence and decision-making skills so it is very important you think about them in advance.
     Examples of situational questions include:
  - You have been given two tasks that have the same deadline. How would you prioritise these two pressing deadlines?

- A client is very unhappy with a product she has recently bought following your purchase advice. How would you deal with her dissatisfaction?

Now watch the following video clip of a simulated job interview. As you watch it, try and identify the types of questions asked and jot down a few examples.

https://www.youtube.com/watch?v=OVAMb6Kui6A

Question Type	Examples	Key Vocabulary
1.	1.1	
	1.2	
2.	2.1	
	2.2	
3.	3.1	
	3.2	
4.	4.1	
	4.2	

Handout 2: Asking Questions at a Job Interview

Watch the video clip once more. This time, focus on the applicant's questions for the interviewer. Try to identify the information that the applicant may have used to make the questions (e.g., company's website, company's values) and note down any specific vocabulary used to phrase the questions.

Question	Information used to make the question	Specific vocabulary
1.		
2.		
3.		
4.		
5.		

3.4.2 Engaging with interview tasks

Handout 3: Problem-Solving Scenario

Read the following problem-solving scenarios and with another student choose one to focus on. Then discuss the possible ways in which the task can be done, taking into account appropriate language. After you have finished, simulate a job interview in which the task you chose is given to a candidate.

Problem-solving scenarios
1. Could you give us an example of a time you used logic to solve a problem in your present or previous job?
2. You are giving a team presentation in front of group of investors and it's your turn to talk. All of the sudden the projector stops working. You turn it on and off to see if that works, but it doesn't. What would you do?
3. You are responsible for giving a bonus to factory workers that have perfect attendance during the month. One worker missed one day due to a death in the family. The worker starts crying in your office and tells you that she needs the bonus desperately since she is behind on her rent. The rules are clear and the bonus is for perfect attendance. However, you do have the authority to make exceptions to the rule. What would you do?

Case Chosen	Possible Answer(s)	Language Items Needed

The following materials offer some other activities you can use to help your students deal with interview questions based on two typical interview formats: one-to-one and panel interviews.

How to Answer Interview Questions

One strategic way of answering interview questions is structuring them following the STAR method. STAR stands for Situation, Task, Activity, and Results. Here is a brief description of each element in the method:

Situation	*Provide a context for your answer* (e.g., **In my previous job**, I.../**At** [name of the organisation], I...]

Task	Explain what you did or were asked to do (e.g., In my previous job, **I was in charge of a small team of 6 people**)
Activity	Provide a brief description of what you did (e.g., As a team leader, **my main responsibility was**...)
Results	Explain what your main achievement was (e.g., As a result of my intervention, **we managed to**...)

Some other tips:

- Do your research on the organisation
- Include some of your research findings in your answers
- Keep your answers concise
- Finish your interview questions on a positive note.

One-to-One Interviews

Some organisations tend to hold one-to-one interviews led by the head of the department or division where the selected candidate will work. This type of interviews allows the interviewer to establish a connection with the applicants more easily to evaluate where they are a good fit for the job. At the same time, it may help the candidate to feel at ease, and perform at their best.

Simulation Task (Pair)

Instructions

Read the job ad, resume submitted by one of the applicants and their research notes on the organisation provided below (see Materials). Student A will be interviewing the applicant. Based on the job ad, you should decide what type of questions you will want to ask them. Then, make a list of relevant questions for the applicant. Student B will play the applicant who has submitted the resume and made the research notes.

Once you have drawn the list of questions and read the resume and research notes, simulate an interview in which Student A is the interviewer and Student B the applicant. After you have finished, you could switch roles.

Materials

Job Ad	Resume (Extracts)	Research Notes
Marketing Graduate Roles at J&J If you are passionate about marketing, this is the perfect opportunity for you! Full-time and part-time jobs are available at our New York office, with start dates available from January onwards. We are looking for someone: • with a record of making a positive impact on projects, events and groups • who collaborates with other people • who can think strategically and generate new ideas • with a recently completed degree in Marketing • with passion and achievements in academic and/or non-academic activities	<u>Qualifications</u>: BA in marketing with advertising & digital communications <u>Languages</u>: French (mother tongue), English (second language), Spanish (advanced level) • excellent IT skills (e.g., MS suite, PPT, social media platforms • excellent soft skills (e.g., good communicator and listener, strong interpersonal skills) • led two projects during internship with local marketing communications company	J&J • are leaders in marketing and digital communication • are leaders in their area, with a deep commitment to delivering leadership results • focus on resources to achieve leadership objectives and strategies • show respect for All Individuals (colleagues, customers and consumers) • place great value on big, new consumer innovations

Job Ad	Resume (Extracts)	Research Notes
• who can demonstrate leadership skills and strong passion for brand management • with excellent communication and social skills • who has strong English spoken and written skills.		

The following Language Corner (LC-3.3) provides a list of items for asking interview questions that your students may have either used or needed for the previous task.

Language Corner (LC-3.3)

There are a number of language items that your students will need for asking the right type of questions. The list below provides some key items but you may want to add a few more which you think will be relevant to your own teaching context.

Possible questions

- Please tell me about ... (e.g., yourself).
- Can you tell me a bit about... (e.g., yourself/your previous job)?
- Why have you applied for... (e.g., this job/this vacancy)?
- What has attracted you the most about... (e.g., this job/this vacancy)?
- Why do you want to work here/at [name of company]?
- Why do you want to leave your (present) company?
- What are you most attracted to/passionate about?
- What are your strengths and weaknesses?
- What would you say are your main... (e.g., strengths/weaknesses)?
- What do you do to overcome (e.g., challenges at work/your weaknesses)?
- Where do you want to be in 3–5 years?

- What do you want to be in 3–5 years?
- What experience have you had of...?
- How much would you say you know about...?
- Do you prefer working on your own or in a team?
- Can you give me an example of a mistake you've made, and how you handled it?
- Can you give me an example when you made a positive impact on a team or a project?

Collocations

- Be attracted to something
- Be passionate about something
- Great/main/real strength (how about collocations for 'weakness'?)
- Overcome a weakness (what else can be overcome?)
- Make a mistake (other collocations for 'mistake'?)
- Know **about**.../have knowledge **of**/be knowledgeable **about**

Structural elements

- **Modals** (e.g., can, could)
- **Simple present**- future reference (e.g., what/where do you to be in 3–5 years?)
- **Would** – hypothetical meaning (e.g., What would you do if....?)
- **Prefer** + Verb ING (e.g., Do you prefer working...?
- **Prefer** (something) **to** (something) (e.g., I prefer working in teams to working on my own.)

Panel interviews

Panel interviews are becoming more common in many industry sectors. In this type of interviews, a group of people (normally three or four) from different departments or sections of an organisation play different roles and ask different questions. On a panel, you could have, for example, someone from Human Resources (HR), someone from the department or section where the vacancy is located, and someone from general management. Of course, the number and composition of the panel will vary depending on the national and organisational cultures. It is very important that you are aware of this, so doing your research on the company is vital.

Types of questions by role

- the HR representative on the panel will tend to ask questions about your previous experiences, your hopes for the new job, and salary expectations
- people from the department or section where the selected candidate will work will ask more technical questions, specific to the role the new employee will be holding. These could include your previous experience, your knowledge of the area, projects you were involved in and how you worked in teams.
- the panel member representing the management team will tend to ask less technical questions. They are normally interested in knowing your reasons for applying, work philosophy, work ethics and culture, and how you would fit into the organisation in general.

Simulation Task (Group of 4)

Instructions

Read the following job ad in the Materials section below. You will simulate a panel interview to fill in the vacancy advertised. Decide who is going to play the role of general management representative (Student A), who will be the person from the department where the job is located (Student B), and who will be the HR representative (Student C). The remaining student (Student D) will play the applicant. After you have decided who will play each of the four roles, Students A, B and C complete the table below with appropriate questions and decide the order of the questions (normally from general to specific). In the meantime, Student D thinks of the answers he/she can give to each of the questions.

Materials

Job Ad
Kub-ready Inc. is seeking to appoint a data engineer to organise, cleanse, align and correlate our clients' raw data into usable information that can lead to better business insights and faster, more accurate solutions. You should have: • A degree in any field of computer sciences • Strong problem-solving skills • Strong communication skills, both oral and written • Strong collaboration skills • Flexible on location as our consultants often work across the country

Questions by role		
Management representative (Student A)	Person from department/section (Student B)	HR representative (Student C)
1.	1.	1.
2.	2.	2.
3.	3.	3.
4.	4.	4.

Language Corner LC-3.4 complements LC-3.3 by offering a list of items for answering interview questions that your students may have either used or needed for the previous task.

Language Corner (LC-3.4)

There are a number of language items that your students will need for answering questions strategically. The list below provides some key items but you may want to add a few more which you think will be relevant to your own teaching context.

Answering interview questions (remember the STAR method)

- In my previous job, I... (what you did/were asked to do)
- At [name of the organisation], I... (what you did/were asked to do)
- My main/key responsibility was/included
- As a team leader, I managed to...
- As a team, we managed to...
- I'd say my biggest/most important/main...
- I've been a/an (role) for about (number) years, and I'm currently working as a/an (role) at (company name).
- I've been at (company) for (number) years, and previously worked at (company) for (number) years.
- My present job/position doesn't offer (e.g., an opportunity [for me] to...)
    Note: Avoid criticising your present/previous organisation or line manager. Instead, focus on what you'd like from your future job which your present doesn't offer.
- In (number) years' time, I'd like to... (something you'd like to learn or achieve).

Asking for clarification (Also see Language corner LC-3.1)

- I'm not sure I understand your question. Can you please clarify?
- Are you asking me if/whether...?
- I'm sorry, but just so I know I'm answering the right question, could you repeat that/the question?
- Can you clarify what you mean by...?
- I'm not exactly sure what you meant by your question. Would you mind rephrasing it?

Collocations

- Main/key responsibility (What other adjectives can be used with 'responsibility'?
- I'm not sure/certain/positive...
- To repeat/clarify/rephrase a question

Structural elements

- **Simple present** (e.g., I'm not sure I understand the question.)
- **Present progressive** (e.g., Are you asking...?)
- **Present perfect** (e.g., I have been at (organisation) for (number) years.)
- **Simple past** (e.g., I managed to improve sales by 5%.)
- **Mind** + VerbING (e.g., Would you mind rephrasing it?)

The next Reflection Activity (RA-3.4) provides you with an opportunity to reflect how relevant and useful these materials could be to teach your students interview skills. Although they were designed for the lesson plans in Tables 3.2 and 3.3, they could be also used to design lesson plans that meet your students' needs more closely.

Reflection Activity (RA-3.4)

- How would you evaluate the materials presented in the handouts above?
- How well do they meet the criteria for materials outlined in the Introductory Unit (see Section 1.4)?
- How would they need to be modified to be more appropriate for your teaching context?

The last Culture and Technology Note (CTN-3.2) of the unit presents some further interview-related considerations you may want to share with your students.

Culture and Technology Note (CTN-3.2)

These are other culture-related notes that you may want to share with your students:

- In some work contexts (for example, in countries such as Japan) staying with the same company for long periods of time can be seen as an asset. In these contexts, seniority in the same company is regarded highly. In others (such as the USA, the UK), mobility is sometimes considered to be a sign of ambition. This is connected with the long-term orientation or the short-term orientation of the respective cultures. Students need to factor these orientations into the answers they may give to questions such as 'Where do you see yourself in 3 years?'
- In many countries, interviewers would make sure not to advantage or disadvantage any candidate by asking them different questions. They would also try to be neutral in their responses, avoiding positive or negative comments on the applicants' replies. This makes it easier for them to evaluate all the candidates on the basis of their answers only and to be able to make comparisons. In this way, interviewers find themselves in a better position to be able to appoint the best candidate for the job.

It is also important to remind students that they can use technology-based tools to research and expand their knowledge of different cultures, especially those they would like to work in. This, as discussed in Unit 2, will provide them with both culture-general and culture-specific knowledge (Tuleja, 2021). As we have also already discussed and illustrated in the previous section, searching for a company's culture, goals and values can prove very useful when preparing for an interview. This will also help students to anticipate some of the interview questions they may be asked.

3.5 Assessing learning

This section of the unit presents a self-assessing task (3.5.1) and a job interview simulation (3.5.2) that you can use to assess whether and to what extent your students have achieved the LOs set out for the unit.

3.5.1 Self-assessing skills and competencies for interview skills

Self-Assessing Skills and Competencies for Job Interviews				
Use the following list of Can-Do statements to self-assess the skills and competencies you have learnt in this unit. In case you are not sure or think you have not yet acquired the skill or competency referred to, make a note on what you can do about it.				
I can	Yes	No	?	I'm planning to
1. understand the key types of interview formats.				
2. identify the different types of interview questions.				
3. ask for clarification on a question with confidence.				
4. identify the different types of interview tasks.				
5. use appropriate vocabulary to answer interview questions and engage in interview tasks with confidence.				

3.5.2 Assessing skills and competencies for interview skills

The following integrated task provides students with an opportunity to show the skills and competencies they have learnt in this unit. You could use it to complement the self-assessment exercise in Section 3.5.1, as a formative assessment exercise or for summative assessment. Alternatively, you can use it as a model for designing another task that would be more suitable for your students and teaching context.

3.5.2.1 Job interview simulation task

Divide the class into 2 groups. Group A will be the applicants and Group B the interviewers. Students in each group can work together and support one another in preparing for the interview. After all students in Group A have been interviewed, the students can swap roles so that they all have an opportunity to be interviewed. Teacher and peers provide feedback after each simulation.

Group A	Group B
Instructions: Read the following ad for a job with **VL GmbH** you will be applying for. There is no need for you to write a CV or resume for it, but pay attention to the requirements mentioned in the job ad and do a quick SWOT analysis to be able to speak about what you would be bringing to the job if hired.	**Instructions**: Read the following job ad which your company has just advertised and for which you will be interviewing a group of short-listed candidates. Considering the types of interview questions you have discussed in this unit, make a list of 2–3 questions of each type. Add as many types as necessary.

VL GmbH
Part-timers, Kurfürstendamm- Berlin
VL GmbH Berlin is seeking to appoint highly motivated part-timers with a real passion for personal fashion advice. They will become VL GmbH personal advisors to a high-class worldly clientele. Highly motivated, creative and willing to learn, the newly appointed VL GmbH personal advisors will work in a prime location in the exciting city of Berlin, Germany.

Profile
YOU will be

- responsible for building a true relationship with our exclusive clientele by assessing and meeting their shopping needs
- the first port of contact for a selected group of VL GmbH clients and in charge of setting the tone for their shopping experiences as they remain our selected clients
- a recent graduate with strong communication and interpersonal skills, and
- fluent in German (or willing to be in a considerable length of time), English and another language which can be your mother tongue.

We offer	
• industry-leading training with exclusive in-depth insight into the retail fashion sector • great opportunities for local as well as global promotion and • a generous benefits package.	
SWOT analysis S: _____ W: _____ O: _____ T: _____	**Interview questions** Type: _____ Q1: _____ Q2: _____ Type: _____ Q3: _____ Q4: _____

Finally, I'd like to remind you here of the importance of a set of marking criteria for the unit, as we discussed in the Introductory Unit (see Section I.5).

3.6 Summary

This unit has explored the interview formats commonly used across most business sectors and highlighted the underlying skills and competencies students will need for dealing with interview questions and interview tasks successfully.

Based on this, the unit has exemplified how the identified skills and competences needed for job interviews could be turned into LOs, and offered a number of lesson plans, materials, and assessments for teaching and evaluating job interview skills. These have been complemented with lists of effective vocabulary items students will need for answering interview questions and performing interview tasks successfully.

In Unit 4, we will be examining interpersonal communication skills and competencies which are key to making and maintaining good relationships at work.

Further readings: An annotated bibliography

Handling tricky interview questions

https://www.personalcareermanagement.com/career-tips/handling-tricky-interview-questions/

In this blog, Corinne Mills—the joint Managing Director of Personal Career Management—offers a number of considerations and strategies for dealing with tricky questions during a job interview.

Indeed company reviews

https://www.indeed.com/companies

This Indeed webpage allows you to search for companies and obtain information about not only their products, goals and values but also what employees and their competitors think of them. It is a very useful resource when preparing for an interview.

Interview tests and exercises

https://www.prospects.ac.uk/careers-advice/interview-tips/interview-tests-and-exercises

Rachel Swain, editorial manager at Prospects, shares her views and experiences about presentations, social events and group activities that recruiters in a number of sectors use to make sure the most suitable short-listed candidate is selected for the job.

Part III

The new job

Unit 4
Teaching skills and competencies for interpersonal communication

---

Learning Outcomes

By the end of the unit, you should be able to:

- identify key skills and competencies needed for interpersonal communication at work
- turn skills and competencies into learning outcomes
- make pedagogical decisions about designing lessons, selecting materials, and assessing interpersonal communications skills and competencies, and
- select effective vocabulary items required for realising such skills and competencies.

4.1 Introducing interpersonal communication

This unit focuses on the interpersonal skills and competencies your students will need for successful communication at work, and on how you can teach them.

Interpersonal communication generally refers to the process of exchanging information, ideas and feelings between two or more people by means of verbal or non-verbal methods. In the workplace, interpersonal communication, whether it happens face-to-face or online, includes daily internal communication with other employees (see Units

DOI: 10.4324/9781003283515-8

5 and 6), employee performance reviews (see Unit 7) and project discussions. Interpersonal communication skills can help your students be productive in the workplace, and build strong and positive relationships with colleagues from their first day at work.

The unit begins by identifying key interpersonal skills and competencies. These can be applied to a number of situations and contexts. However, as you gain more teaching experience and become more familiar with your teaching environment, you will probably want to adapt the skills and competencies set out in the unit to better meet the needs of your own students.

The unit also provides you with strategies you can deploy to turn these skills and competencies into the LOs for a lesson on interpersonal communication skills for the first day at work. It then revisits the pedagogical considerations we discussed in the Introductory Unit to help you identify which theories, teaching approaches and classroom activities are the most suitable for teaching these skills and competencies to your students.

In Section 4.3, you will find sample lesson plans for teaching two of the skills for interpersonal communication for the first day, followed by sample materials that you can use to teach such lessons (Section 4.4). The last section of the unit (Section 4.5) shows possible tasks that you can use to assess the skills and competencies of the unit.

Let's then start by identifying some core skills and competencies for effective communication on the first day at work.

4.2 Key skills and competencies for interpersonal communication in the workplace

Before teaching your students these skills, you will have to keep in mind whether they are new to the workplace. If this is going to be their first job, you will probably want to begin by exploring communication skills in general with them. If they are job-experienced students but have just been offered their first job in an international company, you would probably start with those skills that are key to their first day at work. Whichever the case may be, your students will need to be able to introduce themselves to new colleagues, as well as talk about themselves, and possibly about their previous work experiences and workplace.

In any case, there is a group of core skills and competencies that your students will need to develop so that they are better prepared to communicate effectively in their new work environment. These skills are:

- making introductions and first impressions
- managing interpersonal communication effectively
- building positive relationships at work, and
- using appropriate language and conventions to speak about themselves, their jobs and previous work exp eriences.

Let's reflect on these skills for a moment. Activity RA-4.1 aims at guiding you through your reflection.

Reflection Activity (RA-4.1)

- How important do you think these skills and competencies are for your students?
- Based on your previous experience, are there others you would like to add?
- How do you think your students will best develop these skills and competencies?
- How would you go about teaching them?

As you can see from the reflection activity, your choice of what skills to teach will always be determined by who you are teaching (your students) as we have discussed previously. By the same token, you will always have to consider how they can best learn such skills and how you can teach them most effectively (learning theories and teaching approaches).

Another vital decision you will have to make is how you can turn the skills you have identified into LOs. This is an important step for translating decisions into teaching actions. Whether you have conducted a Needs Assessment (NA) exercise, as we discussed in Unit 1, or you have made your decisions based on your own experiences, the outcomes of your analysis or decisions need to be formulated into LOs.

As we discussed in previous units, LOs are the goals that you want your students to be able to achieve by the end of a lesson. In the case of the skills and competencies we have identified for this unit, Table 4.1

Table 4.1 Turning Skills into Learning Outcomes for Interpersonal Communication

Skills	Questions	Resulting LOs
Making introductions and first impressions	Will they need to introduce themselves to other people? What conventions for making introductions should they follow? How do they want to be perceived (e.g., serious, professional) by their new colleagues?	At the end of the lesson, students should be able to introduce themselves to new colleagues using appropriate conventions. At the end of the lesson, students should be able to decide how they want to be perceived by new colleagues.
Managing interpersonal communication effectively (including small talk)	What are the key components of interpersonal communication that the students need to know? Why is it important for them to understand interpersonal communication practices? How can they use small talk for interpersonal communication at work?	At the end of the lesson, you should be able to identify key components of interpersonal communications. At the end of the lesson, you should be able to understand and follow interpersonal communication practices to function in your work environment effectively.
Building positive relationships at work	How can positive relationships be built at work? What strategies can students use to build positive relationships?	At the end of the lesson, you should be able to deploy specific strategies to build positive relationships at work.

Skills	Questions	Resulting LOs
Using appropriate language to speak about yourself and your (new) company	What appropriate language items will they need? Are there key grammatical structures they will need? What specific vocabulary items will they find useful for such purposes?	At the end of the lesson, you should be able to use appropriate language to make introductions. At the end of the lesson, you should be able to speak about your company using appropriate structures and specific vocabulary.

illustrates how they can be turned into LOs. As before, the questions in the middle column exemplify the thinking process involved in the transformation.

Now that we have explored how to turn skills into LOs, it is time to think about how those skills can be best taught so that your students are able to achieve the LOs.

Given the nature of the skills we have identified, two learning theories (see the Introductory Unit) seem to be most appropriate: **constructivism** and **connectivism**. As interpersonal communication is something that obviously happens when people interact with other people, learning by interacting with others through tasks and activities that encourage students to work in pairs or small groups seems the most appropriate in this case. These are basic principles we discussed in relation to **constructivism**. By the same token, it is important that you encourage students to become active participants of their learning process by self-discovery within their formal and informal (e.g., colleagues, friends and family) networks. So, you may want your students to ask their networks about their previous work experiences and how they managed introductions on their first day at work, for instance. These are learning principles behind **connectivism**.

As it will be illustrated in the section on lesson planning, learning to communicate effectively in the workplace is all about working with others and learning by self-discovery. This, as discussed in the next Culture and Technology Note (CTN-4.1), is highly influenced by cultural norms.

Culture and Technology Note (CTN-4.1)

In some cultures, learning is a collective activity. Students prefer to learn by doing tasks and activities in small groups rather than individually. If this is the kind of culture in which you are working, it may be important to always start the lesson by asking students to work in pairs or small groups. It is equally important to ask the students to choose a "spokesperson" who will be responsible for reporting back to the whole class. The role of spokesperson should rotate to give different students the opportunity to individually report back to the class. In this way, you will be keeping a balance between collective and individual student performance in a culture-sensitive manner. It is also important to keep in mind to vary the interaction patterns in class. To this end, you could present students with a mix of activities, some of which will require them to work on their own, others in pairs and still others in small groups. Alternatively, the same task could gradually move from individual to collective. The first activity in the task may require students to reflect upon their own previous experiences (individual), then share activities with a partner or small group and even report the results of their activities or discussion to the whole class (collective).

When asking students to do their own formal or informal research (e.g., asking family members about their first day at work), there are a number of applications such as Padlet (https://padlet.com) that your students can use to report and share the results of their research with the rest of the class. This technology-mediated task also involves both modes of interaction: individual and collective.

At the point, it would be useful to reflect a bit about the culture of your teaching environment. Reflection Activity RA-4.2 includes some questions to guide your reflection.

Reflection Activity (RA-4.2)

- How would you define the culture you're teaching in? Individualistic, collectivist or both?
- What characteristics of individualistic or collectivist cultures does yours exhibit?
- Do they influence your teaching practices? If so, how? If not, why not?

The first Insights from Research (IR-4.1) discusses recent research on the role of interpersonal communication and relationships in the workplace. It also presents a brief description of the typical language items which are normally used to establish and maintain interpersonal relationships.

Insights from Research (IR-4.1): Interpersonal relationships at work

As Cheng et al. (2019: 28) have demonstrated, establishing and maintaining "interpersonal relationships is an important aspect of social interaction in general and of workplace communication in particular". It is also considered a desirable quality in employees in most organisational contexts as it contributes, among other things, to "building solidarity and rapport" and "facilitating collaboration and problem-solving".

Obviously, language plays a central role in establishing and maintaining interpersonal relationships. In her corpus-driven study, Koester (2010: 156-158) proposed four areas that contribute to interpersonal communication in English-speaking workplaces, with clearly identified language used in each area. The language and linguistic devices used to realise each area are shown in the following table.

Interpersonal area	Language/linguistic devices used
Expressing stance (e.g., Giving opinions, making judgements, evaluating)	Conditional structures (e.g., if there was), evaluative adjectives (e.g., nice) idioms (e.g., come back to haunt us), and modal verbs
Hedging and **Expressing politeness**	Adverbs, modal verbs, past tense, and vague language (e.g., stuff, sort of)
Showing and **building shared knowledge**	Interactive expressions (e.g., you know, of course), and vague language (e.g., things like that)
Showing empathy and solidarity (e.g., Expressing agreement, positive evaluation)	Colloquialisms and idioms, evaluative adjectives, emotive verbs (e.g., like, love), humour, and positive feedback signals (e.g., Great!)

Depending on their proficiency level, you may want to share these notes with your students or use them to develop classroom activities. For example, you could ask them to listen to examples of interpersonal communication in the workplace and ask them to discuss what speakers are doing in the examples (e.g., showing and building shared knowledge, showing empathy and solidarity). Then, you could ask them to identify and analyse the particular language items used in each instance.

4.3 Designing lessons for interpersonal communication

In this section, we will explore sample lesson plans to teach two of the skills and competencies we have identified for this unit. There are also some ideas for you to consider when developing your own lesson plans for the other two skill sets in this unit. The first lesson plan has been designed to teach "making first impressions" and the second to teach "managing interpersonal communication effectively".

Table 4.2 A Lesson Plan for Making First Impressions

Course: Communication Skills for the International Workplace	Year Group:	Date:
Learning outcomes for making first impressions		
At the end of the lesson, students should be able to: • consider the importance of first impressions in a new workplace • reflect on how they form impressions of people when they meet them for the first time, and • decide how they want to be perceived by others.		
Progression of teaching & learning		**Strategies/Materials**
Duration: 5 minutes	Introduction T asks Sts to work in pairs to make a list of Dos and Don'ts on the first day in a new job	Eliciting Sts' previous knowledge on what one should do and not do on the first day in a new job.

Duration: 15 minutes	Activity 1 1. T presents Sts with a short written or spoken text (e.g., HR perspective on first day) and asks them to read/ listen to it and amend/ complete their lists of Dos and Don'ts in light of the new text. 2. Sts discuss whether/ to what extent the HR expert advice applies to their context.	1. Reading/listening to the perspective of an HR expert/ Handout 1 2. Comparing expert advice it to Sts' lists of Dos and Don'ts/Handout 1
Duration: 15 minutes	Activity 2 3. T presents students with 3 photos of different individuals and asks them to write down the adjectives that come to mind when they see each photo. 4. Sts compare and discuss their views in pairs, in particular with reference to how deceiving appearance can be. 5. Class discussion on 3 and 4.	3. Considering a set of photos individually/ Handout 2 4. Pair discussion/ Handout 2 5. Reflecting upon the importance of appearances and how these can be deceiving/ Handout 2
Duration: 20 minutes	Activity 3 6. Sts individually make a list of characteristics they would like to project on their first day in a new job, and consider how appearances and attire can reinforce such characteristics.	6. Writing a list of characteristics/ Handout 3 7. Reflecting upon and dividing the characteristics into Keep/Amend/ Replace/Handout 3

(Continued)

	7. Sts individually consider if the characteristics from 6 are a true reflection of themselves and get to divide them into three categories: Keep/Amend/Replace. 8. Sts write down the updated list of characteristics. 9. Sts are asked to reconsider their impressions on the 3 photos presented in activity 2. They can apply the same 3 categories: Keep/Amend/Replace.	8. Writing down the list of characteristics Sts want to project/Handout 3 9. Reconsidering views on the 3 photos presented in activity 2/Handout 3
Duration: 5 minutes	Conclusion Class discussion on what to wear, say or do in order to reflect the characteristics identified in the previous activity, and consider strategies to suspend prejudice based on appearances.	Sts to consider and write down what they think they should wear, say or do on their first day at work.
Success criteria	• To be able to evaluate the importance of first impressions in a new workplace • To be able to reflect on how they form impressions of people when they meet them for the first time, and • To be able to decide how they want to be perceived by others.	**Assessment** None at the moment
Next steps	Sts will interview a family member about their first day at work, considering what impressions they wanted to make and how they achieved that.	

4.3.1 Lesson plan 1

As we mentioned in Section 4.2 above, learning to manage workplace interpersonal communication successfully requires a set of important skills, such as building positive relationships by using appropriate language, that students need to learn and develop. Table 4.3 shows a sample lesson plan which aims at helping students to develop such skills.

Table 4.3 A Lesson Plan for Building Positive Relationships

Course: Communication Skills for the International Workplace	Year Group:	Date:
Learning outcomes for building positive relationships		
At the end of the lesson, students should be able to: • identify a number of strategies for building positive relationships at work, and • discuss and select appropriate language to realise such strategies.		
Progression of teaching & learning		**Strategies/Materials**
Duration: 10 minutes	Introduction 1. T introduces the topic "building positive relation- ships at work" to the students by means of questions such as 'How would you define a positive relation?' 'Does that also apply to a work context?'	1. Eliciting Sts ideas and previous knowledge/ experiences/ Handout 4
Duration: 20 minutes	Activity 1 2. Sts read a text on the importance of build- ing positive relation- ships at work. 3. Sts answer questions on the text.	2. Reading a text/Handout 4 3. Answering ques- tions/ Handout 4 4. Discussing answers/Handout 4

(Continued)

	4. In pairs or small groups, Sts discuss their answers to the questions.	
Duration: 25 minutes	Activity 2 5. Sts analyse the key vocabulary items relating to each strategy. 6. Individually, Sts complete a table with the selected items 7. In pairs, Sts compare their completed tables. 8. Sts write reflective entries into their diaries about what they have learnt in today's lesson.	5. Analysing vocabulary items/Handout 5 6. Completing a table/Handout 5 7. Comparing results/Handout 5 8. Writing reflective entries/Sts' diaries
Duration: 5 minutes	Conclusion After Sts have entered their reflective notes into their diaries, T invites them to read a few out loud to share with the rest of the class.	Sts' select entries from their learning diaries and share them with the rest of the class.
Success criteria	• To be able to identify key strategies for building positive relationships at work, and • To be able to select appropriate language to realise such strategies.	Assessment A True/False quiz on the key strategies they can deploy to build positive relationships at work.

Next steps	Sts will interview family and friends about their own experiences of building positive relationships at work, noting any instances that led to conflict because of the lack of such relationships. They should be prepared to discuss the results of their interviews with the rest of the class the following week. Sts can use PowerPoint or Padlet (See CTN-4.1) to report results.

Another important skill in relation to interpersonal communications that your students will probably have to develop is how to identify key language that they will need to

1.   talk about themselves, and
2.   describe their new workplace.

Teaching language that is related to particular skills can be quite interesting and empowering for the students. This can be done by exposing them to video or audio clips that you can find on the internet. You can also ask them to do some research for themselves to identify (good as well as poor) examples on the Internet.

It is important to remember is that your students will need to focus on:

- set phrases and expressions: Chunks of language (e.g., "first day at work") that will help them to express themselves with confidence and fluency
- typical sentence structures (e.g., subject + verb + object) that are frequently used in a particular situation (e.g., introducing yourself to colleagues),
- typical collocations (see LC-4.1) relating to the LOs and the activities in the lesson plan, and
- key grammatical items: Items such as nouns, adjectives and verb tenses that recur when using a particular skill or discussing a particular topic. For example, the simple present tense will be useful when describing their new workplace.

A whole lesson on language may become rather boring and repetitive, especially if you have long classes such as 2-hour slots. However, starting with an example to analyse, such as a video clip, a reading text or an audio recording, will always motivate students by focusing on content and ideas first, followed by a detailed analysis of the language used in them. This can be then followed by asking them to do a task similar to the one they have just analysed.

This idea of exposing students to how other people do things or a particular task reflects the key principles of Task-Based Language Learning (TBLL). The framework for TBLL suggested by Jane Willis (1996) can prove very useful when teaching skills and competencies for the international workplace. This framework of pre-task, task and post-task lends itself very well to moving from content and ideas for a task to the particular language items needed to do similar tasks successfully.

The following task for practising introductions is offered as an illustration of TBLL. You can use it as is or modify it to better suit the needs of your own students.

Pre-task
(This could simply show students a written or video/audio-recorded example of how people introduce other people at work. Students can then 'model' their performance on the pre-task.)
Read the following examples of self-introductions. As you read each example, think of the context (who's speaking, where and to whom), the register (e.g., formal, informal), and the language they used.
A. Hi, my name is Jorge and I come from Spain. I am the new assistant to Billy Stanton, the operation manager. B. Hello. May I introduce myself? My name is Margaret and I am the new graphic designer for the marketing department. C. Nice to meet you. I am Agata, the new game computer designer. I worked at an Italian company back home for two years before joining J&J.
Task
You have just joined QM Limited, a company specialising in digital marketing, as a junior data analyst.
1. How would you introduce yourself to another colleague in the same department at an informal gathering? 2. How would you introduce yourself to the general manager before the start of a company meeting?

Post-task
Now, reflecting upon your self-introductions, think of the following questions: • What language items did you use? • How do they compare with those used in the examples in the pre-task? • What do you think you would need to feel more comfortable with introducing yourself to other people at work?

As shown in this task, your students will probably need a specific set of language items for effective introducing themselves or responding to being introduced at work. Language Corner LC-4.1 presents some such items.

Language Corner (LC-4.1)

There are a number of vocabulary items that your students will need on their first day at work. The list below provides some of these, you may also want to add a few more which may be relevant to your own teaching context.

- ([Title] + name), this is ([Title] + name).
- May I introduce you to...? (one person to another)
- Please allow me to introduce you to...?
- Can I introduce....? (one person to many)
- I'd like to introduce...
- Please meet...
- Hello, may I introduce myself? My name is... and I am...
- (Name) is our new... (title/role)
- ([Title] + name), I'd like to introduce ([Title] + name) our (role).
- Hello. I don't think we've met. I am (name) and I am (role).

Etiquette notes

Introductions in most settings tend to follow a specific etiquette. In English-speaking workplaces, for example, the etiquette for introduction is as follows:

- State the (title and) name of the person being introduced to. This is the higher-ranking person. For example, "Mr Atkinson, may I introduce you to...

- Depending on the formality of the occasion, your relation to the person being introduced to, the age of the people being introduced, use an appropriate introductory phrase "I would like to introduce...", "May I introduce...", "Please meet...", "This is...".
- State the name of the person being introduced. This is the lower-ranking person.

It is also a good idea to add some (but not too many) details about each. These could include common job roles, similar departments, or simply shared interests. Remember always introduce a younger or lower-rank person to an older or higher-rank person. The latter should be mentioned first.

Obviously, etiquettes for introductions are shaped by cultural norms and orientations. What etiquette is followed in your context? How does it compare with the one followed in English-speaking workplaces?

Collocations

- Formally/properly introduced (e.g., We haven't been formally introduced.)
- May/can I introduce you to...

Structural elements

- **Prepositions** (Introduce you <u>to</u> (name) = use 'to' before the name of the person being introduced (e.g., Can I introduce you to George?); BUT introduce (name) = no preposition before name (e.g., May I introduce George?))
- **Modals** (e.g., May I introduce...?; Can I introduce...?)

Another important soft skill that your students will have to develop is **making small talk** in the workplace. Small talk has been described as superficial, non-task-related communication which is nonetheless a key component of most employees' experience in the workplace. It includes topics such as the weather, sports, and weekend or holiday plans. It had been shown to serve a variety of purposes, such as building and maintaining relationships, socialising with new employees and building a positive workplace climate. Small talk can also help to soften difficult conversations among employees or between a manager and their team members.

There a number of key features that characterise small talk. Small talk is:

- a way of initiating a conversation with someone you've just met (e.g., at a conference or a business meeting)
- a friendly, usually short, dialogue about a common topic (e.g., the weather, a particular talk at a conference)
- a way of breaking the silence to avoid an awkward or uncomfortable situation
- a friendly way of starting a more serious topic or event (e.g., a business meeting).

It is important for your students to understand that being unable to make or engage in small talk may give other people the impression that they are overformal, unconfident or even socially inept (see also Making First Impressions, Table 4.3).

Language Corner LC-4.2 presents the key language items that your students will need to make small talk at work.

Language Corner (LC-4.2)

The following list includes some of the language items commonly used for making small talk. You may want to add others which you think would be appropriate for your students.

- (Are) you alright?
- Hi, (so) hot/cold/cloudy/humid today, isn't it?
- How was your weekend?
- Welcome back! How was your holiday/break?
- How was the weather/the food?
- How was your journey to work?
- Nice talk, right?
- Are you enjoying/did you enjoy the talk/conference/meeting?
- How's your morning/afternoon/day been so far?
- Busy day?
- My afternoon's been kind of busy. How's yours been?
- (Are you) enjoying your new job/the conference?
- What did you do in your last job?
- Any plans/have you got plans for the weekend/holidays?
- What are your plans for the weekend?
- (Are you) doing something interesting this weekend?

Collocations

- hot/cold/cloudy/humid weather (What other adjectives collocate with 'weather'?)
- a(n) long/interesting/quiet weekend (What other adjectives collocate with 'weekend'?)
- a(n) long/busy/interesting/boring morning/afternoon/day

Structural elements

- **Simple past** (e.g., How was your weekend?)
- **Present perfect** (e.g., How's your day been?)
- **Present progressive** (e.g., Are you enjoying...?)
- **Prepositions** (e.g., at weekends; at the weekend)
- **Vague language** (e.g., kind of; sort of; stuff; a bit)

The following Insights from Research (IR-4.2) discusses emotional intelligence, another competency that recruiters value highly as it contributes enormously to interpersonal relationships.

Insights from Research (IR-4.2): Emotional Intelligence (EQ)

Another soft competency highly regarded and sought after by international recruiters is emotional intelligence, also known as EQ. EQ refers to a person's ability to understand and manage both their own and others people's feelings, and be able to use this understanding to build positive and productive connections.

EQ allows us to deal with conflict and setbacks in a productive manner, negotiate to get things done, and encourage others when they are down.

Psychologist D. Goleman (2020) has divided the skill sets for EQ into four domains: self-awareness, self-regulation, social awareness, and relationship management.

The first two domains relate to 'the self', that is, being able to understand, manage and regulate our own emotions. The remaining two domains relate to 'the other', in other words, how well we perceive and understand our colleagues' emotions, and use this knowledge to build productive and supportive relationships with them.

Task

Read the following scenarios. How would you apply EQ to deal with the situation presented in each scenario?

- You are in a meeting which has overrun. You are feeling very frustrated and have started to lose interest and the motivation to be at the meeting.
- You feel excluded by your line manager as she never keeps eye contact with you at meetings or speaks to you directly.
- One of your colleagues is always complaining with you about their excessive workload and how demotivated they feel at work.

It is now a good time to pause for a moment and reflect upon what we have discussed and analysed in this section about lesson planning. Activity RA-4.3 aims at helping you with such reflection.

Reflection Activity (RA-4.3)

- How do you think your students will best learn the skills identified in this unit?
- How useful do you think your students will find seeing others do the task they will be asked to do later on?
- Would you use the framework for tasks proposed by Jane Willis in your class activities?

4.4 Materials for teaching interpersonal communication skills and competencies

The following sets of materials aim at illustrating what you can use for the lesson plans shown in the previous section. The first set (4.4.1) is provided as an example of the materials you can use to teach "making first impressions" and is meant to accompany the lesson plan in Table 4.1. The second set (4.4.2) was designed for "building positive relationships at work" to realise the lesson plan shown in Table 4.2.

4.4.1 Materials set 1

Handout 1: Things You Should Do on Your First Day of Work

Read the text written by an HR specialist and then complete the table of Dos and Don'ts following the text.

For many people, the first day at work may be very memorable but also rather stressful, mostly due to the heightened pressure to impress. As the saying goes: **The first impression is the last impression.** In other words, the first day at work will set the tone for the rest of your career. But fear not, planning ahead for the day and following the few tips provided below can help you to reduce anxiety.

Here are 10 tips you could follow on the first day of your new job:

1. **Visualise.** Visualise yourself in your new company, smiling and enjoying meeting your new colleagues. By picturing yourself on your first day at work, you will help to reduce your anxiety and feel more relaxed.
2. **Prepare.** Think about a few things to say about the company and questions you can ask. This will help you to show you are curious about your new job and the company.
3. **Show up early.** It is important to be at the site 10 to 15 minutes early so as to get ready for the day and be there at the time you

were asked to. Think about what the commute for your interview was like and add some extra few minutes. If you were interviewed online, you may want to practise the commute a couple of times.

4. **Relax**. Make sure you feel relaxed. Having some good sleep the previous night will help you to feel rested, prepared and relaxed.

5. **Smile**. Remember that the first impression is the last impression, so smile as much as possible when you meet people or introduce yourself. This will show them you are happy to be at work. Above all, be happy and enjoy the experience.

6. **Interact with others**. Talk to as many people as possible, show them you are friendly and they can talk to you whenever they need or want to. This way you will be starting on the right foot in establishing trust.

7. **Listen, listen and listen**. Together with smiling and being friendly, you also need to listen to everything they say, whether they are talking about the goals and values of the company, their projects or your new line manager describing the department and your new responsibilities. If possible, take a few notes; this is when your phone comes in handy.

8. **Show interest**. When you are introduced to other people or you introduce yourself, show interest in others by asking them what they do and their role at the company, for example. This will be a first step into establishing good relationships at work.

9. **Phone on silent**. Use your phone to jot down your notes but remember to keep it on silent. You need to show people you are present!

10. **Be yourself**. Above all, be happy, enjoy the day and meeting new people, and project yourself as who you are.

Dos and Don'ts for the First Day at Work			
In the Text		By Me (Based in My Experience)	
Dos	Don'ts	Dos	Don'ts

To fully exploit the text presented in Handout 1, you could draw your students' attention to the key language items in it. The following Language Corner (LC-4.3) includes some of them.

Language Corner (LC-4.3)

The following vocabulary items have been chosen from the text in Handout 1. You may also want to draw your students' attention to others which may be relevant to their context or proficiency level.

- First day at work/at your new job
- On the first day
- To be meticulous in planning
- To be prepared for
- Pressure to impress
- To set off/start the day
- Position-specific responsibilities
- To project high energy
- Your work ethics
- To put your phone on silence

Collocations

- A memorable/stressful day
- To secure a position/job
- A passive/proactive // response/attitude
- To set the tone
- To spend the day/time + VerbING
- To land/get a (new) job

Structural elements

- **Simple present** (e.g., Most of us remember...)
- **Modal verbs** (e.g., You can reduce your anxiety. You should ask questions)
- **As many as** (e.g., as many people as possible)
- **As much as** (e.g., as much time as possible)
- **Prepositions** (e.g., In the beginning/end; At the beginning/end)

Handout 2: First Impressions

Look at the following 3 photos and write down the adjectives that come to mind when you see each photo. Then, answer the questions below.

I think this person is: I think this person is: I think this person is:

_____   _____   _____

_____   _____   _____

_____   _____   _____

_____   _____   _____

- Now compare the adjectives you used with those of another student. How do they compare?
- Did the adjectives you chose reflect the first impressions the other student had?
- How has their appearance contributed to your choice of adjectives?
- Would you need to change the adjectives you chose if you knew that the first person is a successful technology entrepreneur, the second is a world-famous writer, and the third is unemployed and desperately looking for a job?
- What have your learnt from this exercise?

Handout 3: Projecting the Desired Image

Use the following table to list the adjectives you would use to describe yourself. Add more rows if necessary. Then discuss your choices with another student and make necessary changes if needed (keep it, replace it with, or amend). Finally, answer the questions below.

Characteristic	Keep	Replace with	Amend

Questions

- How could you project the characteristics you have listed?
- Would things like your general appearance, attire and use of language help?
- Now, revisit the adjectives you used to describe the 3 photos in Handout 2. Would you still keep them, replace them or make amendments?

Handouts 2 and 3 can be accompanied by language items your students will need to make the most of them. Language Corner LC-4.4 includes some such items.

Language Corner (LC-4.4)

The following vocabulary items can be used together with Handouts 2 and 3. You may also want to draw your students' attention to other items which may be relevant to their context or proficiency level.

- She/he/they look(s)/appear (s) professional/formal/(too) informal to me.
- They come across as...
- I believe they are...
- They must be [for deduction] (profession, e.g., lawyers/description = e.g., very attentive)
- I'd like to keep/replace (something) with (something new)/ amend
- I've changed my mind actually.
- I still think she/he/they look(s)/appear (s)...

Collocations

- Attractive/distinctive/strange appearance (What other adjectives collocate with 'appearance'?)
- Strong/convincing/false impression (What other adjectives collocate with 'impression'?)

Structural elements

- **Simple present** (e.g., She appears very professional to me.)
- **Present perfect** (e.g., I have changed my mind about him.)
- **Modals** for giving opinions (e.g., I would say..., I should say...)

4.4.2 Materials set 2

As specified in lesson plan 2, there are 2 handouts. Handout 4 includes a text on building positive relationships at work, followed by a set of questions students will answer individually. After they have answered the questions, they will compare their answers with those of another student. Handout 5 guides students through examining the language of positive relationships at work.

Handout 4: Building Positive Relationships at Work

Instructions
Read the following text on building positive relationships at work from **BetterUp** (betterup.com). As you read it, think of the questions in the following section.

https://www.betterup.com/blog/building-good-work-relationships

Questions

- Why are positive relationships important in the workplace?
- Do you think they are more important in international workplaces? Why? Why not?
- How are positive relationships beneficial in the workplace?
- What makes a relationship in the workplace positive?
- Can you mention 3 strategies for building positive relationships in the workplace that you consider most important?

After you finish answering the questions above, compare your answers with those of another student.

Language corner LC-4.5 provides some of the language items that your students will need for Handout 1.

Language Corner (LC-4.5)

For students to able to build positive relationships at work, they will need a particular set of vocabulary items. The following list provides some of such items, but you may also want to add other items which may be relevant to your students' context or proficiency level.

- To build good work relationships
- To have a (huge) impact on

- To thrive at work
- To face challenges/difficulties
- To respect each other
- To micromanage someone
- To harm someone's job satisfaction
- To hold someone back
- To get support from your line manager/colleagues
- To make time for colleagues/others
- To delegate tasks/projects/responsibilities
- At the end of the day

Collocations

- A good/solid/strong/difficult/troubled relationship (What other adjectives can you use with 'relationship'?)
- A professional/collaborative/positive/toxic workplace
- Mutual/deep/great respect

Structural elements

- **Present perfect** (e.g., the COVID-19 pandemic has changed the way..., with the challenges we've faced over the past few years...; Anyone who's worked in a toxic workplace knows...)
- **Modal verbs** (e.g., can have a huge impact on...; your co-workers might not be your best friends...; you can evaluate how good the relationship is by...)
- **Conditional structures** (e.g., if you have solid relationships with your team,...; if you have a boss you don't get along with...)
- **Prepositions** (e.g., have an impact on; the feeling of efficiency; over the past few years; to get along with (someone); to be on tight deadlines; to have trust in someone or something [but to trust someone or something)

Handout 5: Analysing the Language of Positive Relationships

Instructions

Read the text on positive relationships again. This time, focus on specific language that has been used to discuss such relationships at work. As you read, complete the table provided. The first one has been done as an example. Add more rows if necessary.

Aspect of the Relationship	Language Used to Discuss It	Comments
Benefits	"Can Have a Huge Impact On"	To Have a/an (Huge) Impact **ON**

Now that we have explored possible materials for lesson plans, we can pause for a minute to reflect upon them. The next Reflection Activity (RA-4.4) presents you with an opportunity to think more carefully about the materials that we have just analysed. After you finish with the activity, you may want to revise the principles for selecting and adapting materials set out in the Introductory Unit (Section I.4).

Reflection Activity (RA-4.4)

- How useful do you find the materials presented here?
- What would you need to change in them in order to make these materials appropriate for your classroom context?
- Why do you feel you would need to make these changes?

In some teaching contexts, students are encouraged to bring along their own electronic devices such as smart phones, pads or laptops so that they can be used to complement the activities in class. If this is the case in your context, always remember to make room for these extended activities in your lesson plans and to consider the benefits this could bring about as we discuss in the next Culture and Technology Note (CTN-4.2).

Culture and Technology Note (CTN-4.2)

Depending on whether your students have easy access to the Internet while in class, consider if you need to print the handouts or you could just email them to your students before the class. This will ensure a smaller carbon footprint for the lesson and make sure the students will not lose the handouts.

In this respect, and as we have discussed before, it is always a good idea to check the cultural practices of your teaching institution. Do they encourage students to bring their own devices? How about privacy guidelines? How strong is the connectivity level of the institution? These and other context-specific considerations should be taken into account before making decisions about students' own electronic devices in class.

If Internet access is not an issue, and institutional policies allow it, you could also include multimodal communication tasks as well as multitasking skills (see Gimenez, 2014 for a discussion) as part of the internal communication practices of a company. These will be further explored in the next unit.

4.5 Assessing learning

As we discussed in the Introductory Unit, while formative assessment should take place throughout the class, it is important to consider different options for summative assessment. Remember that LOs, teaching activities and summative assessment should all be aligned. Therefore, before considering assessment options, it is important to revisit the LOs set out for a lesson or unit.

Below are examples of Can-Do statements that students can use for self-assessment (4.5.1), and actual assessment tasks for some of the LOs of this unit as well as suggestions for developing your own assessment tasks for the others (4.5.2). You can use the tasks provided in class for formative assessment or for summative assessment at the end of the lesson or course. Alternatively, you may want to adapt the tasks you have used for formative assessment to be re-used as summative assessments.

In order to assess "making introductions and first impressions" as an LO, a role-play task is probably a good option. Students can consider and visualise how they would introduce themselves, but it is not until they actually do it that they can demonstrate they understood how to make a strong first impression (and build up the necessary confidence).

4.5.1 Self-assessing skills and competencies for interpersonal communication

Self-Assessing Skills and Competencies for Interpersonal Communication				
Use the following list of Can-Do statements to self-assess the skills and competencies you have learnt in this unit. In case you are not sure or think you have not yet acquired the skill or competency referred to, make a note on what you can do about it.				
I can	Yes	No	?	I'm planning to
1. make introductions, introduce myself and create good first impressions.				
2. manage interpersonal communication effectively.				
3. build positive relationships at work.				
4. use appropriate language and conventions to speak about myself, my jobs and previous work experiences.				

4.5.2 Assessing skills and competencies for interpersonal communication

Task: Prepare and Practise Your Answers to the Following Three Questions	
Group 1	Group 2
• Who are you? • Where do you come from? • What did you do before joining our company?	• How would you introduce yourself? • How would you describe where you come from? • How would you describe your previous job?

Notes for the teacher: Divide the class into two groups. The students from Group 1 play the role of the colleague that has been with the company for a while—they ask the three questions above. The students from Group 2 play the role of the new colleague—they answer the question using the answers they prepared. Pair up one student from Group 1 and one from Group 2. You can allow them to practise the introductions several times. Then ask them to swap roles.

Another activity that you could use to assess the LOs of this unit involves a short group presentation. This is illustrated in the following activity.

Task: The company you recently joined is hosting a new employees' event.

Think about how you would like to introduce yourself at such an event. As this is a face-to-face introduction, no PowerPoint will be available but you can have a few notes (however, you are expected to speak freely rather than read your introduction).

Notes for the teacher: Ask the students to give their introductory presentations in front of the class or in small groups. Be strict with the time. You can allow other students to provide positive feedback (what they liked about the presentation) but no negative comments should be allowed. You, as the teacher, are the only one that can point out what could be improved in the introductory presentation.

While the assessment tasks and suggestions presented above have been designed to assess individual LOs, you can design summative assessment tasks which assess several LOs at once. For example, a task could be designed for the students to read a text related to one of the LOs of the unit, then they have to either write an email to somebody else with the key ideas from the text or discuss it with another student or make a presentation to the whole class.

As we have already discussed, it is always important to also consider the assessment practices of the institution in which you are or will be teaching. To help you with this, the next reflection Activity (RA-4.5) provides context-related questions as a guide.

As discussed in the Introductory Unit (see Section I.5), these assessment tasks can be accompanied by a corresponding set of marking criteria. These criteria should clearly indicate the skills and competencies the students should demonstrate proficiency in, and how their performance in such skills and competencies is going to be assessed.

Reflection Activity (RA-4.5)

- What is the assessment tradition of the school system you work in?
- What would you have to change in the suggested assessment materials so that they can be used in your educational context?
- What other types of assessment would be appropriate given the LOs of this unit?

4.6 Summary

In this unit, we have examined a number of key skills for interpersonal communication in the workplace and ways in which they can be taught and assessed. Possibly, not all the skills exemplified in the unit are the ones that your students will need in their present or future jobs. You will possibly have to add a few others depending on their needs. The NA exercises we have discussed in Unit 1 will guide you into making appropriate choices.

What is important to remember is that teaching skills for the international workplace will require you to make decisions based on the:

- skills that you think your students already have and those they will need in the future
- LOs that you want your students to achieve and the theories and methods that you think are most appropriate to go with the LOs you have set out for the lesson
- lesson plans and the materials that you need to design or adapt to help your students achieve such LOs, and the
- assessment opportunities for your students to demonstrate whether and to what extent they have achieved those LOs.

As you can see these decisions follow the teaching-and-learning cycle that we presented in the Introductory Unit. This cycle should also guide you as to the procedures you can follow to teach these skills more effectively as we have illustrated in this and previous units.

In Unit 5, we will explore how to teach skills and competencies for written communication which will be complemented with teaching skills and competencies for spoken communication in Unit 6.

Further readings: An annotated bibliography

A task-based approach

https://www.teachingenglish.org.uk/article/task-based-approach

This article on the British Council website offers a brief overview of the task-based learning approach (TBL). It also highlights the advantages of TBL over the more traditional Present, Practice, Produce (PPP) approach, which is sometimes described as the opposite of TBL.

Gimenez, J. (2014). Multi-communication and the business English class: Research meets pedagogy. *English for Specific Purposes*, 35, 1–16. https://doi.org/10.1016/j.esp.2013.11.002

This article discusses multi-communication (MC) practices in four multinationals based in London, UK. Apart from key theoretical considerations of the role of MC in corporate communication, it presents a number of pedagogical applications deriving from the findings of the study. These can be used to exemplify communication practices in multinational corporations.

Willis, J. (1996). *A framework for task-based learning*. Longman.

This text offers a very useful combination of the methodology and practice of task-based language (TBL) teaching. It provides clear examples of a typical task-based lesson (setting up a new task, the task cycle, and language-focused work) and offers useful outlines that show how the framework can be used to plan lessons. Although its main focus is on teaching English through TBL, its framework can be applied to teaching communication by means of learning tasks.

Unit 5
Teaching skills and competencies for written communication

Learning Outcomes

By the end of the unit, you should be able to:

- identify key skills and competencies needed for managing internal communication and producing effective written communication
- turn skills and competencies into learning outcomes
- make pedagogical decisions about designing lessons, selecting materials, and assessing written communication skills and competencies, and
- select effective vocabulary items required for realising such skills and competencies.

5.1 Introducing written communication in the workplace

In the workplace, people communicate for different reasons and with a number of publics. We normally differentiate between written communication (the topic of this unit) and spoken communication (see Unit 6). Examples of written communication include: emails, memorandum (or memo for short), newsletters, short message service (abbreviated to SMS), website and posts. Spoken communication examples comprise: meetings, telephone conversations and presentations. There are, however, other communication events, such as training events and product

DOI: 10.4324/9781003283515-9

launching activities that mix both written and spoken communication. They may also include multimodal communication.

Multimodal communication looks at communication from a more holistic perspective. It does not focus on one area or mode of communication (e.g., the written or spoken word) but considers all forms of communication such as body language, facial expression, gesture, writing, speaking, images, and digital, usually simultaneously. This look at communication in the workplace requires multimodal competencies which we will discuss in more detail later on in the unit. As stated by Hartle, Facchinetti and Franceschi (2022, p. 5) "Multimodal awareness and competence are also paramount in intercultural and interpersonal communication, which has become increasingly common in today's global workplace."

Another common difference made is between communication with internal (within the organisation) and external (outside the organisation) publics. This is an important difference as depending on whether you need to communicate with a colleague (internal) or a supplier (external), you will have to make a number of choices in content, language and register.

Typical examples of internal communication include: meetings, telephone conversations, presentations, emails, newsletters, memos and training sessions. Because the members of an organisation know one another, internal communication tends to be more implicit in the references it makes as members share much knowledge about other people or situations. The language used in internal communication also reflects this and so it tends to be simple and less explicit. For example, expressions such as "as you all know" and "following our tradition" are typical of internal communication.

On the other hand, external communication refers to communication with members outside the organisation. External publics may include clients or customers, suppliers, other companies or organisations, and government officials or authorities. Typical examples of external communication include: meetings with suppliers or other companies, telephone calls from or to customers or suppliers, press conferences, advertisements or commercials, annual reports, brochures and feedback forms.

Studies on the language of organisations (e.g., Gimenez, 2005; Johnson & Chang, 2000; Kollectif, 2019) have, however, pointed out that things are never as clear-cut as the descriptions presented above seem to suggest. For instance, the communication with long-established external publics may resemble some of the features of internal communication as time has helped to establish a more friendly relationship between the communicators who, at the same time, share a great deal of common ground.

Recently, communication experts have suggested that organisations should consider an integrated approach (Kollectif, 2019), which would allow them to plan and manage both internal and external communications more strategically rather than as two distinct phenomena. They emphasise the importance of, for example, making sure that both types reflect the same values and support the same messages to ensure consistency within and outside the company. This approach would ensure that the image projected by a company (externally) and how it is perceived by its own employees (internally) is consistent. Similarly, an integrated approach will make sure that the reputation of the company among external publics is reinforced by what its employees think and say about it.

Before we explore skills for internal and written communication for the workplace, you may want to read more on multimodal communication in the workplace. This is suggested in Extension Task ET-5.1. After you finish, you may also want to read Hartle, Facchinetti and Franceschi's (2022) article on the topic.

Extension Task (ET-5.1)

Use the URL provided below to read a blog on multimodal communication in the workplace and think about the following:

- How has multimodal communication influenced organisational communication?
- In what circumstances could multimodal communication be beneficial for organisations?
- How useful would knowing about multimodal communication be for your students?
- Would you include it into your lessons?

https://worldsofenglish.com/workplace-skills-extension-tasks/

The first Insights from Research (IR-5.1) expands the ideas about multimodal communication we have already explored.

Insights from Research (IR-5.1): Multimodality

Developments in ICT have also had an impact on the way people in organisations communicate. In the contemporary workplace people make use of different channels and media—sometimes packaging two or more together (Gimenez, 2014)—which has been called 'multimodality' (Bremner, 2018; Hartle, Facchinetti, & Franceschi, 2022). Multimodality allows communicators in the workplace to mix a wider range of resources (e.g., text, sound, images, gestures, hyperlinks). As Hartle, Facchinetti, and Franceschi (2022: 3) explain, multimodality "implies an awareness of how visual images (still and moving) and spoken/written language are used, as well as an awareness of layout and space and the impact that both language and image may have on the audience". This is particularly relevant for the international workplace as how a message may impact the audience is much higher stake than in everyday contexts. It is then especially important that students are made aware of not only how multimodality works (mixing resources) but also which resources work well with which, that is how media can be packaged together (Gimenez, 2014), and the role that context plays in multimodal communication. Students also need to be reminded that in the international workplace, contexts may also include a variety of cultures and languages, something that also applies to organisations when devising communication artefacts for their internal and external publics (Ravazzani, 2015).

It is equally important to design multimodal materials (see materials in this unit) to help students increase their awareness of and familiarity with multimodality, which is sometimes referred to as "multimodal literacies", and provide them with opportunities to experiment with a wider range of semiotic resources that go beyond the written word. This, at the same time, will equip them with the skills required in "the 21st-century work environment" (Laadem & Mallahi, 2019: 34).

5.2 Key skills and competencies for internal and written communication in the workplace

This unit will focus on internal and written communication for the workplace. We start by identifying the key skills and competencies for internal written communication. These include:

- Recognising internal practices for written communication
- Identifying strategies for adopting internal communication practices

- Understanding company values and mission statement, and
- Writing communication documents (e.g., emails, memos, reports) effectively.

Let's reflect on these skills and competencies for a moment. Activity RA-5.1 aims at guiding you through your reflection.

Reflection Activity (RA-5.1)

- How important do you think these skills and competencies are for your own students?
- How do you think your students will best develop these skills?
- How would you go about teaching them?

Now we are in a position to think about how we could turn these skills and competencies into LOs for a lesson on internal and written communication for the international workplace. Table 5.1 shows the identified skills and competencies, a few of the questions that have facilitated the thinking process involved in transforming skills into LOs, and the resulting LOs.

Table 5.1 Turning Skills into Learning Outcomes for Internal and Written Communication

Skills/Competencies	Questions	Learning outcomes
Recognising internal communication practices	How can students recognise key internal communication practices in their new workplace?	At the end of the lesson, you should be able to recognise the core communication practices of your workplace.
Identifying strategies for adopting internal communication practices	What strategies can students deploy to adopt the internal communication practices of their new workplace?	At the end of the lesson, you should be able to identify strategies you can deploy to adopt the communication practices of your new workplace.

(Continued)

Skills/Competencies	Questions	Learning outcomes
Understanding company values and mission statement	How can the students explain company values and mission statement? What key vocabulary is needed?	At the end of the lesson, you should be able to speak about your company values and mission statement with confidence. At the end of the lesson, you should be able to explain values and mission statement to others.
Writing communication documents (e.g., emails, memos) for internal communication effectively	What are the main characteristics of written workplace documents? How can students learn to write such documents effectively?	At the end of the lesson, you should be able to write a number of documents effectively.

Now that we have looked at how to turn skills and competencies for internal and written communication into LOs, we could start thinking about how to design lessons for such LOs. This is what we will do in the next section.

5.3 Designing lessons for internal and written communication

This section shows two lesson plans. This first has been designed to teach how to manage internal communication (5.3.1); the second to teach internal written communication for the workplace (5.3.2).

5.3.1 Lesson plan for managing internal communication

Table 5.2 Lesson Plan for Managing Internal Communication

Course: Communication Skills for the International Workplace	Year group:	Date:
Learning outcomes for managing internal communication		
At the end of the lesson, students should be able to: • identify key components of internal communication • understand internal communication practices of a particular workplace, and • adopt such practices for their own written communications.		
Progression of teaching & learning		**Strategies/Materials**
Duration: 10 minutes	Introduction T shows Sts a short video clip about the internal communication practices of a (real) company. Pre-watching activity (if necessary, T pre-teaches associated vocabulary): 1. description of the main components of the internal communication practices of the company 2. concerns the company had about such practices 3. actions taken about such concerns, and 4. an evaluation of the new practices in place.	Watching video and analysing communication practices (George Aitken, Head of Communications at Vodafone UK)/ Handout 1

(Continued)

Duration: 15 minutes	Activity 1 1. Sts discuss vocabulary sets 2. In pairs, Sts discuss points 1–4 in the pre-watching activity, and anything else they found interesting 3. Sts report back to the class the results of their discussion 4. Sts summarise key characteristics of the company's internal communication practices.	1. Discussing vocabulary items/ Handout 1 2. Discussing internal communication practices/ Handout 1 3. Reporting back to the rest of the class 4. Summarising
Duration: 10 minutes	Activity 2 5. Sts examine an example of internal multimodal communication practices and answer questions about it.	5. Analysing example by means of questions/ Handout 2
Duration: 20 minutes	Activity 3 6. Sts read about and discuss strategies for adopting existing practices for internal communication. 7. Sts reflect on what has been learnt in today's lesson and make brief entries into their learning diaries.	6. Reading and discussing / Handout 3 7. Completing own learning diaries
Duration: 5 minutes	Conclusion After students have entered their reflective notes into their diaries, T invites them to read a few out loud to share with the rest of the class.	Sts' read aloud their selected entries from their learning diaries.

Success criteria	• To be able to identify key components of internal communication • To be able to identify the internal communication practices of a workplace • To understand and be able to follow such practices.	**Assessment** A True/False quiz on the key elements of internal communications and strategies for adopting internal communication practices.
Next steps	Sts are asked to search for samples of internal communication practices of (real) companies on the internet. They should then choose one sample and analyse it following what was discussed in class. They should also be prepared to discuss the results of their analysis with the rest of the class the following week. Sts can use PowerPoint or Padlet (see CTN-4.1) to report results.	

5.3.2 Lesson plan for written communication for the workplace

Table 5.3 Lesson Plan for Effective Written Communication

Course: Communication Skills for the International Workplace	Year Group:	Date:
Learning outcomes for effective written communication		
At the end of the lesson, students should be able to: • analyse the main characteristics of written communication for the workplace, • search for typical examples of corporate written communication and evaluate their effectiveness • discuss the results of your research with the rest of the class.		

(Continued)

Progression of teaching & learning		Strategies/Materials
Duration: 10 minutes	<u>Introduction</u> 1. Sts read a short text on the characteristics of effective written communication for the workplace.	1. Reading a text / handout 4
Duration: 20 minutes	<u>Activity 1</u> 2. In pairs, Sts discuss with another student their views on the list of characteristics provided in the text, taking into account: • how important they think these characteristics are • others that the text mentions • others they would like to add 3. Sts make a new list of bullet points with all the characteristics they discussed in the pairs.	2. Discussing viewpoints / handout 4 3. Writing a list of characteristics
Duration: 10 minutes	<u>Activity 2</u> 4. Sts search the Internet for examples of written corporate documents. 5. Sts analyse and evaluate the documents they found following the list of characteristics they created.	4. Doing research 5. Analysing and evaluating

Duration: 15 minutes	Activity 3 6. Sts present the results of their analysis and evaluation to the rest of the class.	6. Presenting
Duration: 5 minutes	Conclusion After the presentations, Sts agree on what are the key features they should keep in mind for writing effective workplace documents.	Sts make a new list with all the features discussed in class.
Success criteria	• To be able to analyse the main characteristics of written communication for the workplace	**Assessment** A True/False quiz on the key characteristics of effective written communication in the workplace.
	• To be able to search for typical examples of corporate written communication and evaluate their effectiveness • To be able to discuss the results of their research with the rest of the class.	
Next steps	Sts may be asked to exchange the documents they have found on the Internet or create a repository of documents where all contribute with their samples and the results of their research.	

After having examined two possible lesson plans, we are now in a position to reflect upon how useful they could be for your own teaching context. The next reflection activity (RA-5.2) provides you with three questions to facilitate your reflection upon lesson plans 5.3.1. and 5.3.2.

Reflection Activity (RA-5.2)

- How useful for your own students do you find lesson plans like the above?
- Do you think you will need to adapt them to make them more appropriate for your teaching context?
- If so, how would you go about adapting them?

These two lesson plans exemplify some LOs for the unit but do not cover all of them. You may want to use these examples to design other plans to cover, for example, writing documents effectively. This could be a follow-up lesson after the students have presented the results of their research and shared the samples they have found.

5.4 Materials for teaching internal and written communication skills and competencies

This section includes two sets of materials. The first one relates to "managing internal communication" (5.4.1) and the second (5.4.2) deals with "written communication for the workplace".

5.4.1 Materials set 1 (to accompany Lesson plan 1)

As specified in Lesson plan 1, there are 3 handouts. Handout 1 includes a set of vocabulary items, possibly needed to be revised and even taught before watching the video clip. Handout 2 shows an example of internal multimodal communication practices, followed by a set of questions to help students to analyse the example provided. Finally, Handout 3 introduces the students to a list of strategies that they can deploy in order to adopt the existing internal communication practices of their new workplace.

Handout 1: Exploring Internal Communication Practices

Watch the interview that **Fuse Universal (https://www.fuseuniversal.com)**
did with George Aitken, Head of Communications at Vodafone UK
https://www.youtube.com/watch?v=vXHCJfd2K9Q&t=117s

Aims

This handout presents you with opportunities to

- explore key language items used to talk about internal communication of a real company
- describe the main components of the internal communication
practices of the company, and
- identify concerns and ways of dealing with them.

Before you watch the video

How familiar are you with the following language items?

- The traditional communications (comms) landscape
- Email-driven and paper-centric
- The primary way of communicating/people communicate in
groups
- Communicating to the frontline
- Overreliance
- Cascading communication
- Layers of management
- Inconsistencies in communication
- To give email access to (someone)
- On the shopfloor
- To miss out
- Sprinkles of colour
- To get rid of
- To pick up the information
- To remove barriers
- To make communication mobile
- To produce richer content
- Videos and interactive PDFs
- A more friendly and engaging way of communicating content

- A reward scheme
- A new strategy to deliver
- To relay a message
- Every single bit of content
- How a message lands
- To go through the right protocols
- To share information/ideas/stuff with an external audience

As you watch the video, think of the following points mentioned. You will be asked to discuss them later on:

1. description of the main components of the internal communication practices of the company
2. previous concerns they had about such practices
3. what they did about such concerns, and
4. why the new practices are considered to be better.

To be able to do the activities in Handout 1, your students will need a specific set of language items. Language corner LC-5.1 shows some items which your students may need.

Language Corner (LC-5.1)

The list below provides some relevant language items relating to internal written communication. You may also want to add others to match your own teaching context.

- To communicate well/effectively/efficiently
- To understand/contribute to the organisation's mission
- To do one's best work
- To help others to succeed
- To go the extra mile for customers
- To align oneself with the organisation's aims and values
- To boost customer experience
- To feel disconnected from the organisation
- To be/feel unengaged

Collocations

- To contribute to
- The extra mile

- To align with
- To feel disconnected from

Structural elements

- **Simple past** (e.g., the main concern was how...)
- **Simple present** (e.g., now we have a more positive approach)

The following is the second handout, which focuses on a piece of internal communication from a real organisation.

Handout 2: Launching a New Product Line

Aims

This handout presents you with opportunities to

- explore a new and dynamic way of communicating internally within a company, and
- discuss the advantages and drawbacks of such practices.

Instructions

Look at the following example of the internal communication practices of a real company and

1. describe the practice being illustrated in the example
2. read the questions below the example and think how you'd answer them, and
3. be prepared to share your answers with the rest of the class.

Questions

1. What type of internal communication do you think this is an example of?
2. How effective do you think this way of communicating to internal publics is?
3. Do you think it helps with employee motivation and sense of belonging?
4. What drawbacks do you think there are in communicating new organisational developments like this?

Launch of a new product line...　 Share　Like

Posted: 17 Nov 2022 11.45　🗹 14　👍 26

This week we are celebrating the launch of our newest product line after months of hard work by the product, design, and marketing teams to get the idea off the ground.

The new product line was the brain child of Laura Percy from the marketing team who presented the original idea on the **forum for ideas and innovations**.

A big congratulations to Laura and the teams involved in the project on getting this up and running. This is clear proof that you, our employees, can shape the present and future of our business. Keep your ideas coming!

Comment on this post

17th Nov　| Write a comment... |

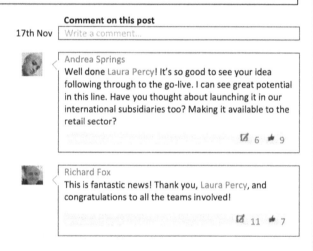

Andrea Springs
Well done Laura Percy! It's so good to see your idea following through to the go-live. I can see great potential in this line. Have you thought about launching it in our international subsidiaries too? Making it available to the retail sector?

🗹 6　👍 9

Richard Fox
This is fantastic news! Thank you, Laura Percy, and congratulations to all the teams involved!

🗹 11　👍 7

Figure 5.1 Launch of a New Product Line

Handout 3: Do You Want to Fit In? Then You'll Have to Adopt Their Practices....

Aims

In this activity, you'll be asked to:

- analyse different strategies to adopt a company's internal communication practices, and
- discuss such strategies with the rest of the class.

Instructions

Read the following strategies and discuss what you think about them with another student first. You will then be asked to report your discussion to the rest of the class.

Five strategies to adopt a company's internal communication practices: A list for new employers who want to fit in.

- First, analyse the media that they frequently use for internal communication. Do they rely on written media such as email and SMS? Or do they prefer spoken media like face-to-face or telephone communication?
- Secondly, pay attention to the format of the documents (e.g., emails, reports, SMS) that you receive as part of your company's internal communication practices. Do they follow a particular format? Does the format vary depending on the document?
- Thirdly, examine the style in which these documents have been written. Have they been written in formal (e.g., Dear Mr Brown) or informal (e.g., Dear Jack or just Jack) style?
- Then, consider the length of the messages. Are emails, for example, long? Are they very short and to the point? Or are they both, depending on what they are about?
- Finally, it is equally important to pay attention to the participants of the internal communication event. Are other people copied into the messages you receive? Who are they? Do they vary depending on the media or the content of the message?

5.4.2 Materials set 2 (to accompany Lesson plan 2)

Handout 4: Main Characteristics of Effective Written Communication

Aims

In this activity, you'll be asked to:

- analyse the main characteristics of written communication for the workplace
- search for typical examples of corporate written communication on the Internet and evaluate their effectiveness
- discuss the results of your research with the rest of the class.

Part 1: Written communication in the workplace

Instructions

Read the following text on the main features of effective written communication in the workplace. How important do you think these characteristics are? Discuss your views with another student.

Written Communication Skills in the Workplace

Written communication in the workplace requires a number of high-level skills so that it is effective and professional. This form of communication is conducted routinely in organisations and corporations, so it is important that employees have a good grasp of the key features of effective written communication, in particular for those working in the international workplace. Effective written communications should be:

- **Accurate and precise**: Information included in written communication (e.g., facts, figures, dates) should be accurate and precise. It should also be free from spelling and grammar mistakes. Accuracy and precision add to the professional quality of written communication.
- **Clear**: Written communication should be clear, straightforward and understandable. This will prevent misunderstandings and reinforce the sense of connection among employees.
- **Concise and complete**: Written communication should succinct and should avoid repetition, but should include all the necessary information for the reader to understand the message.
- **Professional and formal**: Written communication should be courteous. This will contribute to establishing and maintaining a respectful, and culturally sensitive, communication with all readers.

To achieve the high-level skills that effective written communication requires, you could:

- Begin by stating the goal of the communication as early in the document as possible; be clear and concise, and above all stay on topic
- Establish as clearly as possible the aims of the communication and provide supporting evidence and relevant information
- Practise writing different written messages and documents as often as possible and remember to proofread your texts in search of possible spelling and grammar mistakes.

Part 2: Researching and evaluating written documents

Now, search on the Internet examples of written documents and evaluate how effective they are using the criteria you've just read and discussed. You will then be asked to report your results to the rest of the class. For your class report, you can use PowerPoint or any other presentation software you are familiar with.

The next Language corner offers some key language items your students may need to do the activities in Handout 4.

Language Corner (LC-5.2)

The list below provides some relevant language items relating to written communication. You may also want to add others to match your own teaching context.

- Today's fast-paced business world
- Strategies to enhance your written communication skills,
- To deliver effective messages
- Basic/essential/important rules of business writing
- To edit and proofread communications successfully
- To write professional/effective emails
- To analyse one's audience
- To select the right (communication) medium
- To include (only) relevant information
- To write concisely and clearly
- To eliminate common/typical spelling and grammar errors/ mistakes
- To identify/write/include appropriate subject lines
- To communicate properly and with efficiency

Collocations

- A high/significant/substantial level of
- A continual/strong motivation (What other adjectives collocate with 'motivation'?)
- Clear/direct / straightforward/understandable communication
- A courteous/formal/informal tone
- Stay on topic

Structural elements

- **Simple present** (e.g., Written communication requires a high level of skills; This form of communication is very common in business)
- **Modals** (advice) (e.g., Effective written communications should include...; Individuals within a business may choose to follow...)

Besides these materials, you could also use published research on internal communication to complement these activities and even use examples presented in the published reports (e.g., Gimenez, 2005; 2014).

It is also important to include multimodal communication materials so that your students become more aware of the role multimodality plays in corporate communication. The following is an example of such materials.

Video Updates for Internal Communication

Use the URL provided below to watch Ryan Spanger from **Dream Engine (https://www.dreamengine.com.au)** talk about how to improve internal communication by using **video updates**. As you watch, think of the following statements to decide whether they are true (T) or false (F).

https://worldsofenglish.com/workplace-skills-extension-tasks/

Statements	True	False
1. Internal communication is important for keeping employees updated about the company.		
2. Video updates are more engaging than emails and written documents.		
3. However, most internal communication experts do not believe in the power of video as an essential part of internal communications.		
4. It makes sense to use video updates as most people are used to processing information and entertainment by means of video.		

Statements	True	False
5. But the use of video updates for internal communications is limited to mostly online training.		
6. The key to successful video updates lies in keeping them short, informal and engaging.		

Now discuss your answers with another student. Jointly decide what changes are needed to make the false statements true. Once you have decided, re-write the true statements below.

Six True Statements about Video Updates for Internal Communications
1.
2.
3.
4.
5.
6.

The next Insights from Research (IR-5.2) of the unit deals with emails as internal communication in the international workplace. You may want to share or teach the insights to your students. Following the insights, there is a task based on embedded emails.

Insights from Research (IR-5.2): Emails in the international workplace

One of the key documents that many international organisations use for internal communication is emails. Email communication in business contexts have attracted the attention of researchers and teachers of organisational communication for more than 20 years now (e.g., Bremner 2018; Gimenez, 2006; Nickerson, 2014).

Emails have evolved in form and function from the office memo. Many of the communication capabilities of emails (e.g., To, From, Subject, CC-Carbon Copy) as well as their key functions (e.g., convey information, make and respond to requests) are similar to those of the office memo.

However, advances in IT have provided emails with new functionalities (e.g., Reply, Reply All, BBC- Blind Carbon Copy), making them a more flexible tool for internal and external communication. At the same time, they have become more dependent on intertextuality.

"Intertextuality, the notion that texts are linked to other texts, is a pervasive element of workplace writing" (Bremner & Costley, 2018: 1). As other research studies (e.g., Gimenez, 2006) have also argued, embeddedness in workplace emails, i.e., emails as chains rather than individual messages, makes communication more efficient through implicit referencing. The developments in email technology (e.g., the "Reply" and "Reply all" functions, hyperlinks inserted into messages) and the willingness of its users to make full use of such developments have also created a more intertextual and multimodal experience for workplace writers (see also Insights from Research IR-5.1).

As discussed in this unit, students should ideally become researchers of the internal communication practices of their own workplaces. This also applies to how emails are used for internal and external written communication. Despite the particular practices of each workplace, there are some general guidelines that students should know. The following are guidelines that students can follow when writing emails:

- Different from more formal written genres in the workplace (e.g., letters, policies), **emails tend to be informal** in register, and depend more heavily on contextual features (e.g., participants, shared knowledge, previous messages) to make complete sense. The relationship between texts and their contextual features has been called "intertextuality" (Bremner, 2018: 41), which is a key feature of embedded emails (Gimenez, 2006).
- Embedded emails produce a chain of messages that contains a first main message, which I called the 'chain initiator' (this is the message that starts the communication process), one or several internal messages and a 'chain terminator', the final message that brings the communication to an end (Gimenez, 2006).
- The longer the chain of embedded emails is, the more implicit the elements of the message become as the chain initiator provides enough context for the rest of the messages. Although the chain initiator is written first, it appears last in the chain of messages. This is illustrated in Figure 5.1 (taken from Gimenez (2006: 160).
- Nowadays, emails are addressed to two different audiences: active users and witnesses. The former are included in the TO address box, the latter in the CC address box. Witnesses are not expended to respond or take part in the conversation.

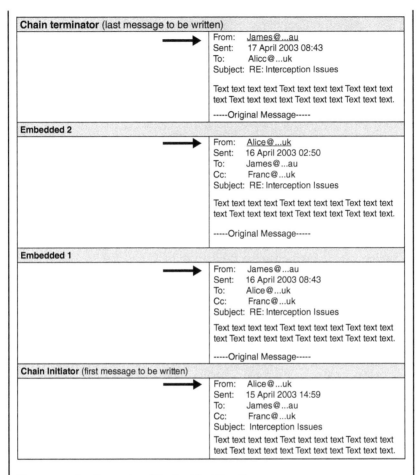

Figure 5.2 An Example of Embedded Emails

- This type of email is frequently used in international communication to discuss complex topics that require team decision-making by geographically dispersed groups.
- When used for internal communication among members of a team who have been working together for a considerable time, they tend to be short and to the point, and to contain many abbreviations (e.g. Brgds [Best regards], Fyi [For Your Information], Tks [Thanks]) which are known and shared by the participants.

You may want to share or teach your students the features of embedded emails included in the research insights. Following that, you could present them with the following task that requires them to analyse a real-world example taken from Gimenez (2006).

Task: Analysing Emails for Internal Written Communication

Read this authentic email and analyse the following elements in it:

- Recipients (their role in the communication)
- Format (e.g., single message, embedded)
- Implicit elements (things left unsaid but understood by the participants)
- Language (e.g., register, vocabulary items, personal abbreviations)

From: Franc
Sent: 06 January 2003 11:57
To: Danny@_____
CC: Ann
Subject: RE: (name) documents
(Embedded document)

Hi Danny,
Following my brief telephone conversation with your colleague (name), I attach a table indicating the information you have requested for the (name) terminal. I will be sending your shortly a web link about (model) in case you want to check the conformity assessment procedure set out in Art. 10 and related annexes.
Kind regards,
Franc

- - - - - - - - -Original Message- - - - - - - - - -
From: Danny
Sent: 06 January 2003 08:06
To: Franc@_____
CC: Ann
Subject: RE: (name) documents

Hi Franc,
Thanks for the form, however we require in addition the following elements to be
described more specifically in a certificate or detailed statement.
– Frequency
– Modulation
– Power
– Bandwidth
Best regards,
Danny (+ surname)

- - - - - - - - -Oorspronkelijk bericht - - - - - - - - -
Van: Franc
Verzonden: vrijdag 3 januari 2003 13
Aan: Danny
Onderwerp: FW: (name) documents

Dear Mr. (+surname)
Following our phone conversation, please find attached a document that
should allow you to clear (name) terminals through customs.
Should more information be needed, please do not hesitate to give me
a call.
Regards,
Franc

- - - - - - - - -Original Message- - - - - - - - - - -
From: Ethan
Sent: 02 January 2003 20.09
To: Franc
CC: Ann
Subject: RE: (name) documents

Franc,
As you will be back sooner than I, and we both have similar experience
in the issue of clearing (name) terminals through customs, could you
field this question from (name of partner company)?
Ethan

- - - - - - - - -Original Message- - - - - - - - - - -
From: Danny
To: Ethan
CC: Ann
Sent: 1/2/03 11:53 AM
Subject: (name) documents

Hi Ethan,
Happy new year to you. Could you please be so kind and help me out on,
import documents for (name) terminals for the following (countries).
This is required to allow the terminal entering legally these countries.
These documents must indicate all specific details on the terminal and
its origin.

> Looking forward to your reply.
> Best regards,
> Danny (+surname)
>
> Taken from Gimenez (2006: 168–170)
> Now, make a list of the elements you have spotted and compare it with that of another student. Then add those elements you spotted, and make a new list. Finally, compare your results with the rest of the class.

Another written document, typical of many business sectors, is the **business report**. There are a number of purposes for writing a report and each purpose gives the document its name. The most common types of reports include:

- 'periodic reports' which aim at providing management with regular information about an area or some aspect of the organisation
- 'progress reports' which provide information about the progress of a project, idea or initiative and outline future developments, and
- 'evaluation reports' which present an assessment of a course of action, project or product supported by evidence, and provide some future action based on the assessment made.

They all have a similar overall structure (introduction, body, and conclusion) but each section may vary slightly depending on the purpose of the report. This is shown in Table 5.4.

Table 5.4 Comparison of Report Types by Section

Section	Periodic report	Progress report	Evaluation report
Introduction	Purpose of report and relevant facts	Purpose of report and current state of project/idea/ initiative	Purpose of report and course of action
Body	Information about achievements and problematic issues	Information about key features, problems faced and solutions found, and schedule	Information about the present situation, need for change, and benefits of change

Section	Periodic report	Progress report	Evaluation report
Conclusion	Summary and recommendation	Future developments	Evaluation of changes and recommendations

The third Insights from Research of the unit (IR-5.3) discusses multi-communication in the workplace. As with the previous insights, there is a task to help your students develop 'media packaging' one of the skills needed for multi-communicating in the workplace.

Insights from Research (IR-5.3): Multi-Communication in the Workplace

The international workplace has gradually become a complex communicative space (Gimenez, 2014), which demands business people to develop new communication skills. One such demand is the ability to multi-communicate. Multi-communication (MC) has been defined as the ability to hold "multiple, face-to-face and electronically mediated conversations at the same time" (p. 2). For example, while speaking to a customer or colleague on the telephone, a person may be at the same time writing an email and/or a text on instant messaging. So, what skills are required for MC in today's international workplace? And, how can these skills be best promoted?

Gimenez (2014) has identified four key such skills:

- **Thematic threading**: Bringing together communication tasks that deal with the same topic
- **Presence allocation**: Spreading presence over a number of communication events
- **Media packaging**: Deciding what media work well together (e.g., emails and phone conversations)
- **Audience profiling**: Grouping diverse audiences by similar needs or requests.

The following task encourage students to develop skills in media packaging. As discussed in the research insight, media packaging refers to the ability to package compatible media (e.g., email + IM, email + telephone/mobile, IM + telephone). The task requires students to have access to these different media types to be able to do the simulation.

TASK 3: MEDIA PACKAGING

To the teacher

Preparation: Before you set this task for the students, you should send them two email messages. One email is from the managing director of their company giving details of the new services the company is now offering customers. This has been widely advertised (national radio, television and the press) so they should expect a vast volume of calls and emails enquiring information about the new services.

New services
- Dermatology clinics: Patients are referred to this service via our booking system for the   diagnosis and treatment of common dermatological conditions;
- Dieticians: Our dieticians offer advice, education and support to you and those who care   for you. We assess your needs and work with you to help you manage your condition - including those who are underweight due to an illness or disease, overweight or with high cholesterol;
- The Children Speech clinic: The Speech and Language Therapy for children helps children with difficulties with communication or using language. We work with children, their families, and carers.

The other email is from a customer requesting further information about the dietician services and wishing to make an appointment for [insert date].

Students should also be asked to log into the chat facility to do the task simulation.

Debriefing: A few ideas to discuss with the students after the simulation: 1. Reasons for organising and grouping tasks they way they did; 2. Why the packaged media in that way; 3. What packaging media facilitated.

MEDIA PACKAGING

Context: You work for a well-known health care centre. Your role demands excellent communication and telephone skills and being able to handle two or more tasks simultaneously.

Instructions: Read the tasks below and decide how you would organise them and what you would do together. Then, do the follow-up simulation.

TASKS

1. Email tasks
1.1 Write a reply to an email from a customer requesting further information about the dietician services and wishing to make an appointment.
1.2 Read the email you have just received from the managing director of your company giving details of the new services the company is now offering customers.

2. IM task
Your company offers a chat service for customers who require information about services. There is a customer requesting information about the dermatology clinics.

3. Telephone task
You are on the phone with a colleague discussing how to best deal with enquiries about the new range of services your company has started offering (e.g. how much information to provide, what type of language and register to use-formal and detached, friendly but professional, etc.)

FOLLOW-UP SIMULATION (in groups of three)

Instructions: Decide who is going to perform the following and then do the simulation:

- A. One of you is at work engaged in simultaneous tasks and is the first time you are multicommunicating,
- B. Another is a customer requesting information about the dermatology clinics by IM, and
- C. The other is a colleague, who is highly experienced in multicommunicating with customers, and who is discussing with you how to deal with customers requesting information about the new services.

Simulation: You are on the phone with a colleague at the same time that you're writing a reply to an email you have just received when a customer logs onto the IM service to request information. You don't actually want to stop the telephone conversation with your colleague as he/she will be very helpful in dealing with these tasks simultaneously.

Figure 5.3 Media Packaging Task

Taken from Gimenez (2014: 13).

Now that we have looked at a number of materials that could be used to realise the lesson plans for the unit, it is time for some further reflection. Reflection activity (RA-5.3) provides you with an opportunity to do so.

Reflection Activity (RA-5.3)

- How would you rate the materials presented in this section?
- How would you adapt them if necessary?
- How would you go about teaching them?

At this point, it would be important to make your students aware of how different cultural contexts value the written word. The following notes serve as a starting point for a class discussion you may want to plan for your students.

Culture and Technology Note (CTN-5.1)

Written a nd spoken communication and cultures

- The value of written and spoken communication varies from culture to culture. Many Latin American countries, for example, place greater value on the spoken word than the British or American working cultures do. Similarly, in parts of the Middle East, spoken agreements are seen as binding. In parts of Latin America and the Middle East a person's word is linked to their honour, so verbal agreements are seen almost as legally binding.
- On the other hand, most western working cultures tend to value the written word highly. In countries such as France, Germany, the UK and the US, written contracts tend to be seen as something permanent, possibly following the Latin proverb "verba volant, scripta manent" (literally: words fly, writings remain). In other cultural contexts, such as in Japan, renegotiating the terms of a written agreement is not uncommon as the written word is seen as a point of departure rather than one of arrival.

The discussion of these notes could then be followed by reflection questions such as "How does your own context value the written word?" and "Does the value of the written word change according to the context (e.g., everyday life, in the workplace?).

The final Insights from Research (IR-5.4) of the unit briefly discusses digital skills for the workplace and offers some description of tools that have been designed to support digital collaborative work.

Insights from Research (IR-5.4): Digital Skills and Collaborative Work

Digital skills have become central to organisational culture and therefore organisational communication. This has been, as we mentioned before, made possible by the advent of the Internet and advances in ICT. More recently, co-working tools such as SmartSheet or Google Workspace (see Further readings for a brief description) have changed the work processes of organisations by allowing collaborative projects to take place in online virtual spaces. For this to happen successfully, however, organisational culture also has to change. As Young Cho and Lee (2022: 27) argued, "in order to build such work processes, both employees and managers need to cultivate an organisational culture with a digital mindset".

5.5 Assessing learning

This section of the unit offers two tasks for assessing its LOs. Task 5.5.1 provides students with a set of Can-Do statements for self-assessment. Task 5.5.2 offers students the opportunity to analyse and discuss the components of an international corporation's mission statement, **Apple Inc.** in this case.

5.5.1 Self-assessing skills and competencies for internal and written communication

Self-assessing skills and competencies for internal and written communication				
Use the following list of Can-Do statements to self-assess the skills and competencies you have learnt in this unit. In case you are not sure or think you have not yet acquired the skill or competency referred to, make a note on what you can do about it.				
I can	Yes	No	?	I'm planning to

1. recognise the key internal communication practices of a particular work setting.				
2. identify and deploy specific strategies for adopting the internal communication practices of a particular work setting.				
3. read and understand the values and mission statement of a specific corporation.				
4. write a number of communication documents (e.g., emails, memos) effectively				

5.5.2 Assessing skills and competencies for internal and written communication

A good task for assessing "understanding values and mission statements" requires students to read real mission statements from the corporate world. The following is an example taken from **Apple Inc.**, https://www.apple.com/feedback/

Task: Understanding values and mission statements
1. Read and identify how the values that **Apple**'s mission statement is trying to project have been written. Pay close attention to the choice of words such as verbs and adjectives. "Apple strives to bring the best personal computing experience to students, educators, creative professionals, and consumers around the world through its innovative hardware, software, and internet offerings."

> 2. Now answer these questions
> There are three parts to the **Apple**'s mission statement: Action (what), people (who), and mode (how).
>
> - What is the communicative function of the first part of their mission statement (what)?
> - Why have they included who they do that for (who)?
> - What is the communicative function of the third part of the statement (how)?
>
> **Notes for the teacher**: It is also important to use mission statements from local companies for this activity. The Internet can help you find the mission statements of known companies in your area.

It is always a good idea to use genuine pieces of organisational communication. Consider using one of the emails sent to all the teachers in your school, for example, but make sure the sample you choose does not contain any sensitive information and remove any names from the example (see Gimenez, 2005, 2014 for examples). You can also use a newsletter for this activity. You can ask the students to analyse these internal communication artefacts and also to consider if and how they would reply. For the analysis, you may want to ask your students to revisit Handout 3 on strategies for internal communication.

> **Reflection Activity (RA-5.4)**
>
> - What tasks would you design to assess the other LOs of this unit?
> - What materials would you need to design such tasks?
> - Would you use the designed tasks for formative or summative assessment? For both? If so, how would you change the formative task for summative assessment?

Finally, as we discussed in the Introductory Unit (see Section I.5), it is always a good idea to develop a set of marking criteria for the unit if possible. Alternatively, you could design a set for the whole course.

5.6 Summary

This unit has introduced general concepts and ideas about internal organisational communication, with an emphasis on written communication. Together with this, multimodal communication was also discussed.

Based on this brief introduction, the unit has identified the key skills and competencies needed for managing internal organisational communication and writing effective written communication, and then turned them into LOs.

Next, we have looked at possible lesson plans and teaching materials to help students achieve the LOs identified, and selected specific vocabulary they would need. Finally, we examined ways in which the LOs for the unit could be assessed.

This unit was designed in conjunction with Unit 6, the next unit, which focuses on spoken communication. Together, the units present a general picture of the types of communication instances common to many workplaces.

Further readings: An annotated bibliography

Gimenez, J. (2014). Multi-communication and the business English class: Research meets pedagogy. *English for Specific Purposes*, 35, 1–16. https://doi.org/10.1016/j.esp.2013.11.002

This article discusses multi-communication (MC) practices in four multinationals based in London, UK. Apart from key theoretical considerations of the role of MC in corporate communication, it presents a number of pedagogical applications deriving from the findings of the study. These can be used to exemplify communication practices in multinational corporations.

Gimenez, J. (2005). Unpacking business emails: Message embeddedness in international business email communication. In Gotti M. and P. Gillaerts (eds.), *Genre variation in business letters*. (pp. 235–255). Peter Lang.

In this chapter, I review the evolution of email as a key tool for business internal written communication. The chapter presents many authentic examples that can be used to further illustrate the activities in the handouts in this unit.

Google Work Space: https://workspace.google.com/

Google Work Space is a flexible solution that allows teams to connect, create and collaborate.

Hartle, S., Facchinetti, R., & Franceschi, V. (2022). Teaching communication strategies for the workplace: A multimodal framework, *Multimodal Communication*, 11(1), 5–15. https://doi.org/10.1515/mc-2021-0005

In this article, Hartle, Facchinetti and Franceschi describe a series of pedagogical activities to help students of English for Professional Purposes to develop a number of multimodal competencies and strategies for effective communication in the contemporary workplace.

Johnson, J.D. & Chang, H.-J. (2000). Internal and external communication, boundary spanning and innovation adoption: An over-time comparison of three explanations of internal and external innovation communication in a new organizational form. *Journal of Business Communication*, 37(3), 238–263. https://doi.org/10.1177/002194360003700303

This article compares three explanations of the dynamic interrelationships between internal and external communication: the functional specialisation, the stars, and the cyclical model explanations. In the functional specialisation explanation, individuals tend to focus on the mix of internal and/or external communication given by the positions they occupy in the corporation. The communication stars explanation suggests that most individuals demonstrate similar levels of communication in both internal and external networks. Finally, the cyclical model describes a more dynamic pattern in which individuals shift back and forth between internal and external communication, influenced by the results of their privious communication behaviour.

Kollectif (2019). Measurement. Linking internal communication to business results. Report available at https://www.ickollectif.com/linking-ic-business-results

This report emphasises the importance of making sure that both internal and external communication reflect the same values and support the same messages to ensure consistency within and outside the company. The integrated approach suggested in the report would ensure that the image projected by a company (externally) and how it is perceived by its own employees (internally) is consistent.

SmartSheet: https://www.smartsheet.com/

SmartSheet is a powerful collaboration tool that allows users to task manage and collaborate in order to manage projects, automate processes, and scale up by using only one platform.

Unit 6

Teaching skills and competencies for spoken communication

Learning Outcomes

By the end of the unit, you should be able to:

- identify key skills and competencies needed for effective spoken communication
- turn skills and competencies into learning outcomes
- make pedagogical decisions about designing lessons, selecting materials, and assessing spoken communication skills and competencies, and
- select effective vocabulary items required for realising such skills and competencies.

6.1 Introducing spoken communication in the workplace

Together with written communication (see Unit 5), spoken communication, also referred to as oral communication, is another important component of corporate internal and external communication. Examples of spoken communication include meetings, telephone conversations, and presentations. These can be used for both internal (e.g., team meetings) as well as external (e.g., telephone conversations with suppliers) communication.

The key elements of spoken communication are both linguistic (e.g., words) and paralinguistic (e.g., accentuation, intonation) elements.

DOI: 10.4324/9781003283515-10

Although these elements vary in importance and function in different languages (e.g., intonation is more important in stress-timed languages like English), they tend to be the pillars upon which spoken communication is built.

At the same time, purpose is another important element in spoken communication. In the workplace spoken communication may serve different purposes:

- **Persuading**: Spoken communication can be used to persuade someone to do something. You may need to persuade a colleague to join up a project (internal communication) or a client to buy a particular product or service (external communication).
- **Sharing ideas**: One key aspect of spoken communication in the workplace is that it offers an excellent means for communicating within other colleagues, a team or within and outside the company. Spoken communication is central for, for example, sharing ideas in internal and external meetings or while working together on a project or idea for developing a new product or service.
- **Creating positive relationships**: As we discussed in Unit 4, when someone new joins a new company they will need to speak to others about themselves and their previous job and experiences. This is the first step in creating a positive relationship with colleagues. Spoken communication can also be used to create positive relationships with external publics such as customers and suppliers.
- **Increasing productivity**: Together with effective communication that gets the right message through with colleagues and team members, spoken communication facilitates the achievement of maximum outputs. It is generally accepted that better results are usually brought about by, for instance, group discussions.

Most of the spoken communication events (e.g., meetings, presentations) that commonly take place in the workplace will have at least one of these purposes.

6.2 Key skills and competencies for spoken communication

From the brief description in Section 6.1, we can see there are a number of skills and competencies relating to spoken communication that students would need to develop for effective spoken communication in the workplace. The key skills and competencies we are focusing in this unit are:

- Using paralinguistic features (e.g., accentuation, voice pitch, intonation) for effective spoken communication
- Selecting appropriate language in relation to audience, content and purpose of delivery
- Making effective presentations, and
- Participating in meetings.

These are a few skills and competencies that may be applicable to a wide range of situation and contexts. However, you may want to think of others that you consider more appropriate to your students and the context where you are teaching.

It is now time to do Extension task ET-6.1. This task requires you to watch a video clip and be able to select specific information from it.

Extension Task (ET-6.1)

Use the URL provided below to watch **video clip ET-6.1** on spoken communication in the workplace. As you watch, think of the following points being made:

- The role of English in international workplaces
- Factors influencing the required oral skills
- How oral skills may develop in the workplace
- The oral skills and competencies students may need to develop for the international workplace

https://worldsofenglish.com/workplace-skills-extension-tasks/

Now, it is time for our first reflection activity. Activity RA-6.1 provides some pointers to help you to reflect on what we have discussed so far.

Now that we have explored some key skills and competencies in relation to spoken communication in the workplace, we can think of ways of translating them into LOs. Table 6.1 exemplified such a process.

> **Reflection Activity (RA-6.1)**
>
> Considering what we have discussed so far, what are your views on the following:
>
> - How relevant for your teaching contexts are the skills and competencies listed above?
> - What other skills and competencies would you like to add?
> - What specific language items would these skills and competencies require?

Table 6.1 Turning Skills and Competencies for Spoken Communication in the Workplace into LOs

Skills/Competencies	Questions	Resulting LOs
Using paralinguistic features (e.g., accentuation, voice pitch, intonation) for effective spoken communication	How can students become (more) aware of the role of paralinguistic features in effective spoken communication?	By the end of the lesson, you should be able to use a number of paralinguistic features for effective spoken communication.
Selecting appropriate language in relation to audience, content and purpose of delivery	How can students choose appropriate language for spoken communication according to audience, content and purpose of delivery?	By the end of the lesson, you should be able to choose appropriate language for spoken communication according to audience, content and purpose of delivery.
Making effective presentations	What are the key characteristics of effective presentations for the workplace? What presentation skills and competencies do students need for the workplace?	By the end of the lesson, you should be able to make effective presentations for the workplace.
Participating in meeting	What strategies can students deploy to participate in meetings?	By the end of the lesson, you should be able to deploy a number of strategies to participate in meetings effectively.

Together with written (Unit 5) and spoken communication (this unit), there is an increasing use of social media in the workplace. This has been called 'enterprise social media' or ESM for short. The first Insights from Research of the unit (IR-6.1) discusses the key aspects of ESM.

Insights from Research (IR-6.1): Enterprise Social Media (ESM)

Social media (e.g., blogs, microblogging, social network sites) are increasingly being adopted by organisations for both internal and external communication. This emerging tendency in organisational communication, which has been termed enterprise social media (ESM), seems to facilitate knowledge sharing among employees, strengthen employee connection, as well as increase their awareness of cultural behaviours and preferences of others (Treem et al., 2015). Externally, they also allow organisations a more flexible communication pattern not only with their customers but also with other corporations and businesses with the aim to persuade rather than sell (Hartley & Chatterton, 2015), which, as Darics (2015, p. 1) argues, "means that this new [...] communicative situation has led to a change of paradigm in the ways businesses address and respond to their audiences". However, Treem et al.'s (2015) study concluded that how employees in the American organisation they researched saw the value of ESM for internal communication may have been influenced by their experiences of social media outside the organisation. Those with significant experience in social media, mostly younger participants, were rather sceptical of its value for organisational communication and sometimes saw it as a distraction. However, culture has to be brought into the picture when considering these findings. Research investigating employees' preference of and satisfaction with ESM in other cultural contexts have yielded different results. Mehra and Nickerson (2019), for example, found that the younger employees in the Indian organisation they investigated were "more likely to take advantage of a wide range of media to interact with suppliers, customers and employees, including computer mediated communication and mobile phones" (p. 1590).

As the use of ESM becomes more ubiquitous in organisational communication, attitudes to it are another aspect that you may want to discuss with your students. To this end, you could design a short survey to explore their attitudes to social media in general and ESM in particular, explore the similarities and differences in attitude between pre-experience and work-experienced students, and also ask them to conduct a brief survey among family and friends, the results of which could be reported back to the rest of the class.

Taking the LOs presented in Table 6.1 into account, we are in a position now to make some pedagogical decisions to design lessons for helping students to achieve such outcomes. This is what we will be doing in the next section.

6.3 Designing lessons for spoken communication

This section of the unit offers two possible lesson plans for the LOs we outlined in the previous section. The first lesson (Table 6.2) focuses on selecting appropriate language for spoken communication events, and the second (Table 6.3) deals with making effective presentations.

Table 6.2 A Lesson Plan for Selecting Appropriate Language in Relation to Audience, Content and Purpose of Delivery

Course: Communication Skills for the International Workplace	Year group:	Date:
Learning outcomes for selecting appropriate language for spoken communication		
By the end of the lesson, students should be able to: • identify how audience, content and purpose influence communication, and • select appropriate language accordingly for specific spoken communication events.		
Progression of teaching & learning		**Strategies/Materials**
Duration: 10 minutes	Introduction T asks Sts to form pairs to discuss their knowledge and experiences of how communication may change due to audience, content and purpose, with a particular focus on how this affects language choices.	Eliciting Sts' previous knowledge/experience

Duration: 25 minutes	Activity 1 1. Sts read an origi- nal story and dif- ferent subsequent versions of it to discuss what and why certain ele- ments in the sub- sequent versions have changed, with special atten- tion to language. 2. Sts complete a table with their answers to the questions about the text. 3. Sts report their an- swers to the class.	1. Discussing dif- ferent versions of the same story/Handout 1 2. Completing a table/Handout 1 3. Sharing answers with the class.
Duration: 15 minutes	Activity 2 4. Following from Activity 1, Sts make a list of what they need to change when the audience and purpose of their communication are different. 5. In pairs, Sts com- pare their lists and agree upon a final list containing all the items from the two lists. 6. In pairs, Sts read a given story and decide to re-tell it to either a differ- ent audience, or with a different purpose, or both.	4. Writing a list/Handout 2 5. Comparing and agreeing in pairs/Handout 2 6. Making decisions in pairs/ Handout 2 7. Re-telling a new version of a story

(Continued)

	7. The pairs practise how they would re-tell a new version of the given story, considering the items they have agreed upon for their final list.	
Duration: 10 minutes	Conclusion Sts reflect on the activities of the lesson and summarise what they have learnt in bullet points.	
Success criteria	• To be able to identify how audi-ence, content and purpose influence communication, and • To be able to select appropriate language accord-ingly for specific spoken communi-cation events.	Assessment A list of statements for Sts to decide whether they are T or F. Sts to re-write the F statements to make them T.
Next steps	Sts will re-write a given short story so that it meets the expectations of different audiences and fulfils different purposes.	

Table 6.3 A Lesson Plan for Making Effective Presentations

Course: Communication Skills for the International Workplace	Year group:	Date:
Learning outcomes for dealing with interview questions		
By the end of the lesson, students should be able to: • identify the key elements of effective workplace presentations, and • prepare an effective presentation for the workplace.		

Progression of teaching & learning		Strategies/Materials	
Duration: 10 minutes	Introduction T asks Sts to discuss in small groups their knowledge and experiences of presenting either in class or at work.	Eliciting Sts' previous knowledge/experience	
Duration: 25 minutes	Activity 1 1. T presents students with a video clip on how to give a presentation at work. 2. Sts watch the video, paying attention to particular aspects mentioned in Handout 3. 3. In small groups, Sts discuss the particular aspects they have identified and make a common list. They then report their results to the class.	1. 2. 3.	Introducing a video clip/Handout 3 Watching a video clip and identifying key aspects/ Handout 3 Discussing aspects, making a common list and sharing results with the class.
Duration: 15 minutes	Activity 2 4. Sts read a blog with more information about workplace presentations, paying attention to particular aspects of workplace presentations.	4. 5. 6.	Reading and selecting information/ Handout 4 Discussing information and agreeing in pairs/Handout 4 Choosing a topic and making plans/Handout 4

(Continued)

	5. In pairs, Sts discuss what new information they have learnt from the blog, and agree upon key aspects of pre-sentations they should remember when presenting at work. 6. In pairs, Sts choose one topic for a presenta-tion and plan how to go about researching and preparing for their presentation.	
Duration: 10 minutes	<u>Conclusion</u> Sts reflect on the activities of the lesson and summarise what they have learnt.	
Success criteria	• To be able to identify the key elements of ef-fective workplace presentations, and • To be able to pre-pare an effective presentation for the workplace.	**Assessment** Sts watch a presentation on video and evaluate it, taking into account the key characteristics of effective workplace presentations identified in class.
Next steps	Sts will prepare a presentation (this could be done in pairs) on a given topic to be delivered in the next class.	

Now that we have considered possible class plans for two of the LOs we identified for spoken communication in the workplace, we can stop for a moment to reflect upon them. Reflection activity RA-6.2 provides you with 3 questions in support of your reflective process.

Reflection Activity (RA-6.2)

Considering the two lesson plans above, what are your views about the following:

- How relevant are they for your teaching context?
- What should be the next lesson plan in the sequence?
- How much practice in making workplace presentations would your student need?

Your students may be familiar with academic presentations so they represent a good starting point to discuss workplace presentations. You may want to start by eliciting their knowledge, experiences and views on presentations in general. Next, you could present to them with more specific information about workplace presentations. The following classroom activity has been designed to illustrate this point.

Presentations, Presentations, Presentations

As you are probably aware, there are different types of presentations (e.g., academic, workplace, sales pitches). You may be more familiar with some than with others.

1. **Discussion**: With another student, discuss your views and experiences of academic presentations. You may want to make notes on your discussion which you may share with the rest of the class when you have finished.
   1.1   Have you ever presented in class?
   1.2   If so, how was the experience for you?
   1.3   What, in your view, are the key features of effective academic presentations?
   1.4   Any challenges? If so, how did you deal with them?

2. **Reading**: Now, read the following text about workplace presentations. As you read, pay attention to the following features of workplace presentations:
   - The role of context
   - Their key purposes
   - Defining factors for preparing them
   - Challenges
   - Strategies to deal with challenges

Workplace presentations

Context (e.g., topic, relationship between presenter and audience) will always play a role in how workplace presentations are planned, designed and delivered. For instance, Evans's (2013) research on a number of businesses located in Hong Kong discovered that externally as well as internally-oriented presentations have three clearly defined purposes: *providing* (e.g., information about new or existing products), *updating* (e.g., reporting on the progress of a project) and *coordinating* (e.g., the efforts or activities of different department). Also, in contrast to other types of presentations (e.g., academic, conference), workplace presentations take less consideration of background information about the presentation and the presenter as the audience already know the presenter, the company and the topic of the presentation, resulting in most presentations being brief and to the point. It is essential, therefore, that students of workplace communication are familiarised with the fact that 'content selection' and 'time management' are more important factors defining workplace presentations than 'introducing themselves to the audience' and 'providing background information'.

Like in other types of presentations, 'answering questions' was found in Evans's research to be a challenging aspect of workplace presentations. In international workplaces, a related linguistic challenge is posed by unfamiliar accents which may add to the difficulty of handling questions from the floor or interacting with the audience. Teachers could help their students by equipping them with strategies such as finding out who will attend their workplace presentation beforehand to anticipate whether anyone would speak in an accent they are not very familiar with. Students could then listen to video clips (e.g., on YouTube) of other people with similar accents.

Research has also shown that not all workplace presentations use design software (e.g., Microsoft PowerPoint) as business people tend to be always very busy and cannot always afford the time most software requires to design a presentation. In such cases, most business people would consider other media (e.g., flipcharts) more appropriate.

3. **Completing**: Next, complete the following table with the information about workplace presentations you have just read.

Workplace Presentations: Key Features	Your Notes
Role of context	
Key purposes	

Workplace Presentations: Key Features	Your Notes
Defining factors	
Challenges and strategies	

4. **Further reading**: Read the following text about sales pitches. As you read, think about the following elements:

   - What pattern did Steve Jobs follow for most of his sales pitches?
   - What key elements should a sales pitch include?

Sales pitches

Sales pitches are another very common type of presentations in business which share some of the futures and purposes of academic and workplace presentations. According to Gallo (2009), Steve Jobs, former CEO at Apple Inc., had mastered the art of presenting with theatrical precision. His sales pitches were designed following the pattern of a classic story:

   - create a story: Craft an exciting story for your presentation
   - deliver the experience: Turn your presentations into visually appealing experiences
   - refine and rehearse: Practise your delivery until it sounds natural and conversational

Similarly, Gallo has described most of Jobs' presentations as following the problem–solution pattern:

   1. Deliver a story that arouses your audience's interest
   2. Pose a problem that has to be solved
   3. Offer a solution to that problem
   4. Describe the specific benefits of adopting such a solution
   5. State a call for action

The key elements in a sales pitch include:

   1. **Headline**: The headline or title should encapsulate the big idea you want to share with your audience, written in a short and memorable way.
   2. **Passion statement**: This statement should show your audience how passionate you are about the topic of the presentation (e.g., I am excited about this (topic) because...)

3. **Three key messages**: Decide which three messages you want your audience to remember.
4. **Metaphors and analogies**: Think about what metaphors or analogies you will use to describe the topic of your presentation.
5. **Demonstrate**: Instead of just describing it, demonstrate as far as possible the topic of your presentation.
6. **Evidence and endorsement**: Use evidence (e.g., figures, sales) and endorsements (e.g., customer's evaluations) to support your demonstrations.
7. **Video clips**: If possible, include brief video clips as visual support.
8. **Use multimodal communication**: People process information in different ways: visually, auditory and kinetically. Use multimodal communication to cater to the different processing preferences (see also Unit 5).

5. **Comparing**: Now that you have read and discussed different types of presentations, you are in a position to draw comparisons between them. Use the following table to highlight how academic, workplace and sales pitch presentations compare.

Features of Presentations	Academic	Workplace	Sales
Purpose			
Role of context			
Audience			
Relationship between presenter and audience			
Content			
Structure			
Challenges			

Another activity to further explore presentations relates to how they are evaluated. To this end, you could design evaluation schemes to rate your students' performance (see also Section I.5, Introductory Unit). The schemes would serve a number of purposes. First, they would make clear to the presenter what is expected of their performance. Secondly, they would make students more aware of the features of effective presentations they need to consider when preparing their presentations. Finally, they would guide your assessment while your students are presenting in class.

The following are provided as examples of schemes to evaluate 1. Academic presentations and 2. Workplace presentations. These two schemes could also be used to compare how the two types of presentations are evaluated.

1.   Academic Presentation Evaluation Scheme
E= Excellent
VG= Very Good
G= Good
R= Needs revision

Evaluation Scheme for Academic Presentations	Student's Name:			
Features	E	VG	G	R
1. Delivery				
1.1 Clear and easy to follow				
1.2 Appropriate timing				
1.3 Engaging				
2. Content				
2.1 Relevant				
2.2 Research-based				
2.3 Key ideas/issues included				
3. Structure				
3.1 Logical organisation				
3.2 Signposted				
3.3 Clear, balanced argument and evidence presented				
4. Questions from the floor				
4.1 Appropriate responses				
4.2 Signs of preparation				
4.3 Handled strategically and knowledgeably				

For group presentations, you could add a fifth feature: Teamwork.

Features	E	VG	G	R
5. Teamwork				
5.1 Well-prepared and evenly distributed				
5.2 Coherent presentation				
5.3 Well-integrated delivery				

2.   Workplace presentations
E= Excellent
VG= Very Good
G= Good
R= Needs revision

Evaluation Scheme for Workplace Presentations	Student's Name:			
Features	E	VG	G	R
1. Delivery				
1.1 Clear and engaging				
1.2 Brief and concise (to the point)				
1.3 Appropriate timing				
2. Content				
2.1 Relevant to the purpose				
2.2 Well-selected				
2.3 Supported with evidence (e.g., figures, sales, testimonies)				
3. Structure				
3.1 Clear patterning (e.g., problem–solution)				
3.2 Signposted				
3.3 Multimodality (e.g., visuals, video clips)				
4. Questions from the floor				
4.1 Appropriate responses				
4.2 Signs of preparation				
4.3 Handled strategically				

As with academic presentations, you could add a fifth feature (Teamwork) for group presentations.

Features	E	VG	G	R
5. Teamwork				
5.1 Evidence of collaboration				
5.2 Coherent presentation				
5.3 Well-integrated delivery				

Presentations may be a daunting experience for new presenters. Besides the considerations and tips your students have read and watched in this lesson, there is a set of related language items that they will need to be familiar with and which should help them feel more in control of their presentations. Language Corner LC-6.1 presents some such language items.

Language Corner (LC-6.1)

There are a number of language items that your students will need for presenting in the workplace. The list below provides some key items but you may want to add a few more which you think will be relevant to your own teaching context.

- (Good) Morning/Afternoon (everyone)
- Welcome to...
- The topic of this presentation is...
- (Today/this morning/afternoon) I'd like to talk to you about/talk you through
- This presentation will look at/show you/share with you
- OK, let's start with/by ...
- OK, let's get started.
- Let me start by telling you...
- You may be wondering why...
- So, why am I telling you this?
- This presentation will (+ goal or objective)
- Some time ago, we discovered that...
- In the last six months, (topic/issue) has (increased/decreased/rocketed) to unprecedented levels.
- What's the biggest problem that we face today?
- Imagine that....
- Please, feel free to ask questions as I speak.
- There will be plenty of time for questions at the end.
- As you can see from this chart/graph,
- The following chart/graph (shows)
- As I mentioned before,
- Summarising,
- To finish, let me...

Collocations/Expressions

- Make a presentation
- Make a presentation to somebody

- A presentation on...
- Persuade someone to do something
- Encourage someone to do something
- Inform someone about something
- Show someone something
- Start with (+a problem/an issue/a situation)
- Start by (an action = Verb+ING)
- Finish off
- Round up
- Off the cuff

Structural elements

- **Simple past** (e.g., Last year we noticed an increase in...)
- **Present simple** (e.g., Today, I want to refer to....)
- **Present perfect** (e.g., In the past few years, the trend has moved towards...)
- **Simple future** (e.g., As we can see, this tendency will tend to slow down in the next...)
- **Sequence indicators** (e.g., first; next; the last thing...)
- **Section markers** (e.g., to begin (with); summarising; to finish)

6.4 Materials for teaching spoken communication skills and competencies

In this section, we will look at a number of handouts that could be used to deliver the lesson plans we discussed in the previous section. Handout 1 provides materials for analysing language for different audiences, Handout 2 deals with story re-telling, Handout 3 focuses on the elements of effective presentations for the workplace, and the final handout (Handout 4) discusses tips for preparing a work presentation.

Handout 1: Analysing Language for Different Audiences

1. Read the following story which has recently been published in a local Argentinian newsletter. Then read versions 1, 2 and 3 and in each version identify:

- **what** has changed (e.g., language, sentence structure)
- **why** it has been changed (e.g., purpose), and
- **who** it is now intended for (e.g., different audience)?

Story

R&R, the leading cosmetic brand in Argentina, have decided to stop testing their products on animals after animal rights campaigners have called for a national boycott on their cosmetics to stop their "lethal dose" testing on mice. The main argument against animal testing lies in the pain and suffering inflicted on animals. However, in their press release, R&R have argued that their decision was made after confirming that, due to the fact that the physiology of animal species is different from that of humans, animal testing has proven to be a flawed method of assessing product safety.

Version 1

You know what? You know R&R, right? Well, they have decided to stop testing on animals. They say they have discovered that animal testing can't guarantee the safety of their products. And that animals are different from humans. For me, they've decided to stop because campaigners suggested boycotting their products in the past months, that's actually why.

Version 2

Most testing on animals requires repeatedly force-feeding chemicals, to mice especially, for weeks in order to discover any possible adverse health reactions like cancer or other illnesses. As a requirement of some of these tests, 50 percent of the test subjects (e.g., rats) must die. This type of test is called a "lethal dose" test and animals are not given pain relief at any point of the testing process.

Version 3

At R&R, we take animal suffering very seriously. After many years of following standard practice in the industry sector, R&R have decided to stop testing on animals, thus becoming one of the first corporations in the country to seek alternative ways of testing their products. These alternative tests will nonetheless allow us to continue offering our valued customers the same safety standards we have always provided.

2. Now, complete the following table. Provide examples to illustrate your choice when possible.

Aspects	Version 1	Version 2	Version 3
Register (e.g., formal, informal)			
Sentence structure (e.g., co-ordination, subordination)			
Vocabulary items (e.g., technical vocabulary)			
Content (e.g., opinions, facts)			
Audience (e.g., a friend, the public)			
Purpose (e.g., inform, persuade)			

Handout 2: Re-Telling a Story

1. Based on the activities in Handout 1, make a list of what needs changing when the audience and purpose of a spoken communication are different.

My list

- _____
- _____
- _____
- _____
- _____

2. Now compare your list with that of another student. Then, agree upon a final list containing all the items from the two lists.

Our list

- _____
- _____
- _____
- _____
- _____
- _____
- _____
- _____

3. Read the following description of **Nike**'s (https://www.nike.com) design philosophy which was written for Nike's external publics. After you have read it, decide how you can tell the same content to either a different audience, or with a different purpose, or both:

Audience: To a friend, to a newspaper report, etc.

Purpose: To inform a friend about ISPA, to persuade people to buy disassembled products, etc.

Nike's ISPA

ISPA (Improvise, Scavenge, Protect, Adapt) is a Nike design philosophy that challenges creators to experiment, break moulds and reimagine products. The ISPA team considered the circular design principle of "disassembly", or the ability to easily take a product apart to recycle its contents, one of the most challenging principles to implement in footwear design.

Adapted from https://about.nike.com/en/stories/
ispa-link-link-axis

4. Finally, in pairs practise how you would re-tell a new version of the story above, taking into account the items you have agreed upon in "Our list".

Handout 3: Elements of an effective workplace presentation

1. Watch the following video clip about presentations at work:
   https://www.youtube.com/watch?v=okzvYA_tgjo
2. As you watch, pay attention to the headings in the following table and jot down some notes for each:

Opportunities offered	
Tips for a killer presentation	•
	•
	•
	•
	•
Types of presentation media seen on the clip	

3. In your group, discuss the particular aspects of workplace presentations each of you has identified and make a common list. Be prepared to report your results of your discussion to the class.

Handout 4: Preparing a presentation at work

1. Read this blog about work presentations, paying attention to these particular aspects in it:

    https://www.indeed.com/career-advice/career-development/types-of-presentations

    • Purposes of work presentations
    • Types of presentation styles
    • Aspects to consider before choosing a style
    • Tips for an effective work presentation

2. With another student, discuss what new information you have both learnt from the blog, and agree upon key aspects of presentations you should remember when preparing a presentation.

3. Now, choose one topic for a presentation and plan how to go about researching and preparing for it:

    Topic 1: Nike's latest products (You could simulate you work for Nike, or you work for the competition and you're presenting a competitor's analysis)

    Topic 2: **Our latest product/service project**

    Topic 3: **Our new mission and vision**

The next refection Activity (RA-6.3) presents three questions about the materials included above for you to reflect upon.

Reflection Activity (RA-6.3)

Considering the materials above, what are your views about the following:

• How relevant are these materials for your students? If they are not, could you adapt them? If so, how?
• What specific student needs should the new materials meet?
• What sources (e.g., blogs, video clips) would be most appropriate for your new materials?

Let's now turn to some culture and technology notes relating to the LOs of this unit. Culture and Technology Note CTN-6.1 presents some observations you may want to share with your students or use as the basis for developing teaching materials. You may also want to divide your class into groups who can try out the different presentation software described in the notes, and then discuss their experiences of using the software with the rest of the class.

Culture and Technology Note (CTN-6.1)

Different workplaces go about establishing and building their spoken communication practices in different ways. These practices shape and are shaped by the culture of each company or corporation, and sometimes by the culture of the country where they are located. There may be a difference in views and opinions about how things should get done between the culture of the country and that of the company or corporation. This is normally the case when a multinational operates in a country different from that of their headquarters (see Gimenez, 2002 for an example).

Presentations offer a typical example of the possible differences in corporate culture. In many companies, PowerPoint presentations are the norm. In others, they are discouraged as they present a number of disadvantages (Speach blog). Employees may not always have the time PowerPoint presentations require to prepare, or they may find that they are not the best medium for the topic to be presented (see also "Presentations, presentations, presentations" in this unit).

Sometimes, a flipchart may appear a more convenient way of presenting a new project, a situation with sales or how an idea for a new product or service is developing. At other times, only a few pointers on a notebook would be enough, especially when a meeting has been called upon at short notice.

There are a number of presentation software that you and your students may want to explore. Here are a few notes about some of them:

Prezi

Prezi is very popular for non-linear presentations. The software offers a great variety of canvases that you can fill with your content. It also allows you to jump from place to place during the presentation.

SlideDog

This software is excellent for using multiple media formats (e.g., video clips, photos, PDF files). It allows you to combine all the media you need into a single presentation which you can show altogether and in any order.

Haiku Deck

Haiku Deck is an easy-to-grasp interface which is fully web-based. It stores all your materials in the cloud, thus making it possible to retrieve and edit your presentations anywhere you are and on a number of devices.

Another typical spoken communication event in the workplace is meetings. Like presentations, they have very specific objectives, some of which are similar to those we have already discussed in relation to presentations: providing information, upgrading people on recent (project, products) developments, and co-ordinating an activity or a course of action.

One way of teaching meetings to your students is by starting with a discussion of what they already know or have experienced. If you are teaching work-experienced students, they should have had some first-hand experiences of meetings. If your students are pre-experience, then you could lead the discussion. If your class has both types, you could pair them up, making sure there is one work-experienced and one pre-experience student in each pair. Some of the questions you could ask as a warm-up exercise include:

- Have you had any experiences of workplace meetings?
- What is the meetings culture like in your organisation?
- Have the meetings you've attended finished on time?

After your students have discussed these questions, they could share their views with the rest of the class. Next, you may introduce them to the typical structure of workplace meetings. However, it is important to keep in mind that the culture of an organisation will have a strong influence on how meetings are conducted. As Handford (2013) has argued, we need to keep in mind that not all meetings will follow a strict format and order for discussing the items on the agenda and that factors such as national, local and organisational culture, the status and relationship of the attendees and the purpose of the meeting itself will always shape the way meetings are conducted. The second question in the warm-up activity aims at making students aware of this point and you could remind them of what has been said by the different pairs.

Having said that, most meetings will have:

- **A start**: This includes a presentation and agreement on the agenda for the meeting, an agreement to start the meeting, and dealing with pressing issues first
- **The conduct of the meeting**: presentation of the items on the agenda, discussion, agreement and regular updates

- **An end**: This includes a summary of the key issues discussed in the meeting, listing of priorities and action points, any other business (usually abbreviated to AOB) and wrapping up of the meeting.

It is important for students to identify the different parts of the structure of a typical meeting so that they can feel better prepared to take part in it. In this respect, one key section of the meeting, especially for students who are new to business meetings, is when asked to participate to give an opinion or report on something. Equally important for them to feel prepared if to read in advance all the meeting-related documents (e.g., agenda, reports, data) that are normally circulated before the meeting. Together with this, there is a list of language items that are typical of workplace meetings your students will need to be familiar with. Language Corner LC-6.2 presents some such items.

Language Corner (LC-6.2)

Beginning and welcoming

- (I'd like to) welcome you all to today's meeting.
- Now, if we are all here, let's get started.
- If everyone is here, we can start.
- Shall we start?

Announcing the main purpose for the meeting

- I've/we've called this meeting to discuss …
- We're here to discuss…
- The main issue I'd/we'd like to discuss today is …

Apologies for a person's absence

- (name) can't be with us today because…
- (name) has sent his/her apologies. He/She is …

Developments or pressing issues

- (name), could you tell us how (project) is progressing?
- Do we have any news on (project), (name)?

Introducing the first item

- Let's begin start by looking at/discussing ...
- Let's kick off with ...

Looking at the next item

- Next, we have the issue of ...
- Now, let's move on to look at ...
- Ok, moving on ...

Asking for contributions/suggestions

- Has anyone got anything to contribute/suggest/comment on at this point?
- I'd like to hear comments/suggestions at this point.
- Would you like to add anything, (name)?
- What's your opinion on this, (name)?
- Can you tell us more about....?

Giving an opinion

- I think that...
- May I just say/add that....?
- In my view/opinion...
- (I'm afraid) I have a different view.
- (I'm sorry but) I don't think I can agree with that.

Finishing up

- Any other business? Any AOBs?
- If there are no other comments, I'd suggest finishing for today.
- If that's all then, we can finish here.
- (I'd like to) thank you all for attending.
- Thank you all for your participation.

The second Insights from Research (IR-6.2) of the unit explores workplace meetings, and offers some materials and ideas for pedagogical applications based on the research discussed in it.

Insights from Research (IR-6.2): Workplace Meetings

Despite being sometimes described as a necessary evil and a waste of time (Doodle, 2019), when successful, meetings can actually bring about real benefits, including fostering creativity, innovation and relationships. Meetings have been the focus of linguistic research since the early 1990s (e.g., Boden, 1994; Bargiela-Chiappini & Harris, 1997; Poncini, 2004; Stubbe et al., 2003; Yamada, 1990). However, as a result of the central role of technology in the workplace, the field has started to pay closer attention to the competencies and skills needed for successful meetings (e.g., Gimenez, 2020; Ilie et al., 2019; Nickerson & Planken, 2016). Competencies, defined as a cluster of capabilities, and knowledge that facilitate a person's effective participation in a given activity, have been brought to the limelight, especially in business performance research (e.g., Cappelli & Tavis, 2016; García-Zambrano & Rodríguez-Castellanos, 2016). In relation to meetings, such research has identified competencies for collaboration and managing communication technology to be central.

In an international context, the success of a multicultural meeting largely depends on the participants being able to reach common ground about its structure and function. As Pan, Wong Scollon and Scollon (2002:125) observe, "when people of different cultural backgrounds come into a meeting with different assumptions about the structure or the function of meetings, they inevitably encounter tremendous difficulty in comprehending what is going on".

In my recent research on a group of nine meetings at three different European organisations (Gimenez, 2020), I managed to identify the key competencies that students preparing for the international workplace should have and develop. This research was guided by the question "What business-meeting skills and competencies should we be teaching today?". Results from the study have shown that the key competencies required for contemporary business meetings are: analytical thinking, creative collaboration, relational capacity and managing high-end technology. The table below offers a brief description of each of these competencies. Following this, some pedagogical applications to help students develop such competencies are presented.

Competency	Description	Indicators
Creative collaboration	The ability to engage creatively and collaboratively in demanding tasks that require creative thinking and collective intelligence	High levels of engagement with task; creative thinking; strong drive to harness collective intelligence

Competency	Description	Indicators
Analytical thinking	The ability to examine complex challenges and demands by unpacking them, and considering different and sometimes conflicting ideas to deal with them	Open to new and different ideas; willingness to assess own and others' ideas and viewpoints; analyzing the whole by focusing on its parts
Relational capability	The ability to foster collaboration among members of a team in order to develop a sense of belonging, leading to satisfaction and loyalty	Urge for collaboration; strong sense of belonging; high degrees of satisfaction and loyalty
Managing high-end visualisation technology	The ability to integrate visualisation technology (e.g., high-end computers) with communication events (e.g., meetings) effectively	Understanding of the functions of visualisation technology; integration of technology and communication

Ideas to develop the competencies listed in the table above:

Make your students aware of the need to:

- Engage with tasks creatively and collaboratively, integrating both what needs to be talked about and the supporting technological tools. This would help students develop strategies for "creative collaboration"
- Work creatively and collaboratively to find solutions to problems and take follow-up actions which is another way of fostering "creative collaboration"
- Interact with other participating members of the team in a respectful and supportive way, welcoming similar as well as opposing ideas and contributions. This would encourage students to apply "analytical thinking" competencies
- Take responsibility for one's opinions and actions, feeling free to express one's ideas and viewpoints at the same time, which would help them to further develop their "analytical thinking" competencies
- Publicly recognise other people's efforts and contributions in order to increase levels of "relational capability"; and

- Collaboratively find ways of making meetings more efficient by the use of technology, especially when visualisation technology can facilitate and/or support efficient communication. This is particularly important for helping students to learn to manage "visualisation technology" for communication purposes.

6.5 Assessing learning

This section presents a self-assessment table and an integrated task to assess the LOs set out at the beginning of the unit.

6.5.1 Self-assessing skills and competencies for spoken communication in the workplace

Self-Assessing Skills and Competencies for Job Interviews				
Use the following list of Can-Do statements to self-assess the LOs for this unit. In case you are not sure or think you have not yet acquired the skill or competency referred to, make a note on what you can do about it.				
I can	Yes	No	?	I'm planning to
1. use accentuation and intonation for effective spoken communication.				
2. choose appropriate language for spoken communication according to audience, content and purpose of delivery.				
3. make effective presentations for the workplace.				
4. deploy a number of strategies to participate in meetings effectively.				

6.5.2 Assessing skills and competencies for spoken communication

The following integrated task provides students with an opportunity to show the skills and competencies they have learnt in this unit. You could use it to complement the self-assessment exercise in 6.5.1, as a formative assessment exercise or for summative assessment. Alternatively, you can use it as a model for designing another task that would meet your students' needs more successfully.

You may also design a set of evaluation criteria for this particular task (see also Section I.5, Introductory Unit). As previously discussed, the criteria may include: appropriate content, language, audience awareness, appropriate choice of medium, and the like. It is important that you discuss the criteria with your students, making sure they understand how their presentations will be assessed.

Researching for, Designing and Delivering a Work Presentation

Background

You work for a multinational corporation headquartered in New York. You are now visiting the corporation subsidiary in Beijing and have to present to the employees at the subsidiary the corporation's new guidelines for global communication.

Instructions

1. Choose a real (from the Internet) or fictitious organisation to work on
2. If you choose a real organisation, search for information about their communication policies
3. Using the results from your research on the corporation and what you have learnt in this unit, design a presentation on the corporation's new guidelines for global communication. Choose an appropriate medium, content and language for your presentation.
4. Make your presentation to the rest of the class.

6.6 Summary

This unit has discussed key aspects of spoken communication for the workplace. The unit complements Unit 5, which focuses on written communication.

As previous units, Unit 6 has identified the main skills and competencies for oral communication at work and translated these into LOs. Based on these, the unit has presented lesson plans that could be followed to develop two LOs. Next, it has provided four handouts with materials that can be used to deliver the lesson plans offered in the unit. This has been accompanied by reflective activities, selected language for work presentations and culture and technology notes.

The unit has finally offered two assessment activities. The first provides students with an opportunity to reflect upon what they have learnt by means of Can-Do statements; the second includes an integrated task to assess work presentation skills.

Unit 7 will focus on teaching skills and competencies for workplace appraisals following the teaching and learning cycle described in the Introductory Unit.

Further readings: An annotated bibliography

Gimenez, J. (2002). New media and conflicting realities in multinational corporate communication: A case study. *International Review of Applied Linguistics*, 40 (4), 323–343. https://doi.org/10.1515/iral.2002.016

In this research article, I discuss the role of new media in the communication practices between an Argentinian subsidiary and its European head office, and the communication conflicts that arose from the globally-adopted identity imposed by the head office and the socially-constructed identity sustained by the subsidiary. This study clearly shows the conflicts in communication brought about by the difference in culture between the European parent company and its Argentinian subsidiary.

Speach me

https://speach.me/reasons-you-should-stop-using-powerpoint/

This blog presents a few reasons why people should stop using Power-Point and offers alternative software.

Part IV

Appraisal and promotion

Unit 7

Teaching skills and competencies for performance appraisals

Learning Outcomes

By the end of the unit, you should be able to:

- identify the types of performance appraisals usually used across business sectors
- recognise the key skills and competencies needed for performance appraisals
- turn these skills and competencies into LOs
- make pedagogical decisions about designing lessons, selecting materials, and assessing performance appraisals and giving feedback, and
- select effective vocabulary items your students will require for performance appraisals and giving feedback.

7.1 Introducing performance appraisals in the workplace

Performance appraisals, also known as annual reviews, performance evaluations or employee appraisals, are regular reviews of the job performance (e.g., achievements and growth) and contribution to a company by employees.

DOI: 10.4324/9781003283515-12

Performance appraisals may be conducted once a year, or every six or four months, and are used to inform promotions (see Unit 8), monetary incentives (e.g., bonuses) or contact termination.

There are different types of performance appraisals but the most common ones are:

- **360-degree assessment**: This type of appraisal takes into account feedback from an employee's line manager or supervisor, the employee themselves, and sometimes their peers.
- **Management by objective**: This review requires the manager and their employee to identify particular goals for the employee over a given period of time. When the time concludes, the manager evaluates whether and to what extent the goals have been met.
- **Negotiated appraisal**: This type allows a mediator to be present in an attempt to moderate any possible tensions arising from performance appraisals.
- **Peer assessment**: In this kind of appraisals employees evaluate another employee's performance.
- **Self-assessment**: This type requires employees to rate their own performance.

Some companies would combine one or two of these types to make performance appraisals more rounded and productive.

Performance appraisals also help managers and their employees to create a development plan with the skills and competencies needed for employees to reach their goals. This plan could include additional training and new responsibilities. In recent times, performance appraisals have become more dialogic in nature, providing opportunities for frequent conversations and developing stronger relationships.

From these considerations, we can already identify some underlying skills and competencies that students will need to be able to take part in performance appraisals effectively. This is what we will explore in the following section.

7.2 Key skills and competencies for performance appraisals

The key skills and competencies that students should develop to participate in performance appraisals include:

- self-assessing their own work performance
- identifying future goals and training needs
- dealing with negative feedback, and
- evaluating other employees' performance.

These skills and competencies should enable students to manage their own performance appraisals more effectively as well as participate in the appraisal of others. Another skill that students may find useful is 'negotiating'. This will be dealt with together with applying for promotion in Unit 8.

Extension Task ET-7.1, which you can also use as teaching material, provides some further insights into performance appraisals.

Extension Task (ET-7.1)

Use the URL provided below to watch **video clip ET-7.1** about work appraisals. As you watch, think of the following questions:

- How are performance appraisals defined?
- How does this definition compare with the one introduced in the previous section?
- What characteristics are highlighted?
- What is the role of HR in the performance appraisal process?
- What key factors for a successful performance appraisal are mentioned?
- Have you ever taken part in a performance appraisal? How does your experience compare with what is being described in the video clip?

https://worldsofenglish.com/workplace-skills-extension-tasks/

Now, you may want to do the first Reflection Activity (RA-7.1) of the unit. The activity provides some questions to help you to reflect on what we have discussed so far.

Reflection Activity (RA-7.1)

Considering what we have discussed so far, what are your views about the following:

- Are performance appraisals used in the organisations you know or work for?

- How useful for your students do you think the skills and competencies for performance appraisals are?
- If you were teaching pre-experience students, how much information about performance appraisals would they need?
- If there are job-experienced students in your class, how could you capitalise on their previous experiences of performance appraisals?

Now that we have explored some key skills and competencies in relation to job performance appraisals, we can think of ways of translating them into LOs. Table 7.1 exemplified such a process.

Table 7.1 Turning Skills and Competencies for Performance Appraisals into LOs

Skills/ Competences	Questions	Resulting LOs
Self-assessing work performance	How can students learn to self-assess their work performance? What language would they need for self-assessment?	By the end of the lesson, you should be able to self-assess your work performance, using appropriate language.
Identifying future goals and training needs	How can students identify future goals and training needs? What language would they need for speaking about future goals and training needs?	By the end of the lesson, you should be able to identify future goals and training needs, and speak about those using appropriate language.
Dealing with negative feedback	How can students deal with negative feedback given out during performance appraisals?	By the end of the lesson, you should be able to develop key strategies for dealing with negative feedback.
Evaluating other people's performance	What strategies can students deploy to evaluate other people's performance? What language would they need for giving feedback on other people's performance?	By the end of the lesson, you should be able to evaluate other people's performance and provide them with feedback by using appropriate language.

To achieve these LOs, your students will need to be familiar with a number of language items as shown in Language Corner LC-7.1.

Language Corner (LC-7.1)

A number of language items may prove useful for your students to participate in performance appraisals effectively. The list below provides some key items but you may want to add a few more which you think will be relevant to your own teaching context.

- This quarter/semester/year, I have achieved....
- In my view, this has been a positive/productive quarter/semester/year for me.
- One goal I'd like to achieve this quarter/semester/year is...
- To achieve that goal/objective I'd like/need to...
- We need to determine further growth in...
- I'd like to set out a plan for future development.
- What/something you are doing (very) well is...
- You will have to focus more closely on...
- After reflecting (up)on my performance this quarter/semester/year, I think/believe...
- I've finished filling out the form for...
- I'd like to develop the following skills and competencies: ...
- Following the outline/form we've agreed, I'd say...

Collocations/Expressions

- Identify strengths/weaknesses
- Determine areas for improvement

Structural elements

- **Present perfect** (e.g., This quarter, I have achieved...)
- **Modals to express advice** (e.g., I think you could...; In my view you should...; You will have to...)

Culture and Technology Note CTN-7.1 presents some notes relating to the LOs of this unit you may want to share with your students or use to design teaching materials.

Culture and Technology Note (CTN-7.1)

National culture may exercise a great influence on the types of performance appraisal processes that are implemented in companies or corporations. For this reason, organisations should understand the cultural values in which they operate to make sure that their performance appraisals are appropriate and effective.

For instance, individual-based performance appraisals are widespread in cultures that value individualism, such as the United States. Collectivist societies, on the other hand, would tend to adopt performance appraisal practices that focus on collaboration and favour participation such as 360-degree performance appraisal systems.

However, it is always important to keep in mind that a corporation may adopt aspects of the national culture where they operate even when their headquarters are based in a different cultural framework. This could be the case of multinational corporations.

Technology has made performance appraisals much easier and simpler. For example, appraisal software can help a company to save time with automations and templates which can be used before an appraisal meeting. Some also offer review builders and powerful analytics to facilitate the process, and thus make appraisals much more effective. Some such software includes: Leapsome, Factorial and Altamira Performance. A brief description of each follows.

Leapsome: https://www.leapsome.com/
A platform that offers performance management, employee engagement, and learning all together and that can be integrated to calendars and Teams.

Factorial: https://factorialhr.co.uk/
A human resources software for managing and evaluating employee performance reviews, creating personalised questionnaires, assigning reviewers and adding feedback in a portal for employees.

Altamira Performance: https://www.altamirahrm.com/en/
Performance management software for managing skills and performance evaluation as well as for goal setting in a single integrated environment. It also allows delegating performance assessment tasks to managers and employees.

Teaching skills for performance appraisals

After having identified key LOs for performance appraisals, we are in a position to make pedagogical decisions to design lessons for helping students to achieve such outcomes. This is the focus of Section 7.3.

7.3 Designing lessons for performance appraisal

This section of the unit offers two sample lesson plans. The first plan (Table 7.2) has been designed to teach students how to self-assess their work performance. The second lesson plan in this section (Table 7.3) focuses on assessing other people's performance.

Self-assessing work performance requires a particular set of language items your students will need to have or develop. The next Language Corner (LC-7.2) shows some examples of the key items for assessing one's own work performance.

Table 7.2 A Lesson Plan for Self-assessing Work Performance

Course: Communication Skills for the International Workplace	Year group:	Date:
Learning outcomes for self-assessing work performance		
By the end of the lesson, students should be able to: • identify strategies for self-assessing work performance, and • discuss self-assessment work performance to identify strengths, weaknesses and opportunities for growth.		
Progression of teaching & learning		**Strategies/Materials**
Duration: 10 minutes	Introduction T asks Sts to form pairs to discuss their views on what it means to self-assess work performance and how it could be done.	Eliciting Sts' views

(Continued)

Duration: 25 minutes	Activity 1 1. In pairs students draw a list with their views on and strategies for self-assessment. 2. Sts read a text on tips for self-assessment and then compare their views/strategies with those expressed in the text. 3. Sts draw a second list with the tips from the text. 4. Sts discuss how the two lists compare.	1. Completing a table (1)/Handout 1 2. Reading a text/Handout 1 3. Completing a table (2)/Handout 1 4. Discussing lists
Duration: 15 minutes	Activity 2 5. Sts watch a video clip on self-assessment of work performance. 6. Sts compare the views/strategies on the video and those of they identified in Activity 1. 7. Sts discuss and agree on a final list of strategies to follow when writing a self-assessment of their work performance.	5. Watching a video/Handout 2 6. Comparing and agreeing in pairs/Handout 2 7. Discussing and agreeing/Handout 2

Duration: 10 minutes	Conclusion Sts reflect on the activities of the lesson and summarise what they have learnt in bullet points.	
Success criteria	• To be able to identify strategies for self-assessing work performance, and • To be able to discuss self-assessing work performance to identify strengths, weaknesses and opportunities for growth.	**Assessment** None at the moment
Next steps	Sts will write a short self-assessment of their (simulated) work performance over the past semester. If they are pre-experience, they can write on their academic performance over their past semester.	

Language Corner (LC-7.2)

The list below provides some key items in relation to self-assessing work performance. You may want to add a few more which you think will be relevant to your own teaching context.

- I take initiative in...
- I often go above and beyond.../the extra mile to
- I work hard to exceed targets/expectations...
- To be reliable/responsible for
- Cope well under pressure
- This quarter/semester/year, I have demonstrated...
- I have invested significant time/energy in...
- I am a dedicated employee who...
- I am a good communicator who...

- I communicate effectively with...
- I am a creative thinker who can...
- I am well known for my dependability
- Sometimes I do not ask for help when...
- I have never missed a deadline in the past...
- I would like to continue... (Verb + ING)
- I always provide constructive feedback when...
- I make sure everyone on my team is/feels...
- As to my professional growth, I'd like to

Collocations

- Be responsible/accountable for/in charge/control of
- To invest (time, energy) in; to spend (time, energy) on
- To meet a deadline
- To miss a deadline
- To give/provide/offer feedback on (something)

Structural elements

- **Simple present** (e.g., I take initiative in...)
- **Present perfect** (e.g., I have never missed...)
- **Adverbs of frequency** (e.g., I often go above and beyond...; I always provide...)
- **Adverbs of manner** (e.g., I work responsibly.)

Here are some Insights from Research about self-assessment (IR-7.1). You may want to share them with your students or use them to design teaching materials.

Insights from Research (IR-7.1): Self-Assessment

Some students may find self-assessment difficult, especially if they come from an educational tradition where assessment is something only done by teachers and 'to the students'. This has implications for them as students and independent learners, and as future employees. Students will need to develop self-assessment skills as part of their performance appraisals, especially if they are considering working in an international corporation (Hartley & Chatterton, 2015).

Self-assessment is the ability to examine oneself in order to find out how much progress one has made. It requires employees to monitor their own abilities and evaluate strengths and weaknesses as in a SWOT analysis (see Unit 1). One of the main contributions of self-assessment to employees is that it puts them in charge of their own development.

There is a group of questions that can guide self-assessment. These include:

- Where have you excelled?
- What achievements are you most proud of?
- Where do you feel you need more support?
- What goals do you feel you have not yet accomplished?
- What would help you to accomplish them?
- What do you most like and dislike about your job?
- What career goals would you like to accomplish in the next three years?

These questions, together with some guidance from their line manager or HR representative, will provide a good starting point for those employees new to self-assessment.

Table 7.3 A Lesson Plan for Assessing Other People's Performance

Course: Communication Skills for the International Workplace	Year group:	Date:
Learning outcomes for assessing other people's performance		
By the end of the lesson, students should be able to: • follow key principles for assessing someone else's performance, and • provide them with feedback.		
Progression of teaching & learning		**Strategies/Materials**
Duration: 10 minutes	Introduction T asks Sts to discuss in small groups (3-4) their knowledge and experiences of providing (peer) feedback	Eliciting Sts' previous knowledge/experience

(Continued)

Duration: 25 minutes	Activity 1	1. Reading an article/Handout 3
	1. Sts read an article on assessing someone else's job performance and providing feedback.	2. Jotting down notes to complete a table/Handout 3
	2. Individually, Sts complete a table with information about key principles for assessing someone else's performance.	3. Comparing notes/Handout 3
	3. In pairs, Sts compare their notes.	
Duration: 15 minutes	Activity 2 4. Sts read the article again and select information about:	4. Reading and selecting information/ Handout 3
	4.1 strategies for assessing someone else's performance 4.2 strategies for providing feedback on someone else's performance, and 4.3 specific language for assessing someone else's performance and providing feedback.	
Duration: 10 minutes	Conclusion Sts reflect on the activities of the lesson and summarise what they have learnt.	

Success criteria	• To be able to follow key principles for assessing someone else's performance, and • provide them with feedback.	**Assessment** None at the moment
Next steps	Students will search the Internet for information about how culture influences how feedback is provided in their own work contexts.	

Other activities for which you can plan lessons in connection with performance appraisals include: "identifying training needs" and "dealing with negative feedback". A good starting point for identifying training needs is to remind your students of the results of their SWOT analysis (see Unit 1). These should give them an indication of the areas in which they need to work further and whether they would need to take a particular course of action (e.g., take specific courses or training).

The other activity is dealing with negative feedback. This is never easy. However, there are a number of strategies you can discuss with your students to cushion the impact that negative feedback can have on them. These include:

- **Don't rush to react**: instead practise active listening so that you are better prepared to engage in a conversation with your assessor
- **Be appreciative and genuine**: After you have listened actively to what your assessor had to say, thank them for their feedback and take responsibility for anything you have done wrongly or failed to do
- **Summarise the feedback**: Summarising the main points made by your assessor will make sure you understood what they said, and help you to highlight any action points needed to remedy the situation
- **Take action**: Create a plan of action that will help you to improve your performance so that you can turn negative feedback into positive appraisal next time.

Now, we can stop for a moment to reflect upon the plans in Tables 7.2 and 7.3. Reflection Activity RA-7.2 provides you with three questions in support of your reflective process.

Reflection Activity (RA-7.2)

Considering what we have done so far, what are your views about the following:

- The appropriacy of these lesson plans for your students
- The specific language your students will need for self-assessment and assessing other employees' performance
- The cultural elements that come into play in job performance appraisals.

7.4 Materials for teaching performance appraisal skills and competencies

The materials for this unit include Handouts 1 and 2 to support the lesson plan outlined in Table 7.2 and Handout 3 for a lesson plan to teach how to evaluate other people's performance as detailed in Table 7.3.

Handout 1: Top Tips for Self-Assessing Work Performance

1. After you have discussed with another student your views/experiences on how to self-assess work performance, complete the first list in the table below.

Self-Assessing Work Performance	
List 1: Our views	List 2: Views from the text
•	•
•	•
•	•
•	•
•	•

2. Now, read the following text about tips for self-assessment. Then, complete the second list in the table above.

Top tips for self-assessment on work performance

1. **Focus on what you have accomplished**
   Start by making a list of the main tasks and projects that you have been involved in over the period of time of the review. Then, write what you managed to accomplish next to each task and project, highlighting how your accomplishments have benefited the company. Whenever possible, link the tasks and projects to your job description and your accomplishments to the company's values and/ or objectives.

2. **Keep a record of your tasks, projects and accomplishments**
   Apart from your own narrative, it is important to provide some evidence of hard data to show what you have done and achieved. For example, you could refer to an increase in sales or the number of new accounts you are managing.

3. **Be critical**
   Critically assess your performance, highlighting your accomplishments but also pointing out weaknesses that you need to improve and what you have learnt from your mistakes. It is crucial that you strike a good balance between strength and weakness and that you are careful not to criticise yourself too harshly. Remember that critiquing is looking at both strengths and weaknesses whilst criticising is focusing only on weaknesses.

4. **Focus on growth**
   Take an opportunity to turn weaknesses into strengths by focusing on how learning from your past mistakes can help you to grow. Highlight that, despite your weaknesses, you remain committed to growth and improvement. Make this an opportunity to seek a mentor or a coach who can help you to improve an area where you may have been struggling.

5. **Act professionally**
   Give your self-assessment its due attention and have the form ready when you and your appraiser have agreed. Support any claims with evidence or examples (see 2 above), and make sure your writing is free from grammar or spelling mistakes.

   3. Discuss: How do the two lists in the table above compare?

Handout 2: Self-Assessment on Work Performance

1. Watch the following video clip where **Carrie Luxem** (https:// carrieluxem.com/the-show) speaks about self-assessment at work. As you watch the clip, jot down some notes on the tips for self-assessment that Carrie mentions.

    https://worldsofenglish.com/workplace-skills-extension-tasks/

Notes

_____

_____

_____

_____

_____

_____

_____

2. Now, compare the views/strategies on the video clip with those you discussed following your own experience and the reading text in Handout 1.
3. Based on the results of your comparison, work with another student to discuss and agree on a final list of strategies to follow when writing a self-assessment of your work performance:

List 3: Final Tips for Self-Assessing Work Performance
• _____
• _____
• _____
• _____
• _____
• _____

Handout 3: Assessing Someone Else's Job Performance

1. Read the following article published in **Fast Company** (https://www. fastcompany.com) on assessing someone else's job performance

by Art Markman, a professor of psychology and marketing at the University of Texas at Austin. As you read, jot down some notes to complete the following table.

https://www.fastcompany.com/90455272/this-is-the-best-method-for-evaluating-someones-job-performance

Points Made in the Article	Your Notes
Evaluating someone and comparing products	
The importance of considering their trajectory	
The role of context	
What feedback should be based on	
Advantages and drawback of comparative feedback	

2. Now, compare your notes with those of another student. Are the notes the same? How do they differ?

3. What strategies for **evaluating someone else's job performance** have you learnt from the article?

    *   _____
    *   _____
    *   _____
    *   _____
    *   _____

4. What strategies for **providing feedback on someone else's job performance** have you learnt from the article?

    *   _____
    *   _____
    *   _____
    *   _____
    *   _____

5. What **specific language** for evaluating someone else's performance and giving them feedback can you list from the article? The first two have been provided as examples.

    *   *a set of criteria that human resources lays out for a particular job*
    *   *comparing a person's performance now to what they have done in the past*

    *   _____
    *   _____
    *   _____
    *   _____

Giving and receiving feedback is a culture-bound activity. It is essential for your students to become aware of this and also reflect upon how culture will certainly shape the way feedback is given. The next Culture Note (CTN-7.2) aims at providing some insight into the relationship between culture and feedback.

Culture and Technology Note (CTN-7.2)

In international workplaces, the need to develop our cultural intelligence and tune in our communication styles has become a must. Here are a few notes to take into account when giving feedback on someone's performance in the international workplace.

Know as much as possible about your work context

This seems an obvious claim but sometimes we assume that there are correct and even universal ways of doing things. In the case of giving feedback, many people think that there is only one correct way of doing it. But there is not. Different cultures go about providing feedback in different, sometimes very different ways. For instance, in the UK feedback tends to first focus on what someone is doing well to then move on to what needs improvement. Note that the focuses of the first half of that statement is on the person (doing something well), and the second half on the action (what needs to be improved). In many Latin American countries, on the other hand, feedback refers only to what needs improving, usually made personal as in "you need to improve....", as it is generally believed that what the person is doing well "doesn't need to be revised".

Use direct or indirect language accordingly

In some contexts, giving feedback is realised using very direct language, as in "you need to improve....". In others, the concept of saving face is so strong that feedback can only be delivered in a very indirect way as in "something that you may want to consider in relation to dealing with new customers...".

Thus, in indirect cultures people tend to use what we call 'downgraders' (e.g., a little (bit)..., slightly) to soften the tone of negative feedback, whereas in direct communication cultures, 'upgraders' (e.g., always, totally) are often used.

Establish a sincere and honest conversation

Sometimes people have their own expectations about how feedback should be given out. One way of getting to know how they expect to

receive feedback on their performance is to open up a sincere and hon-
est channel of communication with them. To this end, you may ask them
questions such as: how would you prefer to receive feedback? Would you
rather we focus on what you are doing well first? Is there anything you
would like me to take into account before we start?

The next Insights from Research (IR-7.2) discusses how performance
assessment is applied in the real world of work.

Insights from Research (IR-7.2): The theory and practice of performance assessment

Recent research on work performance has found that there is a considerable degree of discrepancy between the theory and the practice of how
work performance is evaluated in the real world. A study by Riratanaphong
and van der Voordt (2015), for example, concluded that in the corporations they investigated, the performance measurement frameworks
existing in the literature (the theory) were adapted when applied in the
workplace (the practice), and the key principles of performance assessment were interpreted according to the internal and external contexts of
the organisation under investigation. This again reminds us of the importance that both culture and contexts have on decision-making processes
in the workplace.

7.5 Assessing learning

In this section you will find a self-assessment table (7.5.1) and an integrated task (7.5.2) which you can use to assess some of the LOs set out
at the beginning of the unit.

7.5.1 Self-assessing skills and competencies for performance appraisals

Self-Assessing Skills and Competencies for Performance Appraisals				
Use the following list of Can-Do statements to self-assess the LOs for this unit. In case you are not sure or think you have not yet acquired the skill or competency referred to, make a note on what you can do about it.				
I can	Yes	No	?	I'm planning to

1. self-assess my work performance critically and professionally.				
2. identify future goals and training needs.				
3. deal with negative feedback to help improve my performance.				
4. evaluate other employees' performance using appropriate strategies and language.				

7.5.2 Assessing skills and competencies for performance appraisals

This integrated task provides students with an opportunity to show the skills and competencies they have learnt in this unit. You could use it a formative assessment exercise or for summative assessment. Alternatively, you can use it as a model for designing other tasks that would meet your students' needs more successfully.

As we discussed in the Introductory Unit (see Section I.5), it would be very helpful to design a set of marking criteria to discuss with your students before the do the task, making sure they understand how their performance will be assessed.

Context

You work for a corporation whose communication culture is highly indirect and have been asked to provide feedback on the job performance of a colleague.

Instructions

Read the following notes that your colleague's line manager has sent you and think how you would like to provide them with feedback.

- Has missed last semester's targets
- Comes to most meetings unprepared

- Is usually late to work
- Is very passionate for their work
- Usually goes the extra mile to help colleagues

7.6 Summary

Unit 7 has discussed key aspects of performance appraisal at work. It has identified the main skills and competencies for performance appraisals and translated these into LOs. Based on these, the unit has presented lesson plans that could be followed to develop two of those LOs. Next, it has offered three different handouts with materials that can be used to deliver the two lesson plans offered in the unit. This has been accompanied by reflective activities, selected language for appraisals and giving feedback and culture and technology notes.

The unit has finally offered two assessment activities. The first provides students with an opportunity to reflect upon what they have learnt by means of Can-Do statements; the second includes an integrated task to assess providing feedback in a culture-sensitive way.

Unit 8, the final unit, deals with teaching skills and competencies for applying for promotion, also following the teaching and learning cycle described in the Introductory Unit.

Further readings: An annotated bibliography

Holpp, L. (2011). *Win–win performance appraisals: What to do before, during, and after the review to get the best results for yourself and your employees.* McGraw-Hill Education.

Holpp's book provides insights and tools to make performance reviews a collaborative process for achieving long-term goals. It deals with key issues relating performance reviews such as writing productive evaluations, holding face-to-face appraisals, and conducting follow-up meetings.

Neal, J. E. (2020). *Effective phrases for performance appraisals: A guide to successful evaluations.* Neal Publications

This practical and very useful phrase book has been written to make the drafting and completion of performance appraisals an easy and accurate task. It contains more than 3,000 phrases related to key rating factors.

Unit 8

Teaching skills and competencies for applying for promotion

Learning Outcomes

By the end of the unit, you should be able to:

- identify the key skills and competencies needed for applying for promotion
- turn these skills and competencies into LOs
- make pedagogical decisions about designing lessons, selecting materials, and assessing applying for promotion, and
- select effective vocabulary items your students will require for applying for promotion.

8.1 Introducing applying for promotion

In this last unit, we will explore the skills and competencies your students will need to apply for promotion. Once we have identified such skills and competencies, we will turn them into the LOs that your students will need to achieve. To realise these LOs pedagogically, we will explore sample lesson plans and teaching materials that could be used for the lessons. Finally, we will discuss and exemplify ways in which the LOs of the unit can be assessed.

We start by considering the **promotion request letter**, a key document that is written when an employee wants to be considered for a higher or different position in their own company.

DOI: 10.4324/9781003283515-13

Many companies and organisations prefer to advertise a new position internally before they consider a pool of external candidates. Others may advertise new positions both internally or externally at the same time. Whichever the case in your students' context may be, they will need to let their line manager or supervisor know of their interest in the new position being advertised. Depending on their advice and possibly the outcome of their negotiation with their line manager, students will need to write a promotion request letter.

A promotion request letter highlights the candidate's value to the company supported by their hard work, professionalism and contributions (see Unit 7). It also explains why they are a good fit for the job by detailing their skills and competencies to succeed in the new role.

From this brief introduction, there are a number of key skills and competencies that we can identify as relevant for students wishing to apply for work promotion. This is what we will discuss in the next section.

8.2 Key skills and competencies for applying for promotion

Before making an application, your students will have to consider whether they have the skills, competencies and experience needed for applying for a higher position. A SWOT analysis based on the job description of the new position would be a good start. Next, they would also benefit from self-assessing their performance at work as we discussed in Unit 7, and considering the outcomes of their latest performance appraisal. Knowing how to negotiate their application with their line manager or supervisor and how to write an effective promotion request letter are also important skills they will need. Therefore, the key skills and competencies for this unit are:

- Having a realistic view of one's capabilities
- Knowing how to negotiate with one's line manager or supervisor, and
- Writing an effective promotion request letter

Your students will need to do some work before deciding whether they are in a position to apply for promotion. As we mentioned above, a realistic SWOT analysis (see Unit 1) is a good starting point. This analysis could then be compared with the requirements for the new position. Self-assessing their past performance in a critical way (see Unit 7) would also provide them with information they can use to inform their decision to apply and for the preparation of the application documents. Finally, the outcomes of their latest performance review (see Unit 7) should also be taken into account to make a final decision. All this information should provide them with a realistic view of their own capabilities and whether or not they are ready to apply for promotion.

Coupled with this, your students will have to discuss their plans to apply for promotion with their line manager or supervisor, and possibly negotiate with them their application. Negotiation skills such as communication, persuasion, planning, and cooperating (see lesson plan in Table 8.2) will be needed, especially if their manager's view is different.

Now that we have identified the key skills and competencies for applying for promotion, let us consider how we can turn them into LOs for the unit. Table 8.1 shows some examples.

Table 8.1 Turning Skills and Competencies for Applying for Promotion into LOs

Skills/Competences	Questions	Resulting LOs
Having a realistic view of one's capabilities	How can students create a realistic description and evaluation of their work capabilities? What tools (e.g., SWOT analysis, self-assessment) can they use?	By the end of the lesson, you should be able to create a realistic view of your own capabilities by using appropriate tools.
Knowing how to negotiate an application for promotion with one's line manager or supervisor	What skills and competencies would students need to negotiate their application?	By the end of the lesson, you should be able to identify key skills for negotiating your application for promotion with your line manager or supervisor.

Skills/Competences	Questions	Resulting LOs
Writing an effective promotion request letter	What are the main characteristics of a promotion request letter? How can students learn to write effective promotion request letters?	By the end of the lesson, you should be able to write an effective promotion request letter.

Before considering possible lesson plans for these LOs, you may want to do Reflection Activity RA-8.1. This activity provides you with some questions to help your reflective process.

Reflection Activity (RA-8.1)

Considering what we have done so far, what are your views on the following:

- How useful for your students do you think these skills and competencies are?
- If you were teaching a mixed group (pre-experience and job-experienced students), how would you teach these skills and competencies?
- How could your job-experienced students help pre-experience students?

Insights from Research IR-8.1 discusses self-efficacy. Self-efficacy has been discovered to play an important role in creating a realistic view of one's own capabilities.

Insights from Research (IR-8.1): Self-Efficacy

The term 'self-efficacy' was coined by psychologist Albert Bandura (1977). Self-efficacy refers to a person's belief in their ability to succeed in a particular situation. Bandura explained "People's beliefs about their abilities have a profound effect on those abilities. Ability is not a fixed property; there is a huge variability in how you perform. People who have a sense of self-efficacy bounce back from failure; they approach things in terms of how to handle them rather than worrying about what can go wrong" (p. 26).

There are a number of strategies that can be put in place to develop self-efficacy.

One of these is **peer modelling** or learning from examples set by those around us (see Constructivism in the Introductory Unit). Modelling or peer mentoring is an efficient way of helping new employees to develop their self-efficacy. A second key strategy is encouraging employees to actively **seek feedback**. When well-implemented, feedback provides people with a rounded idea of what they are doing well and what they need to improve. Therefore, feedback can be one of the most important sources of building levels of self-efficacy. Next, encouraging **active participation** is also important for building self-efficacy. Active participation is essential to the development of not only self-efficacy but also critical thinking skills. Another important strategy is creating opportunities for people to **make their own choices**. This will allow them to take responsibility for their own actions and become more accountable and responsible members of a team.

These key strategies (peer modelling, feedback seeking, active participation, and making choices) can be implemented in class so that students develop skills which they can later transfer to the workplace.

After having identified the LOs and reflected upon their value for your students, we are in a position to look at possible lesson plans to deliver those LOs in class.

8.3 Designing lessons for applying for promotion

This section of Unit 8 presents two possible lesson plans. Table 8.2 shows a lesson plan for learning to negotiate, and Table 8.3 presents a lesson plan for learning to write an effective promotion request letter.

Table 8.2 A Lesson Plan for Learning to Negotiate

Course: Communication Skills for the International Workplace	Year group:	Date:
Learning outcomes for learning to negotiate		
By the end of the lesson, students should be able to: • identify key skills for negotiating, and • provide advice/feedback on making an application for promotion.		

Progression of teaching & learning		Strategies/Materials
Duration: 10 minutes	Introduction T to elicit Sts' views and experiences of negotiating.	Eliciting Sts' views and experiences
Duration: 15 minutes	Activity 1 1. Sts read a text on negotiations and think about a number of statements about it. 2. Sts re-visit the statements and identify which ones are True and which are False. Then, they correct the false statements. 3. In pairs, Sts discuss what they knew and what they have learnt about negotiations.	1. Reading a text/Handout 1 2. Reading and writing/Handout 1 3. Discussing/Handout 1
Duration: 30 minutes	Activity 2 4. Sts watch a video and answer questions on its content. 5. Based on the text and the video, Sts read a scenario about an employee considering applying for promotion. 6. Individually, Sts decide what advice they would give the employee as to how they should go about making and application for promotion. 7. In pairs, Sts compare their advice and make necessary changes.	4. Watching and answering Handout 2 5. Reading and responding/Handout 2 6. Giving advice/Handout 2 7. Discussing and agreeing/Handout 2

(Continued)

Duration: 5 minutes	Conclusion Sts reflect on the activities of the lesson and summarise what they have learnt in bullet points.	
Success criteria	• To be able to identify key skills for negotiating, and • To be able to provide advice/feedback on making an application for promotion.	**Assessment** None at the moment
Next steps	Sts will write a checklist of things they need to remember next time they plan to apply for promotion. They have to be ready to share their list with the other students in the next class.	

Language Corner LC-8.1 lists key vocabulary items connected to negotiations. You can pre-teach them before the lesson in Table 8.2 or explore them with your students after they have finished the tasks in the lesson, following the principles of TBLL (see Unit 4).

Language Corner (LC-8.1)

The list below provides some relevant language items relating to negotiations. You may also want to add others to match your own teaching context and its culture (See Culture and Technology Note (CTN-8.1).

- To negotiate over something
- To reach an agreement on something with someone
- To express oneself clearly/concisely/directly
- To engage one's audience
- To adapt one's communication style
- To recall (specific) details/information
- An application for promotion
- To recognise other people's feelings and emotions

Collocations

- beneficial/continuous/difficult/lengthy/successful/unsuccessful negotiations
- a series of negotiations

- effective/interpersonal/regular/verbal/non-verbal/written/ business communication
- communication with someone/about something
- To build connections/rapport
- To increase understanding
- To develop trust
- To bring/offer/provide benefits
- To promote collaboration

Structural elements

- **Modals** (for suggestions) (e.g., Could we....?; Should we start by....?)
- **Expressions of opinion** (e.g., I think....; In my view,....; I'd say that...)

Culture obviously plays a central role in negotiations. The first Culture and Technology Note (CTN-8.1) presents a few views on the topic.

Culture and Technology Note (CTN-8.1)

Cultural differences should be taken into account when planning a nego- tiation. Contrasting sets of values that determine the hierarchy of negoti- ating objectives, behaviour mannerisms and non-verbal cues could all be a barrier to confidence and trust and make communication more difficult.

National as well as personal perceptions of the negotiation process can have a negative influence on the outcome of any negotiation. The ele- ments of a negotiation, such as the negotiators, their hierarchy within the organisation, the process of communication and the setting where a negotiation takes place, can differ substantially due to culture.

Here are some examples.

- For the Japanese, for instance, a negotiation is a consensus-gener- ating process. They disregard confrontations and favour harmony. This ensures that social relations develop smoothly and that con- sensus is the overarching aim. We could say that most Japanese would approach a negotiation from a positive perspective.
- In comparison, most Americans consider negotiations to be problem-solving exercises, and see the solution to the problem as the ultimate aim of a negotiation. This seems to indicate that for many Americans negotiations are a problem that needs solving.

- For many French negotiators, a negotiation is an established art with a long tradition where the negotiators and the language they use play a pivotal role. For them, negotiators must project a sense of self-assurance and create a sound argument around the logic of their suggestions for actions. Negotiations are like debating fora, with flexibility and accommodation simply for the sake of arguing.

How are negotiations viewed in your cultural context? Are those views reflected in the workplace?

Table 8.3 A Lesson Plan for Writing a Promotion Request Letter

Course: Communication Skills for the International Workplace	Year group:	Date:
Learning outcomes for writing a promotion request letter		
By the end of the lesson, students should be able to: • identify the main characteristics of a promotion request letter, and • write an effective promotion request letter.		
Progression of teaching & learning		**Strategies/Materials**
Duration: 10 minutes	<u>Introduction</u> T to elicit Sts' views and experiences of requesting a promotion.	Eliciting Sts' views and experiences
Duration: 15 minutes	<u>Activity 1</u> 1. Sts read a text on main steps for writing a promotion request letter. 2. In pairs, Sts discuss the possible answers to the questions about the text. 3. Out of class, Sts ask family and friends about their past experiences of requesting or applying for promotion.	1. Reading a text/Handout 1 2. Discussing answers/ Handout 1 3. Doing research/ Handout 1

Duration: 25 minutes	Activity 2 4. Sts read a scenario on a new internal vacancy. 5. Following the steps discussed in Activity 1, Sts draft a promotion request letter for the scenario they have just read. 6. In pairs, Sts provide each other feedback on their draft (see also Unit 7).	4. Reading /Handout 2 5. Drafting a promotion request letter/Handout 2 6. Providing peer feedback
Duration: 10 minutes	Conclusion In pairs, Sts make a checklist of the key steps needed for writing a promotion request letter for their work context. They then share their checklist with the rest of the class.	
Success criteria	• To be able to identify the main characteristics of a promotion request letter, and • To be able to write an effective promotion request letter.	**Assessment** None at the moment
Next steps	Sts will edit the draft they started in class so that they produce a final copy to be shared with other students. Sts will present the results of their survey to family and friends about their past experiences of requesting or applying for promotion.	

For the activities included in the lesson plan in Table 8.3, your students will need to be familiar with a specific set of language items. Language Corner LC-8.2 presents some such items.

Language Corner (LC-8.2)

The list below provides some relevant language items for writing a promotion request letter. You may also want to add others to match your own teaching context.

- a (formal) heading
- a professional greeting
- To send a printed letter to (your manager/team lead)
- To use the subject line to clarify/specify/detail (the content of the email)
- To include necessary details such as...
- To choose a salutation that applies to/is appropriate for (your recipient)
- To state the purpose of the letter/email directly and specifically
- I am writing (this letter/email) to request a promotion to the role of...
- To explain why this role suits you
- I have been working for (name of company)...
- In my past experience, I have...
- The projects and tasks I have been involved in include...
- I have succeeded in... (Verb+ING)
- As to relevant qualifications, I would like to draw your attention to...
- I feel I will do well in the new position as I...
- I would like to thank you for your guidance and contribution towards...
- I remain committed to...
- I would be very happy to assist you in finding a replacement for...
- I would be happy to train/help them to take over
- I would highly appreciate it if we could set up a meeting to...

Collocations

- To request/apply for/gain/win a promotion
- To be/become/remain committed
- A specific/primary/principal purpose
- In my (previous/work/past/professional experience

Structural elements

- **Present simple** (e.g., I remain committed to...)
- **Present progressive** (e.g., I am writing this letter...)
- **Present perfect** (e.g., I have succeeded in...; I have been involved in...)
- **Would** (hypothetical use) (e.g., I would (very) happy to...; I'd appreciate it if...)

Now you may want to learn more about the documents needed for applying for an internal promotion. This is presented in Extension Task ET-8.1. You could also use this task with your students.

Extension Task (ET-8.1)

Use the URL provided below to watch **video clip ET-8.1** on applying for internal promotion. As you watch, think of the following questions:

- What should be included together with the application?
- Why is it strategic to submit such a document?
- What are the benefits of writing such a document?

https://worldsofenglish.com/workplace-skills-extension-tasks/

How about the role of culture in applying for promotion? Here are some notes you may want to consider and also share with your students.

Culture and Technology Note (CTN-8.2)

Companies in some cultures would prefer to advertise internally first. These companies follow a "promotion-from-within" strategy characterised by great investment in education and training to develop existing staff and tend to use performance appraisals such as 360 feedback (see Unit 7).

These companies also prioritise career development and equip their managers with the appropriate mindset, tools and resources in order to identify and work together with employees who actively seek promotion.

They also tend to have a coaching programme that favours collaboration and helping employees interested in promotion to learn how to do things that would help them transition into the new role with the help and support of an expert.

Finally, these companies often hold workshops on 'how to get promoted' facilitated by HR and supported by employees who have already benefitted from the "promotion-from-within" strategy.

How about your workplace? Do they follow the "promotion-from-within" strategy?

What actions do they take in support of that strategy?

The second Insights from Research of the unit (IR-8.2) further discusses work promotions and their relationship with culture and industry sectors.

Insights from Research (IR-8.2): Promotion and job motivation

Research by Otto et al. (2021) has investigated the possible relation between promotion and job satisfaction across a number of business sectors in Germany. It has long been established that job satisfaction can actually increase through wage increases and promotions, collectively called 'gratifications'. However, it is difficult to maintain the same level of satisfaction along time despite the different gratification types available to human resources departments. In their study of job satisfaction over 27 years, Otto and colleagues discovered that "promotions positively affected job satisfaction in the short term but diminished after 1 year" (p. 151). Research conducted in Indonesia (Haryonoa, Supardib & Udina, 2020) found, however, that in the context of national education promotion had a positive effect on work motivation, and in particular on employee job performance. In still another example, Xie and Yang (2021) discovered that, among Chinese junior civil servants, perceptions of promotion opportunities can have a direct influence on performance (task and contextual performance) as well as on their job motivation. These three research studies remind us once more of the importance of considering context (including industry sectors) and culture in relation to people's views on organisational processes such as job promotions.

8.4 Materials for teaching applying for promotion skills and competencies

This section includes four handouts that have been designed to accompany the lesson plans in Tables 8.2 and 8.3. The first set of two handouts was designed to be used with the lesson plan included in Table 8.2, and the second set with the lesson plan in Table 8.3.

8.4.1 Set 1

Handout 1: Key Skills for Negotiations

1. Read the following text on negotiations. As you read, think of the following statements:
    - people negotiate all the time both at home and at work
    - engaging communication, one of the underlying skills for negotiating, requires taking into account your listeners' needs but the speaker's communication styles

- active listening focuses on the speaker in a meaningful way
- emotional intelligence recognises the importance of the speaker's emotions
- influential communication is based on clear and concise information, including the benefits of doing something
- rapport promotes collaboration but may lead to unwanted results in a negotiation.

Negotiations

We always negotiate! To some people, life is a series of negotiations. At home, we negotiate how much screen time to allow the kids, what time we have dinner, who cooks and who washes up. We also negotiate over buying a new car, spending the next holidays, and moving to a new house. At work, we negotiate terms and conditions, deadlines, a new business strategy, creating new partnerships and our next promotion.

Even if we seldom stop to think about it, we learn to negotiate as we experience all or at least some of the decisions mentioned above. In all these situations, we apply a number of skills and competencies that help us to reach an agreement with the other party or parties we are negotiating. Here are a few:

Clear and engaging communication

Being able to communicate your ideas clearly and in an engaging way is key to effective communication. An effective communicator is able to identify verbal and non-verbal (e.g., body posture, eye contact, attire) cues both to express themselves clearly so as to avoid misunderstanding and to engage their audience in meaningful communication. Engaging your audience requires adapting your communication style to meet your listeners' needs and communication style. For instance, do they prefer facts to opinions? Then, do not present them with an argument but show them data generated by your past performance.

Active listening

Active listeners are able to focus completely on the speaker in order to fully understand their message and respond in a thoughtful manner. This interpersonal communication skill (see Unit 4) allows you to engage with the speaker and recall specific details of their message without needing it to be repeated. At work, active listening helps to build connections, increase understanding among colleagues and develop trust. These are important aspects to consider when you negotiate your application for promotion, for instance.

Emotional intelligence (see also Unit 4)

This refers to the ability to control one's feelings and recognise the feelings of other people. During a negotiation, emotional intelligence can allow you to stay calm and focus on the issue being negotiated. The idea is to reach consensus and a beneficial solution for all parties involved in the negotiation. If, for instance, your line manager thinks you are not ready for promotion, you may instead negotiate a plan of action so that you are ready next time an opportunity for promotion arises.

Influential communication

Negotiations depend on the ability of the negotiators to influence others. Influential communication is based on being able to define clearly and concisely why a course of action is being proposed and the benefits resulting from it, so that all parties support such action. When negotiating your promotion, it is important that you define clearly why you are ready based on a realistic view of your performance (see above) and the benefits your promotion will bring not only to yourself by also to your company.

Rapport building

Together with influential communication, the ability to build rapport by showing your understanding of other people's feelings and emotions (emotional intelligence) and engagement with others (active listening) will allow you to strengthen your relationship with others and demonstrate that you understand them and their opinions. Rapport will promote collaboration and increase the likelihood of a positive outcome for the negotiation.

2. Mark the statements above, reproduced in the table below, as True or False. Then correct these False ones.

Original Statements	True	False	Correction
People negotiate all the time both at home and at work.			
Engaging communication, one of the underlying skills for negotiating, requires taking into account your listeners' needs but the speaker's communication styles.			

Original Statements	True	False	Correction
Active listening focuses on the speaker in a meaningful way.			
Emotional intelligence recognises the importance of the speaker's emotions.			
Influential communication is based on clear and concise information, but avoids including the benefits of doing something.			
Rapport promotes collaboration but may lead to unwanted results in a negotiation.			

3. Now discuss with another student:
    - Things that you already knew about negotiations
    - Things you have learnt from reading the text
    - Things that you will do in your next negotiation.

Handout 2: Negotiating a Promotion Application

1. Watch the following video clip about negotiating at work, and think about
    - How is negotiating defined?
    - What first step is mentioned? Why is this important?
    - How do you need to prepare mentally for the negotiation?
    - Why is emotional distancing important?
      https://www.youtube.com/watch?v=Z3HJCQJ2Lmo
2. Based on the text and the video, read the following scenario and follow the instructions below.

Context

Alex has been with *Euromatics* for the past five years and she thinks she has the skills and competencies needed for a new position her company is advertising for internal promotion, but she is not absolutely sure. Her last performance review had a positive outcome and she and her supervisor identified a number of opportunities for her professional development.

Instructions

Think about

1. What Alex should do before she applies for internal promotion (e.g., how she could create a realistic view of herself as an employee)
2. What documents she would need to write for her promotion
3. Once she has done all that, what she should do next
4. What negotiating skills she should possess
5. If she now thinks she is ready, how she should apply for her promotion.

8.4.2 Set 2

Handout 3: Characteristics of a Promotion Request Letter or Email

A promotion request letter or email is a key document that you need to produce when considering applying for internal promotion.

1. **Instructions**
    Read the following article on how to write an effective promotion request letter or email and then do the exercises below.

How to write a promotion request letter or email

1. **Heading**
    Depending on the organisational culture of your workplace, you may choose to send a printed letter or a formal email to your manager.
    Letter: In the case of a printed letter, remember to begin with a formal heading. This should include your name, current job or position, contact details, and the date. Following these, write the name of your manager, their position and contact details.
    Email: If you have chosen to send an email, you do not need a formal heading. As is the case with emails, use the subject line to clarify the purpose of your email.

2. **Opening salutation**
    Begin the body of your letter or email with a formal and professional greeting. This could follow the patter Dear + Title (Mr/

Mrs/Ms/Dr) + Surname. Always follow the conventions for addressing others already established in your workplace. If, for example, the culture of your workplace is relaxed in relation to how people are addressed, you may choose to use your manager's first name, especially if you are sending them an email.

3. **State your request**
   The first paragraph in the body of your letter or email should state your purpose (requesting a promotion) directly and specifically. For instance, you could write something like "I am writing this (letter/email) to request a promotion to (position) internally advertised on (date)".

4. **Explain your reasons for the request**
   The next paragraph in your letter or email should explain why you are suitable for this new role. Make sure you include:

   - The time you have been working for the organisation
   - The work experience that makes you a good fit for the position
   - Evidence that shows your previous performance (e.g., projects in which you performed well, impact of your performance) (see performance appraisal, Unit 7)
   - Courses and qualifications relevant to the new position
   - Your critical evaluation why you think you can succeed (see also Unit 7)

   Finish this section of your letter or email by restating your loyalty to the organisation and your gratitude to your manager for the opportunities you have had so far.

5. **Offer help with the transition**
   One of your manager's main concerns could possibly be who is going to take over your current responsibilities. This is an opportunity for you to offer help with the transition. For instance, you could offer to train the person taking over from you to do your current everyday tasks and responsibilities.

6. **End your letter/email with a 'thank you'**
   End your letter or email by thanking your manager for their consideration. You can also use this last paragraph to request a meeting to further discuss your promotion.

7. **Final salutation**

End your letter or email with a formal salutation such as "Sincerely," or "Respectfully," followed by your name and your signature. This final salutation should match the opening salutation in tone and register.

8. **Discussion**

Discuss with another student:

8.1. Is this type of letter or email common in your work context?

8.2. How appropriate are these steps for requesting a promotion in your culture?

8.3. Is there anything else you would consider adding to the letter or email?

9. **Doing research**

Ask your family and friends how they have been promoted and whether they had to submit any documentation for requesting promotion. Be prepared to share your results with the rest of the class.

Handout 4: Drafting a Promotion Request Letter

1. Read the following scenario on a new internal vacancy. You have just seen the ad in the newsletter of your company.

We are internally recruiting for a Communications Assistant (CA). The new CA will have an opportunity to shape the internal and external communications of the company and make their own contributions to the Communications Team. They will be expected to work independently and take responsibility for driving their own communications projects.

Key responsibilities

The new CA will

- assist in driving communication that engages both internal and external publics around our strategic priorities and values
- produce engaging content for internal and external channels based on research and interviews

- help with communication assignments (e.g., website updates, email marketing) as needed, and
- develop, implement, and conduct regular reporting on communications related targets

We are looking for

We are looking for a confident and energetic person who enjoys the freedom to work independently as well as part of a team, and take pride in delivering quality work. They should have high-level proficiency in both verbal and written English and a passion for communication in writing, visual media and in person. They should also be a multi-tasker, who approaches tasks with a high level of energy and who is open to the day-to-day challenges of our busy, international work environment.

2. Following the steps discussed above, draft a promotion request letter for the scenario you have just read.
3. After you have finished your draft, swop drafts with another student to provide them with peer feedback. Remember to be constructive and start with what they have done well first!

8.5 Assessing learning

This section includes a list of Can-Do statements for self-assessment (8.5.1) and an integrated task to assess the LOs set out at the beginning of the unit (8.5.2).

8.5.1 Self-assessing skills and competencies for applying for promotion

Self-Assessing Skills and Competencies for Job Interviews				
Use the following list of Can-Do statements to self-assess the LOs for applying for promotion. In case you are not sure or think you have not yet acquired the skill or competency referred to, make a note on what you can do about it.				
I can	Yes	No	?	I'm planning to

Self-Assessing Skills and Competencies for Job Interviews				
1. create a realistic view of my work capabilities.				
2. negotiate my application for promotion with my line manager or supervisor.				
3. write an effective promotion request letter.				

8.5.2 Assessing skills and competencies for applying for promotion

The following integrated task aims to give students an opportunity to show the skills and competencies for applying for promotion they have learnt in this unit. You could use it to complement the self-assessment exercise in Section 8.5.1, as a formative assessment exercise or for summative assessment. Alternatively, you can use it as a model for designing another task that would meet your students' needs more successfully.

Writing Necessary Documents for Applying for Promotion

Background

You have worked as a junior marketing assistant for the past six years and have just graduated from university with a degree in digital marketing. A position for a new member of the marketing team has just been advertised for internal promotion. You think you are ready for promotion and have the skills and competencies needed for the new role.

Instructions

1. Create a realistic picture of yourself as a junior marketing assistant
2. List the documents you will need to apply for promotion
3. Suggest a meeting to negotiate with your line manager your application for promotion
4. Draft the documents you identified as needed to apply for internal promotion.

Finally as we discussed before (See Section I.5, Introductory Unit), it is always a good idea to include a set of marking criteria for the students to know what skills and competencies they will be assessed on, and how their performance will be evaluated.

8.6 Summary

This final unit has explored applying for promotion. It has identified the main skills and competencies for requesting a promotion and translated such key skills and competencies into LOs. Based on these, the unit has presented two lesson plans that could be followed to develop the LOs set out. Next, it has provided four handouts with materials that can be used to deliver the lesson plans offered in the unit.

All this has been accompanied by reflective activities, selected language for work presentations and culture and technology notes.

Finally, the unit has offered two assessment activities. The first of these have provided students with an opportunity to reflect upon what they have learnt by means of Can-Do statements; the second has included an integrated task to assess key skills and competencies for applying for promotion.

Further readings: An annotated bibliography

16 Mistakes Employees Make When Trying to Get a Promotion

https://www.forbes.com/sites/jacquelynsmith/2013/10/24/16-mistakes-employees-make-when-trying-to-get-a-promotion/?sh=5d1fff0835f1

This blog explores common mistakes some employees make when applying for a promotion. It discusses mistakes such as asking for too much at once, believing that promotions are based on merit alone, neglecting long-term goals, and trying too hard.

Do You Want to Get Promoted?

https://hbr.org/2021/05/do-you-want-to-get-promoted

This blog, part of the Harvard Business Review collection, takes a different approach to applying for promotion by presenting a list of strategies your students need to consider like documenting their achievements, identifying projects that demonstrate their soft skills, and asking for 360-degree feedback (see Unit 7).

How to get promoted, the dos and don'ts

https://www.betterup.com/blog/how-to-get-promoted

This blog focuses on what your students should do to get promoted. It discusses strategies such as getting to know their line manager's worries and concerns, improving their communication skills, getting feedback on improving their performance, and recognising other people's feelings (see also emotional intelligence in Unit 4).

Postface: Bringing it all together

Teaching Communication, Skills and Competencies for the International Workplace was designed to help you with your journey as either a new teacher or a teacher new to teaching skills and competences in English for the workplace.

When we started this journey together, we said that as a new teacher you may be asking yourself a number of questions, such as where to start to plan lessons and what pedagogical decisions to make in order to help your students with their learning needs. We also established that more experienced teachers sometimes also ask themselves these or similar questions as a way of reflecting upon their teaching practices.

The journey began with the knowledge foundations needed to make relevant pedagogical choices. These foundations then informed the design of lesson plans, choice of learning materials and, finally, the assessment of students' learning. This was graphically represented in what I call *The Teaching-and-Learning Cycle*.

As the orchestrator of what happens in your teaching/learning space, i.e., your classroom, you started each unit of the book by reflecting upon how teaching and learning happens in general (e.g., guided by the theories of learning and the methods for teaching) and in particular (e.g., thinking about your own students and teaching context). These considerations informed the design of lesson plans which aimed to help your students achieve the learning outcomes for each lesson. The book presented a number of sample lesson plans which you could either adopt or adapt, depending on your students' needs and your teaching context. To realise these plans, you were guided through selecting, adopting or adapting the appropriate materials that you could use to support the choices you had made when planning a lesson. The final stage encouraged you to use both formative and summative assessment to evaluate whether and to what extent your students had been able to achieve the learning outcomes of each lesson. As reflection is central to everything we do as teachers, this final stage took you back to the starting point: reflecting upon whether your pedagogical decisions and choices were appropriate for your students and what could be done next time around if they were not.

As explained in the roadmap for using the book, *Teaching Communication, Skills and Competencies for the International Workplace* is a very flexible resource that allows you to use its materials in a variety of ways, depending on the stage you are at in your teaching career, the work-related experiences of your students, and the type and duration of your course.

I hope that at this point you feel more confident about how to answer most of those initial questions that, as a new teacher, you may have had. However, always keep in mind that professional development, in the form of reflection in and on practice, courses, further readings and professional conferences, is an on-going process for both new as well as seasoned teachers.

In this respect, there are a few resources that you can turn to for your own professional development. As listed in the Resources section of the book, there are association, such as the Association for Business Communication (ABC), that organise conferences in different parts of the world. Conferences are a great opportunity for networking with other teachers, and for keeping abreast of the latest developments and research in the field. There are also a few journals that publish articles on workplace communication in general and communication in the international workplace in particular. These have also been listed in the Resources section of the book.

I also hope that *Teaching Communication, Skills and Competencies for the International Workplace* has helped you to achieve the goals you had when you started using the book, and that it will serve as a spring board to your teaching career and future professional development.

Best of luck!

References

Accor Careers, (n.d.) https://careers.accor.com/global/en

Altamira Performance, (n.d.) https://www.altamirahrm.com/en/

Anderson, J. (2017). Peer needs analysis: Sensitising learners to the needs of their classmates. http://www.jasonanderson.org.uk/downloads/peer_needs_analysis.pdf

Anderson, L. W. & Krathwohl, D. (2001). *A taxonomy for learning, teaching, and assessing: A revision of Bloom's taxonomy of educational objectives.* Longman.

Apple, (n.d.) https://www.apple.com/feedback/

Bandura, A. (1977). Self-efficacy: Toward a unifying theory of behavioral change. *Psychological Review*, 84(2), 191–215. https://doi.org/10.1037/0033-295X.84.2.191

Bargiela-Chiappini, F. & Harris, S. (1997). *Managing language: The discourse of corporate meetings.* John Benjamins.

Bargiela-Chiappini, F., Nickerson, C. & Planken B. (2007). *Business discourse.* Palgrave Macmillan.

Barnes, K. J., & Smith, G. E. (2013). Beyond the textbook: An approach to facilitating student understanding of organizational culture in organizations. *Organization Management Journal*, 10(1), 45–65. DOI:10.1080/15416518.2013.781400

Beamer, L. (2000). Finding a way to teach cultural dimensions. *Business Communication Quarterly*, 63(3), 111–118. https://doi.org/10.1177/108056990006300313

Bennet, J. (n.d.). *SWOT analysis: Generating ideas* https://www.teachingexpertise.com/articles/swot-analysis-generating-ideas/

BetterUp, https://www.betterup.com

Bjørge, A. K., Sandvik, A. M., & Whittaker, S. (2017). The recontextualisation of values in the multilingual workplace. *Corporate Communications: An International Journal*, 22(3), 401–416. DOI 10.1108/CCIJ-09-2016-0062

Bloom, B. S. (1956). *Taxonomy of educational objectives, handbook 1: Cognitive domain.* Addison-Wesley Longman.

Boden, D. (1994). *The business of talk: Organizations in action.* Polity Press.

Bremner, S. (2018). *Workplace writing: Beyond the text.* Routledge.

Bremner, S. (2013). "Making sense of workplace experiences: Student perspectives on organizational culture", paper presented at the *78th Convention of the Association of Business Communication*, New Orleans, USA.

Bremner, S. & Costley, T. (2018). Bringing reality to the classroom: Exercises in intertextuality. *English for Specific Purposes*, 52(1), 1–12. https://doi.org/10.1016/j.esp.2018.05.001.

Cambridge Community. (n.d.) Getting started with assessment for learning https://cambridge-community.org.uk/professional-development/gswafl/index.html

Cappelli, P. & Tavis, A. (2016). The performance management revolution. *Harvard Business Review*, 58–67. https://hbr.org/2016/10/the-performance-management-revolution

Classmarker, (n.d.) https://www.classmarker.com/

Cheng, W., Lam, P. W. Y., & Kong, K. C. C. (2019). Learning English through workplace communication: Linguistic devices for interpersonal meaning in textbooks in Hong Kong. *English for Specific Purposes*, 55(1), 28–39. https://doi.org/10.1016/j.esp.2019.03.004

Darics, E. (2015). *Digital business discourse.* Palgrave Macmillan.

Denison, D. R. (1990). *Corporate culture and organizational effectiveness.* Wiley.

Dewey, J. (1910). *How we think.* Heath and Co.

Doodle (2019). The state of business meetings. https://meeting-report.com

Dream Engine, (n.d.) https://www.dreamengine.com.au

Evans, S. (2013). "Just wanna give you guys a bit of an update": Insider perspectives on business presentations in Hong Kong. *English for Specific Purposes*, 32(4), 195–207. https://doi.org/10.1016/j.esp.2013.05.003

Factorial, https://factorialhr.co.uk/

Fink, L. D. (2013). *Creating significant learning experiences: An integrated approach to designing college courses.* Wiley.

Forbes, (n.d.) https://www.forbes.com

Fuse Universal, (n.d.) https://www.fuseuniversal.com

Gallo, C. (2009). *The presentation secrets of Steve Jobs: How to be insanely great in front of any audience.* McGraw Hill

García-Zambrano, L. & Rodríguez-Castellanos, A. (2016). Key relational competencies and business performance: Evidence for Spanish companies. *European Business & Management,* 2(2), 47–53. https://www.science publishinggroup.com/journal/paperinfo?journalid=324&doi=10.11648/j.ebm.20160202.15

Gilster, P. (1997). *Digital literacy.* Wiley.

Gimenez, J. (2020). "Workplace microethnographies: What a week in the communication fabric of organisations can tell us", Paper presented at the *Research in Languages Seminar*, University of Westminster.

Gimenez, J. (2014). Multi-communication and the business English class: Research meets pedagogy. *English for Specific Purposes,* 35,1–16. https://doi.org/10.1016/j.esp.2013.11.002

Gimenez, J. (2006). Embedded business emails: Meeting new demands in international business communication. *English for Specific Purposes,* 25(2), 154–172. https://doi.org/10.1016/j.esp.2005.04.005

Gimenez, J. (2005). Unpacking business emails: Message embeddedness in international business email communication. In M. Gotti and P. Gillaerts (eds.), *Genre variation in business letters* (pp. 235–255). Peter Lang.

Gimenez, J. (2002). New media and conflicting realities in multinational corporate communication: A case study. *International Review of Applied Linguistics,* 40(4), 323–343. https://doi.org/10.1515/iral.2002.016

Goleman, D. (2020). *Emotional intelligence: Why it can matter more than IQ.* Bloomsbury

Google Work Space, (n.d.) https://workspace.google.com/

Gooverseas (n.d.). How to apply for jobs abroad, https://www.gooverseas.com/blog/how-apply-for-jobs-abroad

Gunnarsson, B.-L. (2013). Multilingualism in the workplace. *Annual Review of Applied Linguistics,* 33, 162–189. doi: 10.1017/S0267190513000123.

Haiku Deck, (n.d.) https://www.haikudeck.com

Hall, E. T. (1976). *Beyond culture*. Anchor Books

Handford, M. (2013). *The language of business meetings*. Cambridge University Press.

Hartle, S., Facchinetti, R., & Franceschi, V. (2022). Teaching communication strategies for the workplace: A multimodal framework, *Multimodal Communication*, 11(1), 5–15. https://doi.org/10.1515/mc-2021-0005

Hartley, P. & Chatterton, P. (2015). *Business communication: Rethinking your professional practice for the post-digital age*. Routledge.

Harvard Business Review, (n.d.) https://hbr.org/

Haryonoa, S., Supardib, S. & Udina, U. (2020). The effect of training and job promotion on work motivation and its implications on job performance: Evidence from Indonesia. *Management Science Letters*, 10, 2107–2112. doi: 10.5267/j.msl.2020.1.019

Hewitt, R. (2008). *The Capital's 'Language Shortfall' and Migrants' Economic Survival*. Eco- nomic and Social Research Council, UK Research Report: R000221846.

Hewitt, R. (2012). Multilingualism in the workplace. In M. Martin-Jones, A. Blackledge, and A. Creese (Eds.), *The Routledge Handbook of Multilingualism* (pp. 267–280). Routledge.

Holpp, L. (2011). *Win–win performance appraisals: What to do before, during, and after the review to get the best results for yourself and your employees*. McGraw-Hill Education.

Hymes, D. H. (1972). On communicative competence. In J.B. Pride and J. Holmes (Eds.), *Sociolinguistics: Selected readings* (pp. 269–293). Penguin.

Ilie, C., Nickerson, C. & Planken, B. (2019). *Teaching business discourse*. Palgrave Macmillan.

Indeed – Job search, (n.d.) https://www.indeed.com

International Labour Organization (ILO). (2022). *World employment and social outlook. Trends 2022*. https://www.ilo.org/wcmsp5/groups/public/---dgreports/---dcomm/---publ/documents/publication/wcms_834081.pdf

Johnson, J.D. & Chang, H.-J. (2000). Internal and external communication, boundary spanning and innovation adoption: An over-time comparison of three explanations of internal and external innovation communication in a new organizational form. *Journal of Business Communication*, 37(3), 238–263. https://doi.org/10.1177/002194360003700303

Koester, A. (2010). *Workplace discourse*. Continuum.

Kollectif, IC (2019). *Linking Internal Communication to Business Results.* Research brief. https://www.ickollectif.com/linking-ic-business-results

Laadem, M. & Mallahi, H. (2019). Multimodal pedagogies in teaching English for specific purposes in higher education: Perceptions, challenges and strategies. *International Journal on Studies in Education*, 1(1), 33–38. https://doi.org/10.46328/ijonse.3

Leapsome, (n.d.) https://www.leapsome.com/

McDonough, J. & Shaw, C. (2013). *Materials and methods in ELT.* Blackwell.

Mehra, P., & Nickerson, C. (2019). Does technology divide or unite generations? Testing media richness and communication climate effects on communication satisfaction in the Indian workplace. *International Journal of Organizational Analysis*, 27(5), 1578–1604. DOI 10.1108/IJOA-10-2018-1576

Murray, B. P. (n.d.) The new teacher's guide to creating lesson plans. https://www.scholastic.com/teachers/articles/teachingcontent/new-teachers-guide-creating-lesson-plans/

Neal, J. E. (2020). *Effective phrases for performance appraisals: A guide to successful evaluations.* Neal Publications

Nickerson, C. (2014). The use of English in electronic mail in a multinational corporation. In F. Bargiela-Chiappini & C. Nickerson (Eds.), *Writing business: Genres, media and discourses* (pp. 35–56). Routledge. https://doi.org/10.4324/9781315840246

Nickerson, C. & Planken, B. (2016). *Introducing business English.* Routledge.

Nike ISPA, (n.d.) https://about.nike.com/en/stories/ispa-link-link-axis

Otto, S., Dekker, V., Dekker, H., Richter, D., & Zabel, S. (2021). The joy of gratifications: Promotion as a short-term boost or long-term success – The same for women and men? *Human Resource Management Journal*, 32(1), 151–168. https://doi.org/10.1111/1748-8583.12402

Ozdic, (n.d.) https://ozdic.com/

Padlet, (n.d.) https://www.padlet.com

Pan, Y., Wong Scollon, S., & Scollon, R. (2002). *Professional Communication in International Settings.* Blackwell.

Poncini, G. (2004). *Discourse strategies in multilingual business meetings.* Peter Lang.

Personal Career Management, (n.d.) https://www.personalcareermanagement.com/

Prezi, (n.d.) https://prezi.com/

Prospects, (n.d.) https://www.prospects.ac.uk/

Raptivity – New Age eLearning Interaction Builder, (n.d.) https://www.raptivity.com/

Ravazzani, S. (2015). Exploring internal crisis communication in multicultural environments. A study among Danish managers. *Corporate Communications: An International Journal*, 21(1),73–88. DOI 10.1108/CCIJ-02-2015-0011

Richards, J. C. (n.d.). Communicative language teaching today. https://www.professorjackrichards.com/wp-content/uploads/communicativelanguage teaching-today-v2.pdf

Riratanaphong, C. & van der Voordt, T. (2015). Measuring the added value of workplace change performance measurement in theory and practice. *Facilities*, 33(11/12), 773–792. DOI 10.1108/F-12-2014-0095

Rubdy, R. (2003). Selection of materials. In B. Tomlinson (Ed.), *Developing materials for language teaching* (pp. 37–57). Continuum.

SlideDog, (n.d.) https://slidedog.com

Speach me, (n.d.) https://speach.me/reasons-you-should-stop-using-power point/

Spillan, J. E., Virzi, N., & Garita, M. (2014). *Doing business in Latin America: Challenges and opportunities*. Routledge.

SmartSheet, (n.d.) https://www.smartsheet.com/

Stubbe, M., Lane, C., Hilder, J., Vine, E., Vine, B., Marra, M., Holmes, J., & Weatherall, A. (2003). Multiple discourse analyses of a workplace interaction. *Discourse Studies*, 5(3), 351–389. https://doi.org/10.1177/14614456030053004

Study.com (n.d.). https://study.com/learn/lesson/written-communication-types-examples.html

Sword, R. (16 November 2020). Effective communication in the classroom: Skills for teachers. https://www.highspeedtraining.co.uk/hub/communication-skills-for-teachers/

Task-Based Approach, (n.d.) https://www.teachingenglish.org.uk/article/task-based-approach

Tomlinson, B. (2003). *Developing materials for language teaching*. Continuum.

Treem, J. W., Dailey, S. L., Pierce, C. S., & Leonardi, P. M. (2015). Bringing technological frames to work: How previous experience with social media shapes the technology's meaning in an organization. *Journal of Communication, 65*, 396–422. https://doi.org/10.1111/jcom.12149

Tuleja, E. A. (2021). *Intercultural communication for global business: How leaders communicate for success*. Routledge.

Wen, X., Elicker, J., & McMullen, M. (2011). Early childhood teachers' curriculum beliefs: Are they consistent with observed classroom practices? *Early Education and Development, 22*(6): 945–969. https://doi.org/10.1080/10409289.2010.507495

Wilcox-Herzog, A. (2002). Is there a link between teachers' beliefs and behaviors? *Early Education and Development, 13*(1): 81–106. https://doi.org/10.1207/s15566935eed1301_5

Willis, J. (1996). *A framework for task-based learning*. Longman.

Xie, L. & Yang. L. (2021). The influence of perceptions of promotion opportunities on job performance and its mechanisms: A case study of Chinese junior civil servants. *Journal of Contemporary China, 30*, 118–135. DOI: 10.1080/10670564.2020.1766913

Yamada, H. (1990). Topic management and turn distribution in business meetings: American versus Japanese strategies. *TEXT, 10*(3), 271–295. https://doi.org/10.1515/text.1.1990.10.3.271

Young Cho, H., & Lee, H.-J. (2022). Digital transformation for efficient communication in the workplace: Analyzing the flow coworking tool. *Business Communication Research and Practice, 5*(1): 20–28. https://doi.org/10.22682/bcrp.2022.5.1.20

List of resources

Associations

There are some associations that focus on business or corporate communication. They sometimes have a strand or chapter on international business communication, and organise annual or bi-annual conferences and workshops. The following list provides a selection of such associations.

Association for Business Communication (ABC), https://www.businesscommunication.org/

International Association of Business Communicators (IABC), https://www.iabc.com/

International Communication Association, https://www.icahdq.org/

Journals

There are also a number of journals that publish articles on workplace communication in general, and communication for the workplace in particular. Some of them have a very strong practice/teaching orientation, which makes them very useful sources of research-informed ideas for classroom activities. These are marked (**TO**). Some are open access, that is, you do not need a subscription to access the articles they publish. These are marked (**OA**). A selection of such journals is provided below.

Business and Professional Communication Quarterly, Sage
https://journals.sagepub.com/home/bcq

Business Communication Research and Practice, Korean Association for Business Communication
https://www.e-bcrp.org/ (**TO**) (**OA**)
Corporate Communications: An International Journal, Emerald
https://www.emerald.com/insight/publication/issn/1356-3289
English for Specific Purposes, Elsevier
https://www.sciencedirect.com/journal/english-for-specific-purposes (**TO**)
ESP Today, University of Belgrade and the Serbian Association for the Study of English (SASE)
https://www.esptodayjournal.org/index.html (**TO**) (**OA**)
Global Advances in Business Communication, Eastern Michigan University, the Delhi Business School, and the University of Antwerp
https://commons.emich.edu/gabc (**OA**)
Global Business Languages, The George Washington University
https://gbl.digital.library.gwu.edu/ (**TO**) (**OA**)
International Journal of Business Communication, Sage https://journals.sagepub.com/home/job
Journal of Business and Technical Communication, Sage
https://journals.sagepub.com/home/jbt (**TO**)
Journal of Communication (JOC), the International Communication Association
https://academic.oup.com/joc

Sources of ideas and materials

The Internet is probably the biggest source of ideas and materials that we have as teachers. The materials on the Internet are freely accessible, but you have to keep in mind that not all of them have been designed for teaching purposes; therefore, you will need to adapt them for classroom use. Before making decisions about using Internet materials, you may want to revise the principles for evaluating, selecting and adapting materials we discussed in section I.4 of the Introductory Unit.

Business and company websites are another good source of ideas and authentic materials. Depending on the proficiency level of your students, you can either ask them to look at the websites themselves or adapt the materials on the websites before using them with your students. In the former case, the handouts you design only need to include classroom activities. In the latter, your handouts will have to include the adapted materials as well. Remember always to acknowledge the sources of your materials.

Below you will find a few ideas on how to use information and materials provided on the websites of some international companies for teaching purposes. Reference to the units in *Teaching Communication, Skills and Competencies for the Workplace* has been provided.

Company Website	Particular Sections/Pages	Units in *the book*
Nike https://www.nike.com/ gb/london	**Search jobs** https://jobs.nike. com/?jobSearch=true& jsOffset=0&jsSort= posting_start_date &jsLanguage=en List of available vacancies	Units 1–3
	Careers https://jobs.nike.com/ Good examples of jobs and their associated responsibilities	Units 1–4
	About Nike https://about.nike.com/ Good for examples of company mission and values	Unit 5
Accor https://careers.accor. com	**Accor Careers** An extensive list of vacancies in the international hospitality sector	Units 1–4
Sociabble https://www.sociabble. com/	**Sociabble for internal communications** https://www.sociabble.com/ internal-communications Strategies for engaging employees by means of internal communications	Units 5–6

Company Website	Particular Sections/Pages	Units in *the book*
Indeed https://www.indeed.com	**Top verbal skills** https://www.indeed.com/career-advice/career-development/verbal-skills Definitions and examples of verbal communication skills for the workplace	Unit 6
Globalization Partners https://www.globalization-partners.com/	**Strategies for improving employee retention** https://www.globalization-partners.com/blog/7-strategies-that-improve-remote-employee-retention/ Good set of strategies for retention that include ideas for appraisal and promotion.	Units 7–8

Index

Pages in *italics* refer to figures and pages in **bold** refer to tables.

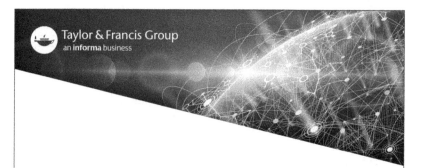

Ingram Content Group UK Ltd.
Milton Keynes UK
UKHW022232070623
423074UK00012B/96